ISBN 978-0-282-40592-2
PIBN 10850566

English
Français
Deutsche
Italiano
Español
Português

www.forgottenbooks.com

Mythology Photography **Fiction**
Fishing Christianity **Art** Cooking
Essays Buddhism Freemasonry
Medicine **Biology** Music **Ancient**
Egypt Evolution Carpentry Physics
Dance Geology **Mathematics** Fitness
Shakespeare **Folklore** Yoga Marketing
Confidence Immortality Biographies
Poetry **Psychology** Witchcraft
Electronics Chemistry History **Law**
Accounting **Philosophy** Anthropology
Alchemy Drama Quantum Mechanics
Atheism Sexual Health **Ancient History**
Entrepreneurship Languages Sport
Paleontology Needlework Islam
Metaphysics Investment Archaeology
Parenting Statistics Criminology
Motivational

THE
MASKS
OF

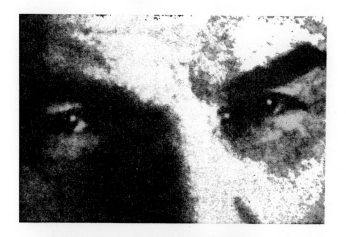

COMMUNISM

DAN N. JACOBS Miami University

1963

6793

The eyes on the cover and the title page are Lenin's.
The photograph from which they were taken
is reproduced in full on page 22.
Photo from the collection of André de Saint-Rat.

INTRODUCTION

Today, the United States is threatened by an enemy dedicated to its destruction. That enemy is Communism, whose leaders promise that in two generations or less they will "bury" the American way of life and the system it represents. There can be little doubt that the men who guide the Communist machine are not only convinced that this can be done, but they are determined that it will and must be done.

It must be done because two rival systems (Communist doctrine claims) cannot continue for long to exist side by side without one being conquered by the other. It will be done, they believe, because their basic philosophy of Marxism-Leninism teaches them that the American system has outlived its usefulness and the Communist system represents the wave of the future.

The Communists believe that history is "with them," that their triumph is inevitable. And, indeed, the events since World War II have strengthened their conviction. When Russia first fell to the Communists in 1917, their leader, Lenin, would have been satisfied if the new government had lasted three months. Lenin had little confidence in the ability of the new regime to survive, surrounded as it was by hostile powers. However, the new government did not collapse, nor was it destroyed. The Union of Soviet Socialist Republics (U.S.S.R.)—the official name of Russia after 1922—emerged from World War II as the second most powerful country in the world.

Since that time, Albania, Yugoslavia, Hungary, Poland, Bulgaria, Rumania, East Germany, North Korea, North Vietnam, China, Cuba, and Czechoslovakia have all fallen under Communist control. These victories, plus the recent accomplishments of Soviet science in sending the first man into orbit around the earth, have helped to convince the Communists and their supporters that Marx and Lenin were right, that the future does belong to Communism. The Communists, then, are out to get the United States. It is not enough for Americans to say that if we leave the Communists alone, they will leave us alone. This will not work, for the Communists *will not* leave us alone. It is one of the basic characteristics of Communism always to push forward, to expand unless blocked and checked. Communism will not stand still; it will overrun and crush those things that we hold dearest if we do not understand it and oppose it with all our force.

One of the great weapons that Communism has fighting for it against the free world is ignorance. Here we have an enemy—Communism—plotting our destruction, sworn to that goal; and yet most Americans know very little about the enemy, its ideas, its methods, and what it is like in practice. Many of us know that it is bad, but often this is because others have told us so, not because of what we ourselves know about Communism. Throughout the lifetime of every person reading this book, a terrible struggle is likely to continue between Communism and the American way. Each of us, in one manner or another, is going to be called upon to fight the enemy. Some of us will probably give our lives in the battle. Therefore, it is necessary that we know what we are fighting for, who and what the enemy is, and why we must oppose him with all our strength. To do less is to be unforgivably careless and contribute to our own destruction.

It is the purpose of this book to inform you about the enemy; why he thinks he will and should take over the world; how he expects to be able to do this; what it is like to live in a country captured by the enemy. It is our hope that through these pages we can alert you to the nature of the enemy's threat, so that the struggle against him can be waged with the strength that comes only from knowledge and understanding.

DAN N. JACOBS

CONTENTS

Karl Marx (1818–1883), the father of Communism, was born in Germany, but was forced to leave his own country because of his outspoken radical ideas. Marx settled in England, where he lived the rest of his life and where his major works were written.

André de Saint-Rat

1

In 1848 a pamphlet was published in London. Its title was *Manifesto of the Communist League* (usually shortened to *Communist Manifesto*). Its author was a German newspaperman named Karl Marx.

At the time, few people had heard of Marx, and few paid any attention to the ideas in his manifesto. He did, however, acquire a few followers; and their number increased after the publication, nineteen years later, of *Capital*, a much longer work that presented his ideas in great detail. After fifty more years, men who called themselves Marxists were able to gain control of the government of Russia. Today the followers of Marx govern more than a third of the people in the world; they have threatened that within three generations they will govern the entire world.

Marx once said that he himself was not a Marxist. He meant that he did not approve of the changes that were being made in his ideas by his followers even during his lifetime. Since his death, Communism has changed so greatly that Marx probably would not recognize it as it exists today. His ideas have been distorted; but they are nonetheless the beginning of Communism, and all Communist theory is based upon Marx.

Background: The Industrial Revolution Creates Problems

One hundred years ago most of the people in every country of the world made their livings by farming. In many countries they still do. But in others—the United States, Canada, Great Britain, Germany, France, Japan, Belgium—a high percentage of the people now live and work in cities. In these countries, immense changes have occurred in almost every other aspect of life as well; the speed with which we can get from one place to another is an example. What has brought about these great changes? Generally speaking, they can be attributed to the *Industrial Revolution*.

Pre-Industrial Society

Before the Industrial Revolution, most people provided for themselves to a much greater extent than any of us does now. They grew their own food, built their own houses, spun their own cloth, made their own clothing. Families were large; usually grandparents, parents, children, and sometimes grandchildren all lived together. By comparison to what we are used to, living standards were low and work was hard.

But everyone had security. Of course disasters, such as drought, flood, or war, could affect anyone. But barring such disasters, everyone could count on having food to eat and a roof over his head; and he knew that if for some reason he were unable to work, the rest of the family would take care of him.

In this pre-industrial society, money was not very important to most people, and they saw little of it. If a farmer had any extra food (after he had provided for his family and paid his rent and taxes) he might take it into town and sell it in the market. He would use the money to buy the few things that he could not furnish himself, such as pots and pans, or salt, or sometimes a few small luxuries.

Of course, not everyone farmed. In Europe, society was organized according to the *feudal* system. Feudalism recognized the division of society into two classes: the peasantry, who grew the food, and the nobility, who ruled, fought, and owned the land. The peasants were the great majority of the population. The nobility governed the country, fought its wars—and lived much more luxuriously than the peasantry.

There was also a third class. In contrast to both the nobility and the peasantry, these people lived in towns. At first this class was small. Its members were mostly artisans; that is, men who made things, such as goldsmiths, blacksmiths, or weavers. As the social level of this class was somewhere between the other two classes, it became known as the *middle class*. As the members of the middle class lived in towns, they also became known as the *bourgeoisie* (from the French word for town, *bourg*).

As the middle class developed, the economic system called *capitalism* gradually grew out of its activities.

Pre-Industrial Capitalism

The first capitalists were traders. The idea of the trader is simple: he buys something in one place, carries it to another place, and sells it at a higher price. The trader takes risks: perhaps his ship, carrying the goods that he has invested a great deal of money in, will be lost; or perhaps no one will want to buy the goods he has purchased. But if he is successful, he will end up with more money than he started out with; he will have made a profit.

The trader illustrates three basic characteristics of capitalism: (1) he takes a risk; (2) his goal is making a profit; (3) he uses capital. *Capital,* in its broadest sense, means *the things that a capitalist uses (and risks)* in order to make a profit. In the case of the trader, the money with which he buys goods is capital. His ships, or carts, or whatever else he carries the goods in, are also capital. *Capital* does not always mean *money,* or even something bought with money; perhaps the trader built his ships or carts himself.

Capitalism also appeared in certain areas where weavers had learned to produce cloth that was particularly beautiful or strong. The weaver discovered that he could sell all the cloth he produced and in so doing make a profit. Sometimes the demand increased to the point where the owner put his wife, his sons and daughters, nieces and nephews to work in his "factory." Sometimes he even hired outsiders. If the business continued to expand, he might eventually employ several dozen people.

Most of these enterprises, however, employed ten people or less. The employer and the employee knew each other and understood each other's problems. Usually the employee could hope that some day he would reach the employer's level, either by inheriting the business or by establishing a business of his own.

Most factories were family owned in this way until the Industrial Revolution, which began in England about 1750 and in the 1800's spread to several other countries, including our own.

The Industrial Revolution Begins

The Industrial Revolution was largely the result of two inventions, the steam engine and the power loom.

These inventions were as remarkable in their own time as the discoveries of fire and the wheel had been in earlier ages. It suddenly became possible for one man to do in a day what formerly had taken ten men a week to do. Jobs that had been performed only with much time and effort were now accomplished more simply and quickly. Hand-made products, which only the wealthy could afford, were replaced by machine-made products that a much greater percentage of the population could afford.

The demand for the output of the new machines grew tremendously and swiftly. New factories sprang up almost overnight, and old factories were equipped with the new power equipment.

The buildings and machinery needed to equip the new factories were often very expensive. By this period in the development of capitalism, however, there were a number of wealthy people with capital to invest; and once the investments had been made, tremendous profits could be expected.

4   *Changes in Society*

As the number of factories increased, the need for manpower to operate them grew as well. The old towns had not been large, and most of the people in them had their regular jobs to perform. As we have seen, the great majority of the people lived in the countryside, and it was there that the largest supply of labor was to be found. Many peasants were willing to break away from the family group, to move into town, and to take up factory work. One of the main reasons for their willingness was that the factories offered cash incomes, which were often irresistible to men who had only rarely seen money and even more rarely owned it.

At first, many factory owners provided for the food and housing needs of their employees. But as new cities arose and more and more people streamed into them, conditions became less and less favorable. Housing, in particular, was inadequate; there simply was not enough space for the rapidly expanding population. And investors preferred not to use their money to build housing, because much greater profits were to be made by investing in machinery, factories, or trading companies.

As a result, the housing that was available brought very high rents. Six, seven, eight, or more people lived in single rooms. Landlords did not care about keeping their buildings in good repair, because they knew that the quarters could be rented under any conditions. When new housing was constructed, little attention was paid to beauty or health or sanitation. Houses were built with no space between them, and often they were in dark valleys where the sun seemed never to shine. Sewers were open, water was polluted. Refuse was piled up in the streets, and heaps of slag from the mines often stood nearby. Working hours, even for children, often exceeded twelve per day in a six-day week; and few people even thought

This street in a slum area of London is typical of conditions in many cities during the early stages of the Industrial Revolution. Dilapidated houses and dark, narrow, dirty streets were a part of the life of almost every factory worker and his family, and few could hope to escape to anything better.

about maintaining safe and healthy living and working conditions. Epidemic, disease, and early death were frequently visitors to the newly-built towns and cities.

The city was a cruel place to live, even in times of prosperity; but when depression hit the community, conditions became even worse. Factories stood idle while the unemployed wandered through the streets with nothing to do. Children cried for food, and beggars were everywhere. At first, those who had moved to the city could return to their former homes in the country in bad times. But eventually the old ties were broken. The factory worker found himself alone with his wife and children; he had no larger family to fall back on and no farm where he could grow his food. He had to rely entirely upon himself, and without a job he was unable to care for his family's needs. It is small wonder that some men turned to stealing and other forms of crime just to keep themselves alive.

The Search for Remedies

To many of those who thought about it, it seemed strange that the factories should stand idle when people needed their products, when there were enough raw materials to supply them, and when there was more than enough manpower to operate the machinery. The problem was that few people had the money to buy the goods that industry had already produced. Yet more money would not be available until the factories began producing and jobs became available. It seemed a vicious circle, and meanwhile the life of the ordinary city dweller became more and more desperate.

During the 1800's a number of men turned their attention to the problems of the new industrialization. Why was it that with such an unlimited need for the products of industry, the factories often stood still? Why was it that industrialization, which should have made a better life for everyone, instead brought increased suffering to a large part of society? Did things have to be this way? What was wrong? Who was to blame?

Those who considered such problems had already suggested a number of explanations and solutions when Karl Marx appeared on the scene in the 1840's.

The Theories of Karl Marx

In developing his theories, Karl Marx built upon the work of many other men. This is not to say that Marx was not an original thinker; but his great strength was his ability to piece borrowed ideas together into a single theory.

The original idea of communism is an old one. The idea of a community whose members shared their possessions can be found in the New Testament (Acts IV: 32–35). In the early 19th century this idea was taken up by several thinkers, most notably Fourier in France and Owen in England. Their followers established communist communities (usually small farming enterprises) in several countries, including the United States. Most of these communities collapsed after a few years.

Marx studied the early communist theories carefully, and he sometimes borrowed from them for his own theories. But Marx borrowed ideas from many other thinkers as well, with the result that his ideas became something quite different from those of the original communists.

Marx developed his theories by studying history. He saw all history through the eye-glasses of what he called the *dialectic*. This, too, was not an original idea, but was borrowed from the German philosopher G. W. F. Hegel.

The Dialectic

All of us probably take for granted that history does not stand still; things are constantly changing. The old gives way to the new, but usually only after a long, hard fight. According to Marx, the fight was *always* going on, and the new *always* won out in the long run. It could be neither doubted nor successfully resisted.

According to the dialectic, changes always follow a certain pattern. The pattern has three stages, called *thesis, antithesis,* and *synthesis*. To start with, there is the *thesis*, which represents the way things are. Soon another idea, the *antithesis*, appears to challenge the thesis. Thesis and antithesis enter into a fight to the death, and both are destroyed; but out of the struggle emerges a new concept, *synthesis*. But synthesis does not hold the field for long; for at the very moment that synthesis wins out, it becomes the next thesis, and the process begins all over again.

According to Marx, everything that has ever happened has followed this pattern, and everything that happens in the future will follow it as well.

Historical Materialism

Closely allied with the dialectic in the Marxian system is *historical materialism,* the idea that everything that happens has economic causes. Marx did not believe that great men, or chance, or political ideals (such as democracy) shape history in any important way. History, as Marx saw it, was almost entirely the result of economic processes.

He also believed that whoever controlled the means of production therefore controlled society. After the Industrial Revolution the factories and mines were the principal means of production; therefore, the capitalists who owned the factories and mines controlled everything and everyone. Only those who *own* have power. Those who must work for others are at the mercy of their employers. They are "exploited" by the owners for the owners' benefit.

According to Marx, the owners control not only the factories and mines but also the means of communication, such as newspapers. As a result, the owners' ideas of right and wrong are the only ideas that are ever printed or spoken. The working class (or *proletariat,*

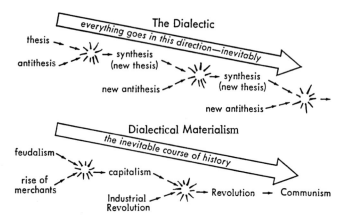

A diagram of Hegel's dialectic and Marx's dialectical materialism, both very greatly simplified. Note that the dialectic is a process that never ends, but that Marx's version ends when Communism, the perfect society, is reached.

to use Marx's term) usually is completely unaware that it is being exploited. By keeping the truth from the proletariat, and by keeping its members working so hard that they have no time to think of anything else, the owners are able to control the workers' minds.

And, Marx says, the owners own not only the factories and mines and means of communication; they own the government as well. Either directly or indirectly they *are* the government. The laws are made in their interest, judges interpret the laws in their interest, police enforce the laws in their interest.

The Dialectic at Work

Marx combined historical materialism and the dialectic into *dialectical materialism,* which provided him with an explanation for everything that has ever happened. Marx believed that dialectical materialism indicated that history worked in a certain way, and he was equally confident that history would continue to operate in that way. As a result, he felt quite able to foretell the future. Marx did not hesitate to predict what was, in his opinion, the future of mankind. But he did not present his ideas as opinions; he firmly believed that they were scientific facts.

According to Marx's interpretation, all history is the history of struggles between social classes. Among primitive men there were no such things as social classes. The division of society occurred when prehistoric man discovered new methods of production. He learned how to farm, how to domesticate animals, how to work with metals. He developed these skills because they were useful to him; but they also provided him with possessions—that is, with private property. He discovered that the products of his work were not only useful to himself but were desired by others as well. Soon there was more to be done than he and the members of his family could accomplish; there was need for additional labor power. The additional labor was obtained by capturing other men in battle (the beginning of war) and turning them into slaves. Slavery was the first division of society into classes, into owners and owned, into "exploiters" and "exploited."

In Marx's analysis, this division has lasted throughout history. After slavery came feudalism; after feudalism, capitalism; and always the fight between the classes has remained. Under slavery the fight was between slaveholders and slaves. Under feudalism the fight was between the nobility and the peasantry. Under capitalism it is between those who control the capital and those who work for wages. The conflict never disappears. Indeed, says Marx, with the passage of time the differences become sharper and the battle more bitter.

Marx found himself living in the period of capitalism, and it was in capitalism that he was chiefly interested. His concern with earlier periods of history was largely an attempt to explain capitalism and determine what might succeed capitalism. According to the dialectic, everything is in a constant process of change. As slavery gave way to feudalism and feudalism to capitalism, so capitalism must in turn fall before the next stage of development. It is the way of history. It is inevitable.

The Nature of Capitalism

According to Marx, the very foundation of the capitalist system is the profit motive. The profit motive meant, to Marx, that every capitalist willingly or unwillingly is completely dominated by greed. His chief interest in life is accumulating as much money as he can.

But, says Marx, the money that the capitalist seeks does not come from his own labor but from the labor of the workmen he hires. It is the laboring man who produces everything. The capitalist produces nothing, but he gathers all the rewards. He is, says Marx, a "parasite" living off the work of others.

When a workman is hired, his pay is as small as the factory owner can get him to work for. The worker must accept the low pay because he needs a job to stay alive. By hiring the workman, the employer actually is purchasing "labor power." He seeks to use that labor power to produce something of greater value than the cost of the labor power. The difference between the selling price of a product on the one hand, and the cost of the labor power (and raw materials and equipment used up in production) on the other, goes to the employer. The extra value is, in Marxian lingo, "surplus value," or capitalist profit.

The idea of "surplus value" can be illustrated with an example. Let us suppose that Product X can be sold for a quarter. The owner of the factory where Product X is made pays a dime for raw materials and equipment used up in production and another dime for the labor power that turns the raw materials into the product. The nickel left over is "surplus value" which, according to Marx, just falls into the employer's lap.

As Marx saw things, the capitalist employer did not deserve that nickel because he had not contributed any labor power. To Marx, the efforts of the capitalist in accumulating capital with which to build the factory, or the risk that the capitalist takes in manufacturing a product that perhaps no one will want, or the talent that he must have to organize production and sales, are all worthless. The man in the factory who puts the product together with his own hands is the only one that counts.

The Decline of Capitalism

According to Marx, the goal of the capitalist is to "maximize surplus value"; that is, to make his profits as large as he can. One way in which he attempts to do this is to buy more efficient machinery. With this machinery, the worker who formerly produced four units of Product X can now produce eight units in the same amount of time. Production will have increased without increasing labor power, and the employer will have greatly increased the "surplus value" left over for himself.

The factory owner now has still more capital to invest in his plant, so he purchases newer machinery that is even more efficient. In time, the man who once produced four units of Product X will be producing ten, twelve, or even more units.

At this point, says Marx, capitalism's greatest problem becomes evident: more goods are being produced than people are able to buy. This is not to say that there are no people who need Product X. The problem is that the employer, always hoping to increase his own profits, does not share the increased profits with his employees by increasing their salaries. They cannot afford to buy any more of the product than they have in the past.

Product X soon becomes a glut on the market. It piles up on the shelves of stores and warehouses. A cut in prices moves some of the goods, but in the long run the only alternative is to produce fewer goods. But a cutback in production means that fewer workers are needed. A large part of the work force is laid off.

This process, Marx says, is not confined to a single factory or a single industry, but occurs everywhere. Even before the cutback in production, some factories had been forced to close because of inefficiency or lack of capital with which to buy modern machinery, so there are already a large number of unemployed. The cutbacks make the problem much more serious.

Of course, Marx continues, the problem all along has been that too many people are too poor to purchase the output of industry. Each man laid off the job means that there is one more family that cannot buy Product X. Again it is necessary to decrease the labor force, and in turn fewer people are able to buy Product X. The process goes on and on.

The workers become more and more desperate. Thousands of unemployed workers offer to work for lower salaries. The employer, still attempting to increase his profits, accepts the offer. In so doing, however, he reduces still further the ability of the workers to buy.

At this point, says Marx, the capitalist may attempt to establish a *monopoly;* that is, to drive out or buy out all of his competitors so that his company alone will make a certain product. The capitalist thinks that without competition he will be able to charge whatever he wants for his product. The monopoly, Marx says, may help temporarily; but the elimination of the previously existing companies again increases the number of unemployed. Now still fewer people can afford Product X.

Conditions grow worse and worse. As the development of capitalism continues, the proletariat finds itself being pushed further and further down. Its members meet with increasing unemployment. They are willing to work for less and less, and their lives become increasingly miserable.

At the same time something is happening to the bourgeois capitalist class as well. The monopolists, those among the bourgeoisie who have the power to force or buy out their competitors, have become richer than the richest king. But the great majority of the bourgeoisie are in a quite different position. Those former owners who have been forced out of business fall into the proletariat. Their parasitic existence has not prepared them for any kind of work, even if jobs were available. Those who have sold their factories for cash soon use up the money. Either they or their children also become proletarians. Most lawyers and physicians meet the same fate: with so many people out of work, no one can pay his legal or medical fees.

The few members of the bourgeoisie who survive become increasingly powerful; but they are aware of what is happening, and they are fearful. As capitalism develops, economic crises occur with greater frequency. Each is more serious than the one before, and each is more difficult to recover from. They see depressions, bank failures, and bankruptcies all around them. While the bourgeoisie lives in corrupt luxury, the existence of its more intelligent members certainly is not carefree.

This process of the division of society into two groups—the bourgeoisie, small and constantly growing smaller, and the proletariat, large and constantly growing larger—is known among Marxists as *polarization*. The polarization of society into these groups, Marx says, is inevitable. At times, the process may be slowed down, but not for very long. The dialectic cannot be resisted.

The Revolution

Of course, says Marx, the bourgeoisie keeps itself in power by controlling the machinery of the state. (In political science, the term *state* refers to what we usually call *the government*.) It also controls the police force (part of the state), the means of communication (such as newspapers), and even the ideas of right and wrong.

Nevertheless, despite its widespread controls, the bourgeoisie cannot survive the repeated economic crises. Recovery from each one becomes more difficult. Finally the day will come when the bourgeois capitalist system cannot recover, and it will collapse.

Perhaps even before this collapse the proletariat will have risen up and delivered the death blow to the capitalistic system. Even if the proletariat does not arise, the system will die—but it will take a little longer. Whether the system will collapse all by itself or be pushed over by the workers Marx refused definitely to say. Probably he favored a bloodless changeover but considered such a changeover rather unlikely.

Where will the revolution occur? According to Marx, in the country where the problems of capitalism have become so great that

Friedrich Engels (1820–1895), like Marx a German living in England, worked closely with Marx for many years. Engels, who came from a wealthy family, provided most of the money that enabled Marx to carry on his studying and writing.

André de Saint-Rat

those in power can no longer deal with them. In other words, the revolution will occur in the country with the highest development of industrial capitalism—at the time Marx wrote, Great Britain. But no matter how or where the revolution is to occur, occur it must. This is inevitable, according to the working out of the dialectic. It may be postponed; it cannot be avoided.

The revolution will be for the benefit of the entire proletariat. However, one part of the proletariat will be more active in bringing the revolution about. Those who take this part will be the "class-conscious" proletariat; that is, those whose eyes have been opened to the "bourgeois lies" and who understand the reasons behind the proletariat's suffering. These knowing proletarians will band together in the Communist party; they will be the "vanguard of the working class" that educates and trains the rest of the proletarians for the revolution to come.

It was Marx's idea that the Communist party should be a large, open organization, in some ways rather like an American political party. It would operate openly and would accept as members all who wished to join.

The Dictatorship of the Proletariat

After the revolution there would still be two classes, but the proletariat would be on top. The proletariat's first step after gaining power would be setting up a *dictatorship;* that is, a government in which one person or group (in this case, the proletariat) has absolute control. The dictatorship of the proletariat would have two purposes: (1) to prevent the bourgeoisie's regaining power by staging a counter-revolution, and (2) to take the means of production from the bourgeoisie; that is, to eliminate private property. As soon as the factories were taken away, the bourgeoisie were no longer to be feared, because they would have lost the source of their power. Without property they would become proletarians, and there would no longer be any social classes.

The dictatorship of the proletariat would not last long, because it would not need to. Earlier it was pointed out that, according to Marx, the only purpose of government is to enable one class to exploit another. He reasoned, therefore, that after classes had disappeared there would no longer be any need for government and it, too, would disappear. Marx called this process "the withering away of the state"; it would occur when the classless society had been reached.

Marx believed that the function of the state was repression. Therefore, after the revolution the state could wither away because the source of greed and selfishness, private property, would have been eliminated. Marx believed private property to be the source of all evil; remove the source and you have removed the evil. He thought that man's basic wants would then be painlessly provided for, and his character would soar to new heights. Men would no longer cheat or steal, because there would be no reason for them to do so. Men would follow the good, because it would never occur to them to do the bad. Men would love their work, because work would become "the primary necessity of life." There would be no need for military forces or police or prisons. The time would come, as one Marxist once said, when the only force that would be required in society would be applied by physicians in mental hospitals.

The Establishment of Communism

Thus, according to Marx, the revolution will be followed by the dictatorship of the proletariat. The dictatorship of the proletariat will not last long, and will be followed by the withering away of the state and the establishment of *Communism.*

Marx was never very specific as to what life would be like under Communism. Communism is sometimes described by using the slogan, "From each according to his ability, to each according to his needs." This means that the time would come when every man would voluntarily work his hardest, not because of high wages or other benefits to be gained but simply because he could not think of acting in any other way. He would *like* working as hard as he could, using whatever abilities he had. He would not be paid according to his abilities or according to the importance or danger of his work, but strictly according to his needs.

Marx, as we have seen, thought that the revolution would occur only when society suffered from disastrous overproduction. Capitalism's problem was that it could produce huge quantities of goods, but it could not get those goods to the people. The masses did not have the money to pay for the goods.

Under Communism, said Marx, there would be no such problem. Every person who needed shoes or an overcoat or a dining-room table or a new pipe would simply go to a warehouse and ask for what he wanted. Men would not ask for more than they needed, because the extra shoes and coats and tables would simply litter up the house. If more shoes were produced than were needed, the factory would cut down on production. The cutback would not mean unemployment, but only a shorter work day for everyone at the shoe factory. Nor would the shortened hours mean smaller pay, for each person would receive whatever he needed, no matter how many hours he might work.

The Flaws in Marx's Thinking

It would be dangerous, when examining the ideas of Marx, to condemn him as an evil man. It would be equally dangerous, perhaps more so, to pass him off as a fool. Marx was neither evil nor a fool; he made some solid contributions to our understanding of the world.

Nevertheless, a twentieth-century observer looking at Marx's theories can easily see a number of glaring contradictions and false assumptions in his thinking.

The Dialectic

Marx states that everything—all of life, nature, the universe, history—acts according to the dialectic. The *Great Soviet Encyclopedia*, the final source of information in the Soviet Union, says that dialectics are "the science of the general laws of motion both of the external world and of human thought."

It is true that many aspects of life can be fitted into the dialectic, for it is the unending story of the old versus the new. For example, it may frequently be seen in relations between generations. Young people are usually more gay and adventurous than their parents. They are likely to accuse their parents of being old-fashioned; the parents accuse them of being wild, foolish, without values. Ordinarily the two generations will try to understand each other and make adjustments to each other.

Eventually the younger generation will grow up and take over. It may be like its parents in many ways. But it will not be exactly alike, because its life experiences will have been different: it will have had television and space flights and the Cold War, whereas its parents had radio and the Depression and World War II. And the new generation will, in turn, grow old, and will some day find its ideas being challenged by the *next* generation.

Obviously much of life can be fitted into this pattern; but the Marxists insist that *all* differences are resolved according to the dialectic. But what about the dispute in which the old emerges victorious and the new dies? What about the committee meeting where there are not two but twelve conflicting ideas—and no one will give up his own idea? What about the fight that ends in a draw? It is a great game to try to prove that everything moves according to the dialectic, but it simply does not.

Historical Materialism

One of Marx's lasting contributions was to point out that there is reason to history. In his day, most historians believed that all history could be explained by studying the lives of the great men, the strong national leaders, such as George Washington or Napoleon. The historians were little interested in what was happening throughout society; such tremendous developments as the Industrial Revolution received little attention from them. Other historians believed that history was shaped almost entirely by chance. According to them, such accidents as the Pilgrims' landing in Massachusetts (instead of Virginia, which is where they thought they were going) are the main cause of the events that follow them. Marx attacked both these ideas—and rightly so—because they insisted on a lopsided way of interpreting history.

But Marx, unfortunately, looked at history in a way that was just as lopsided. It is true that economic factors have had a tremendous influence in history. But so have great men, and so have chance happenings—and so have politics, and geography, and many other factors. To say that history is shaped entirely by economic factors is as wrong and narrow-minded as saying that any other one force is the only one that counts. The story of mankind is much too complicated to have one single explanation.

The entire structure of Marx's thinking rests upon the dialectic and historical materialism. If the foundation is weak, the structure cannot be very sound.

The Class Struggle

The idea of the class struggle has been very useful to Marxists, because it provides them with a convenient scapegoat. According to the Marxist theory, anything that goes wrong, anything that brings unhappiness to men, is a result of the exploitation of one class by another. Such a simple explanation will not stand up to the tests of history or of reason.

Man has always been faced by two great struggles. One is with nature. Since the beginning of time, he has had to defend himself against the unending attacks of cold and hunger, heat and floods, blizzards and hurricanes.

The second has been in his relationships with his fellow man. Here, too, he has had to wage an unending struggle—but *not* against a class enemy. Rather, he has had to struggle, as an individual, against the demands of all society. The struggle is one of each person to think, speak, and act in the way that he himself thinks is right. It is society in general, peopled by rich and poor alike, that decides standards of what is good and what is bad. And it is society that attempts to force individuals to follow those standards. Economic factors usually count for very little in setting up the standards; as a matter of fact, it is usually those at the lower end of the economic scale who are most insistent that the standards be observed.

Society is continually trying to limit the areas in which the individual can exercise his free judgment, can decide for himself what is right and what is wrong. And since most men like to make such decisions for themselves, they find themselves in conflict with the society that wants to make the decisions for them. Here, in the continuing struggle for personal freedom, is where the greatest conflict is found, and not in the class struggle.

Many of the ideas that Marx mistakenly took for granted can probably be traced to one of his basic flaws: Marx simply did not understand human nature. His opinion that all the evil in men is due to a lack of food, shelter, and clothing indicates a sad lack of understanding of his fellow men. There are times, of course, when men rob because they are hungry or because their families need shoes. But today people commit crimes far more frequently because they are angry or unhappy, because they crave attention, because they are bored, or for many other reasons that have nothing to do with a lack of money. It is unfulfilled psychological and spiritual needs, not material problems, that account for most of the unhappiness of mankind.

The Final Test

Marxism, like any other idea that has been put into practice, must stand or fall on its record. And the record shows that the prophecies of Karl Marx simply are not coming true. The horrible conditions of the early industrial cities have largely disappeared. The life of the factory worker has been constantly improving for almost one hundred years. Capitalism has changed with the times and remained quite healthy. The middle class has grown much larger, not smaller. In America several million workers now own shares of American industry and are themselves capitalists; this can hardly be called "capitalist exploitation."

And what of the countries in which the Communist party has gained control? As we shall see, life in these countries is a far cry from the "workers' paradise" that Marx predicted. The "dictatorship of the proletariat" has become a dictatorship *over* the proletariat. The workers (and everyone else) are told what to do by a small group of men who think that they know what is best for everyone. And the state certainly is not "withering away"; rather, it has grown so huge and oppressive that it makes itself felt everywhere.

It is true that the Soviet Union has impressive industrial and scientific advances to its credit; it is now an industrial power second only to the United States. Nevertheless, the average Russian's standard of living is still far below that of the average American (or Englishman, or German, or Frenchman, for that matter). More important, however, is the price that the Russians have had to pay for their industrial power; for every Soviet achievement has been paid for with human suffering and with human freedom. It is a price that no man should be forced to pay.

Marxism as a Religion

It is evident that Marxism is many things: a philosophy, an economic theory, a plan for revolution. Marxism as it is practiced today may also be considered a religion.

Marx denied the existence of God. He called all religions the "opiate of the masses," because he believed that they drugged men

Today Karl Marx is revered by all Communists as the founder of their movement. Above, Soviet premier Nikita Khrushchev, flanked by the leaders of the
Italian and German Communist parties and surrounded by high Soviet officials,
speaks at the unveiling of a statue of Marx in Moscow in 1961.

into being satisfied with their miserable existences. Yet the movement that he founded has developed many characteristics that can
best be described as "religious," though in a special sense of the
word.

Perhaps the use of the word can be explained in this way: a person who believes in Christianity or in Judaism believes in God. He
has no scientific proof of God's existence, but nonetheless he is quite
certain that God exists. He does not *need* scientific proof; the matter
is not open to question. There are other aspects of his faith, too,
that are not open to question. In other words, there are some things

that human intelligence, which is limited, is not capable of proving, but which are accepted by a religious person as part of his faith.

Marxism is a religion in that, to the believing Marxist, the ideas of Karl Marx are no more open to question than is the existence of God to a Christian or a Jew. To a Marxist, the dialectic and historical materialism explain everything. Marxism is not a *hypothesis;* that is, it is not an idea that must be tested in the light of history and experience. Rather, to a Marxist it is *the* truth, revealed by Marx. It explains all the mysteries of the world, and is not open to question.

Many people have come to believe in Marxism because it sounds logical. The shortcomings and oversights that are so obvious to us are not at all obvious to them. After they have adopted Marxism, they usually question it no further; they *believe*. In their religion, the dialectic and historical materialism replace God as the moving spirit of the universe, and the writings of Karl Marx replace the Bible. And many of them are willing to fight as fiercely in the name of their religion as the Crusaders were in the name of theirs.

aids to learning

Check the facts

1. Why is Marx considered the founder of Communism? Why did Marx say that he himself was not a Marxist? How many years elapsed between the publication of the *Communist Manifesto* and the control of the Russian government by Marxists?

2. Why was money of little importance in a pre-industrial society? Besides money, what are some of the things that may be classified as capital? What are the three major characteristics of capitalism?

3. Name the two inventions that were largely responsible for the Industrial Revolution. What were the differences between the factories before the Industrial Revolution and those after it? What were some of the benefits of the Industrial Revolution? What were some of the changes it brought into the lives of the working class?

4. What pattern, according to the dialectic, do changes follow? What is historical materialism? What interpretation of history did Marx derive by the use of dialectical materialism?

5. Why did Marx feel that the capitalist employer should not receive the profits from his factory? What contributions of the capitalist did Marx disregard?

6. According to Marx, what are the stages through which the capitalist system will pass before it collapses? How will this process bring about the polarization of society?

7. Who will be the members of the "class-conscious" proletariat? What will be their function as the "vanguard of the working class"?

8. After the revolution, why would a dictatorship of the proletariat be necessary? What would be the purposes of this dictatorship? Why would it last only a short time? What conditions did Marx predict would result from the elimination of private property?

9. What is Marx's idea of Communism and its operation?

10. What are some of the flaws in Marx's thinking concerning: The dialectic? Historical materialism? The class struggle? Human nature?

11. Make a list of the ideas and prophecies of Marx that have not come true.

12. Name four things that are included in the term Marxism. In what ways is Marxism a religion?

Know word meanings

An accurate knowledge of the meaning of certain terms is essential to an understanding of the material studied. Be sure you can define and use correctly these terms:

manifesto	Industrial Revolution	surplus value
feudalism	thesis	proletariat
bourgeoisie	antithesis	dialectical materialism
capital	synthesis	monopoly
capitalism	dialectic	polarization
exploit	historical materialism	class struggle

Do something extra

1. Compare Marx's ideas of government and private property with those of the anarchist Pierre Joseph Proudhon.

2. Read and report on some of the communist-type communities tried in the United States. Two of them are (1) Robert Owen's settlement at New Harmony, Indiana, (2) Brook Farm in Massachusetts; Emerson and Hawthorne were interested in this one. Are there any similarities between these experiments and Marx's ideas?

3. In what ways do Marx's writings illustrate the adage, "The pen is mightier than the sword"?

4. What measures has the United States government taken to protect the workers from the hardships of unemployment?

5. In what ways have the labor unions prevented exploitation of the workers?

6. Draw an isosceles triangle and indicate on it, at the proper levels, the social and economic classes of society before the Industrial Revolution. On a second triangle indicate the social classes about 1850.

7. Compare the life of a United States frontier or pioneer family with that of a family in Europe before the Industrial Revolution.

8. Read and report on the life of Karl Marx.

9. Read and report on Friedrich Engels and his contribution to Marx.

10. Read and report on the *Communist Manifesto*.

*Vladimir Ilyich Lenin (1870–1924), the man who
brought Communism to power in Russia, was
a fanatic who devoted his life to the idea
of a Marxist revolution. In so doing, he changed
many of Marx's ideas—and founded modern Communism.*

André de Saint-Rat

2

THE IDEA BROUGHT TO POWER

Karl Marx had believed that the revolution that would bring about Communism would occur in the country in which bourgeois capitalism was most fully developed. In other words, it would be most likely to occur in Great Britain, Germany, or possibly the United States. But none of these countries has ever had a successful Marxist revolution. Rather, the first revolution carried out in the name of Karl Marx occurred in Russia.

Why Russia? At the beginning of the twentieth century, Russia had just begun to emerge from feudalism. The country was not highly industrialized. The great majority of her people were still peasants, not factory workers. The middle class was small and weak. How could a Marxist revolution be carried out there?

If there is any one factor that most explains the Russian Revolution, it is that *one man* became devoted to the ideal of a Marxist revolution. Unlike Marx, he was not content to wait for the revolution to occur in its own good time. He wanted to *make* a revolution himself; and as he was a Russian, he made the revolution in his own country. That man was Vladimir Ilyich Ulyanov, who is better known by the alias that he adopted early in his career: Lenin.

Background: Russia in the 19th Century

Russia covers a huge area on the eastern edge of Europe and in northern and central Asia. The European part of Russia has three main divisions: Russia proper, or "Great" Russia, a large area with Moscow roughly at its center; the Ukraine, or "Little" Russia, in the southwest; and Byelorussia, or "White" Russia, to the west.

23

Russia has been expanding steadily for over 400 years. She has spread east as far as the Pacific; south into central Asia, the Caucasus Mountains, and the Black Sea region; and westward into Europe. As a result, the country includes many non-Russian areas: Estonia, Latvia, and Lithuania along the Baltic Sea; Georgia, Armenia, and Azerbaijan in the Caucasus; several smaller European groups; and many Asiatic nationalities. Today there are almost 200 different nationalities in Russia; these non-Russians make up about 20 per cent of the population.

Russian Government and Economy

In the 19th century, Russia was probably the most badly governed country in Europe. Its government was an *autocracy;* that is, a government by one man who has complete and unquestioned power over all the people. There were no such things as legislatures like our Congress; in Russia, the only law was the word of the emperor, or *czar*. The idea that an individual might be entitled to certain rights simply did not exist. Whatever the czar wished, was right, and his will would be done.

In the early and middle 1800's, the majority of the Russian peasantry was still bound by serfdom. The life of a serf was hardly better than that of a slave. He was bound to his master's estate, and could not leave without the master's permission; and under certain conditions he could be sold by one master to another.

In 1861 the czar freed the serfs, largely because he feared a revolution if he did not do so. However, for most of the peasants, life changed hardly at all; for some it became even more difficult. The peasantry remained bound to the land. Agricultural Russia—which meant most of Russia—remained in a feudal state.

As for Russian industry, at the beginning of the 20th century Russia's industrial revolution was just barely under way. It is true that by 1913, just before the outbreak of World War I, Russia was the fifth largest industrial producer in the world. Nonetheless, Russia was still far behind the United States, Germany, Great Britain, and France. Only a small percentage of the Russian people were engaged in industry; the proletariat, which Marx said must be the majority of the population before his revolution could occur, had only begun to develop. The living and working conditions of the workers were exceedingly bad; Russia's industrial revolution had only begun, and conditions were rather like those in England in the 1830's and 1840's.

Sources of Discontent

As the 19th century progressed, discontent with conditions in Russia grew rapidly. The peasant and working classes were not happy with their lives. There was also dissatisfaction among the more well-to-do Russians, especially those who thought about the future of their country. Early in the 19th century Russia had been the most powerful state in Europe, but by the end of the century she had become weak and ineffective. In international affairs, the other countries of Europe did not consider Russia a first-rate power. They knew that Russia was militarily weak and that she would not risk war because war might lead to a revolution.

Among the landowners, there was another cause for discontent. Many of them had fallen on evil days after the emancipation of the serfs. Most of the landowners had never been good managers, and even before the emancipation they were badly in debt. The funds they received from the government in return for their lands were quickly spent. More and more frequently they found themselves selling land for whatever it would bring. The speculators, knowing that the landowners were desperate, drove hard bargains. Thus many of the landowners lost their land and gradually sank into poverty. And even those who managed to hold onto their land usually did not have enough capital—or enough knowledge of farming—to farm it effectively.

There was yet one more group of people who were at odds with the czarist government. These were the intellectuals, or the *intelligentsia,* as they are called in Russia. The intelligentsia came chiefly from the ruined nobility, the badly paid government officials, the poor among the churchmen, and the developing middle class. These people read many western European books; and the more they read, the more they became aware of Russia's terrible backwardness. The more they thought about Russia, the more they hoped for changes in the Russian system.

But the czar and his government were dedicated to the idea that nothing at all should be changed. They were afraid that any widespread reforms might bring about the complete collapse of the czarist system. Therefore, they considered even ideas of change to be a threat, and they did their best to stamp out such ideas.

Where did people get such ideas? The czar blamed books and travel. Therefore, books were strictly censored and travel was restricted. Where did the groups who seek change arise and develop?

In the 19th century Russia was one of the most backward countries in Europe. Conditions in the rural areas were particularly bad. This scene is typical. Note the ramshackle buildings, the unpaved street, and the primitive sled.

The czar blamed the universities. Therefore, universities were strictly supervised by the state. Professors were allowed to teach only what the czar and his advisers approved. Only those students who were "reliable" were admitted to the universities, and even they were closely watched. It has been estimated that at one time half the students in Russian universities were paid by the Secret Police to spy on their fellow students.

Obviously, the intelligentsia was most unhappy with the state of affairs in czarist Russia. Most of the intelligentsia were loyal, patriotic Russians who wished only the best for their country. But the czarist government was doing all it could to prevent any kind of change. As a result, many became convinced that Russia's only hope lay in overthrowing the czar and establishing a completely different system of government and society. In other words, they became revolutionaries.

By the end of the 19th century, there were many groups plotting and scheming to overthrow the czar. Each had its own ideas of what kind of changes should be made and how they should be brought about. Each group was hounded by the czarist police; their members often were thrown in jail, sent into exile in Siberia, or forced to leave Russia. Nonetheless, many of the revolutionaries did not become discouraged; their troubles seem only to have strengthened their dedication to revolution.

Of these revolutionaries, Vladimir Ilyich Ulyanov, otherwise known as Lenin, was the most dedicated and the most successful.

Lenin and the Bolsheviks

Lenin was the son of a respected official in the czarist school system. Thus, like most revolutionaries, he sprang not from the peasantry or the proletariat; he was the son of a member of the lesser nobility. There is little in his childhood that seemingly would have turned Vladimir Ilyich into a rebellious spirit. His family apparently was a happy one; his father was not overly strict; he was not made to suffer by "the system." It is often suggested that what turned Lenin into a devoted revolutionary was the execution of his brother by the czarist police when Lenin was seventeen.

Whatever the reason, when he was in his early twenties Lenin was converted to the idea of a Marxist revolution, and he devoted the rest of his life to that idea. As one man who knew Lenin said of him, "No man has been so willing and able to spend every working moment in pursuit of a single goal as has Vladimir Ilyich." And few men have ever been as sure of themselves. To Lenin, anything that was not Marxist was "bourgeois," and therefore bad; and any Marxist ideas that did not agree with his own were "revisionist," which was even worse than being bourgeois. Lenin was absolutely certain that his ideas were correct, and he shaped the Communist party, the Russian Revolution, and Russia itself according to those ideas.

Lenin's Changes in the Idea of the Party

Lenin believed that he was a loyal follower of Karl Marx, strictly following Marx's writings and totally opposed to any revision of them. Yet Lenin, far more than any other man, is responsible for changing Marxism into a *totalitarian* system; that is, a system in which every aspect of life is regulated by the government. It is a system that Marx, if he were alive today, would almost certainly hate.

The first major point at which Lenin departed from Marx was in the nature of the Communist party. Marx seems to have thought of the party as a political party more or less in the western tradition; that is, a party whose ideas and activities were known to everyone and that might be joined by anyone who wished. Lenin, on the other hand, thought of the party as a conspiracy; that is, a small group operating in secret. He thought that the party should be a small, tightly organized band of professional revolutionaries, men whose lives were completely dedicated to the revolution. In other words, he wanted a party made up of men like himself.

The function of this party, according to Lenin, was to educate, inspire, organize, and lead the masses toward the revolution. Without such direction, Lenin felt, the revolution would never occur—especially in Russia. Marx had said that the revolution would inevitably occur in its own good time; but Lenin, unlike Marx, was not content to wait for the revolution; he wanted it to occur while he was still around to enjoy it. And Lenin was convinced that the Russian masses would never become revolutionary all by themselves. They needed a push and a goal and organization, all of which would be supplied by the party.

Lenin's attitude toward the masses was the origin of one of the basic attitudes of Communism: *contempt for the masses*. Lenin realized that a revolution would never occur if the masses were left to themselves; they would have to be pushed into it. In other words, Lenin was either unable or unwilling to admit that the people have enough sense to know what is best for themselves. They do not even have enough sense to know what they want. Decisions must always be made for the people by the party. The people must be told what their true interests are, and the party will see to it that those interests are satisfied.

In forcing his views on the party, Lenin in effect changed the idea of the Communist party from being the vanguard of the working class to being the *master* of the working class.

Lenin's Changes in the Idea of the Revolution

Lenin was faced by a hard contradiction: he thought of himself as an orthodox Marxist, yet he wanted the proletarian revolution to occur in Russia during his own lifetime.

Marx had said that the revolution would occur in the country with the highest development of capitalism; that is, in the country where polarization was most complete and the suffering of the proletariat most severe. Russia was certainly not such a country. She was just emerging from feudalism, and capitalism had barely established itself. The proletariat was small, and it had almost none of the "class consciousness" that Marx considered necessary for the revolution. It was clear that Russia was far from ready for Marx's proletarian revolution.

But Lenin was not prepared to wait for power, so he developed a rather complicated theory to justify his activities. He reasoned that a "bourgeois revolution" was necessary before a proletarian one could take place; the middle class would have to overthrow the czarist autocracy. But the Russian bourgeoisie was very small and not very revolutionary. Therefore the proletariat, acting together with the peasantry, which in Russia made up the great majority of the population, must take charge and force the bourgeois revolution. After this revolution had been accomplished, the peasant-proletarian alliance would continue to cooperate in developing the economy—so long as it was in the proletariat's interest to do so.

Party Congresses

At this time the official name of the Russian Communist party was the *Russian Social-Democratic Labor Party,* or *R.S.D.L.P.* The leaders of the party held meetings, called *congresses,* at which the party's doctrine and actions were determined. Unlike the party congresses of today, these congresses were open forums; that is, differences could be discussed and ideas fought out without the fear that defeat would mean being thrown out of the party.

The first such congress took place in Minsk, in Byelorussia, in 1898. Lenin was not present: the czar's police had arrested him and sent him to Siberia several years before. Most of those who were able to attend were not important party leaders. They met briefly and accomplished little. Their activities were known to the police, and all but one of the delegates were arrested soon after the congress ended.

The Second Party Congress

The second party congress met in Brussels, Belgium, in 1903. The Belgian police interfered, so the conference moved to London, where its business was completed. This congress was better attended than the first; most of the important leaders of Russian Marxism were present.

The second congress was one of the most important in the history of the party. For the first time, a party program and rules were established. Even more important, the congress brought to the open an important disagreement on the nature of the party. On one side there were Lenin and his followers, who wanted the party to be a tightly-knit band of professional revolutionaries. On the other side were those who wanted the party to be more democratically organized and open to anyone who agreed with its goals.

Lenin and his followers were a minority of those at the congress. But there were a number of "accidents"—some, if not all, of which had been arranged by Lenin. As a result, some members of the opposition withdrew from the congress, and Lenin's followers were *temporarily* a majority. Lenin seized this opportunity to attach the label *Bolsheviks,* which is Russian for "majority-ites," to his faction. His opponents, who were actually more numerous than his followers, he labeled *Mensheviks,* or "minority-ites." Lenin was able to make these labels stick. Thus, even though Lenin and his followers were a majority at only one meeting and for only a brief time, his faction was thereafter referred to as the majority. The name gave Lenin a great psychological advantage in later party struggles; for although his followers were a minority, they were called the "majority."

Lenin's attitude toward the naming of his faction indicates the beginning of another basic attitude of Communism: *contempt for the truth.* The name *Bolshevik* is an obvious lie, but Lenin did not care. He did not hesitate to twist the meaning of a word if he thought that doing so would help bring the revolution. Such distortion of language, intended to make something sound better than it really is, has become a major weapon of Communism. It is sometimes referred to as Aesopian language.

In party relations, Lenin always insisted on the principle of *democratic centralism.* By democratic centralism he meant that anyone could freely express his opinions before a decision was made, but that after the decision had been made absolute obedience to it was required. In practice, however, the emphasis on democracy and its give-and-take of ideas was discarded as Lenin increased his domination over the party. Communist propaganda still speaks of democratic centralism; but the chief freedom that it guarantees is nothing but the "freedom" to obey orders.

The second party congress made it clear that Lenin was determined to shape the revolutionary movement according to his own ideas. If this meant that he must separate himself from other equally dedicated revolutionaries, he was willing to do so. He was quite certain of the correctness of his own position. This complete self-confidence would eventually bring him victory, first in the struggle for control of the party, and later in the struggle for control of Russia.

31

Three revolutionaries pose before a street barricade in St. Petersburg, the Russian capital, during the Revolution of 1905.

The Revolution of 1905

In 1905 a revolution—*not* a Bolshevik-led one—broke out in Russia. To the long-standing reasons for discontent—repression, land shortage, poverty—were added the effects of an unpopular war with Japan for which Russia was badly prepared and in which she was disgracefully defeated. The badly equipped, badly supplied, and badly led Russian army and navy suffered defeat after defeat. Inflation, unemployment, and tales of huge profits being made by war profiteers added to the discontent in Russia. Unrest became widespread and swept up men and women of all classes.

Bloody Sunday

The discontent boiled over in St. Petersburg on Sunday, January 22, 1905. Several thousand workers, carrying religious paintings and pictures of the czar, marched toward the Winter Palace, the czar's residence. The demonstrators meant the czar no harm; they intended only to present a petition listing their grievances. But the young cadets who guarded the palace became edgy as the great crowd approached, and they fired on it. More than a hundred people were killed, and several hundred more were wounded.

"Bloody Sunday," as the day came to be known, succeeded in uniting the workers, middle class, and professional people of Russia against the czar. Demands for reform came from all sides. The czar's advisers, believing that one reform would only create demands for further reforms, advised him to make no changes in the system. But the czar soon realized that he was almost without support. Peace with Japan and reforms within Russia were absolutely necessary if czarism was to be saved.

Accordingly, the czar accepted the offer of President Theodore Roosevelt to mediate the Russo-Japanese War. This resulted in the Treaty of Portsmouth, New Hampshire, in which Russia lost land, influence, and prestige. After the treaty had been signed, the czar issued the October Manifesto, which promised the people an effective *Duma,* or congress; free elections; and respect for rights of individuals.

Results of the Revolution

No one is certain whether the czar at any time meant to keep the promises he had made; however, by making promises he was able to divide the opposition. The middle-class parties were satisfied that their chief demands had been met. The revolutionary parties, and the Bolsheviks in particular, believed that they had the czar on the run and wanted to continue the struggle. But the majority of the people were willing to give the czar's new prime minister a chance to put the reforms into effect. By splitting the opposition, the czar's government was able to regain control and to suppress those who still offered opposition.

In the years after 1905, the czar had second thoughts about the concessions he had made. The czar, Nicholas II, was a weak ruler who usually let his mind be made up by whoever happened to be in the room with him. Under the pressure of revolutionary events he introduced some members of the middle class into his circle of advisers, and he established the promised *Duma,* or congress. Once the danger had passed, however, his older advisers persuaded him to get rid of the new men and their advice and to pay as little attention as possible to the Duma. As a result, the Revolution of 1905 was followed by a period of repression. Russia became quiet—so quiet that Lenin became convinced that he would never live to see another revolutionary attempt.

From the point of view of the revolutionary parties, the most important result of the Revolution of 1905 was the development of the *soviet.*

In 1905 workers and revolutionaries in the Russian capital of St. Petersburg had gathered together in small councils, or *soviets*. These soviets were usually organized within factories. Their purpose was to form organizations that could work effectively for the workers' interests and make their demands heard. All the little soviets were represented on the St. Petersburg Soviet of Workers' Deputies, which was led by Leon Trotsky. At that time, Trotsky was not a Bolshevik; he did not become a close associate of Lenin until a dozen years later.

In 1905 the Bolshevik leadership distrusted the soviets, because the soviets had sprung up by themselves and were not controlled by the Bolsheviks. The soviets were not the product of thorough organizational planning. In short, they were not "professional." But Lenin, even in 1905, recognized that they were popular organizations; and he realized that, if the Bolsheviks could control and direct them, they could aid him in achieving his revolution. Lenin was to put the soviets to good use when the next opportunity occurred.

World War I and the February Revolution

On August 1, 1914, Germany declared war on Russia. World War I had begun.

If there was anything that Russia did not need in 1914, it was war. The Russo-Japanese War had proved that Russia could not hope to defeat even a relatively weak power like Japan; now she was facing Germany, at that time the most powerful country in Europe. Defeat in 1904–1905 had nearly brought an end to czarist Russia; cool heads realized that another unsuccessful war would spell its doom. Nevertheless, in the late summer of 1914 Russia blundered into war.

The Course of the War

The Russian people dearly love their motherland; there is nothing that can arouse and unite them so quickly as an attack upon her. The first few months of the war brought forth this traditional response. All elements of the population, even some of the revolutionaries, rallied around the czarist regime.

In August and September, 1914, the Russian army achieved some quick successes. But this was to prove the high point of the war for Russia. Germany withdrew a part of her forces from France and sent them to the Russian front. The territory that the czar's troops had won was speedily recaptured; and large slices of western Russia, including Poland, Lithuania, and parts of the Ukraine and Byelorussia, were seized as well. From that time on, the course of Russian fortunes ran steadily downhill.

A sense of approaching doom hung over Russia from 1915 on. Food shortages developed—and there was no hope of eliminating them, because most of Russia's able-bodied men were away at the front. The tilling of the fields was left to women, children, and old men. There was also a shortage of military supplies. There were times when only the soldiers in the front line of an attack had guns and ammunition; those behind were armed with axes, knives, and scythes. When a man in front fell, the man behind him would pick up his weapon and continue firing. To increase production, the goverment offered huge bonuses to manufacturers, and a few people made fortunes. Anybody who had anything to sell profited greatly. But for most of the people of Russia, the war meant hard work, long hours, little food—and little hope.

The news from home could hardly encourage the men in the front lines. It fit in closely with what revolutionary agitators were telling them: that this was not their war, but that of the capitalist exploiters; they could expect nothing from it but death, while the fat capitalist industrialists were making millions. Lenin's followers preached that the German soldiers were in exactly the same position as the Russian. Neither had any grievance against the other; both were fighting somebody else's—the capitalists'—war. Let the fighting men of both sides unite, urged Lenin. Let them turn the imperialist war into a revolutionary war. Let the exploited "turn the guns of the exploiters against the exploiters." By 1916 many Russian soldiers, although not turning on their "exploiters," at least were unwilling to continue the war. The number of desertions grew alarmingly.

The Collapse of Czarism

Considering the condition of the Russian economy and the Russian army in 1914, it is doubtful that any Russian government could have waged a successful war against Germany. But the czar's government made it absolutely impossible. Nicholas II, who was not intelligent and could never make up his mind, was surrounded by selfish men of little understanding. Furthermore, he was always under the influence of his neurotic wife, who was in turn under the thumb of an insane monk named Rasputin. Rasputin had convinced the czarina (empress) that only his prayers and magic charms could

Brown Brothers
Czar Nicholas II

Brown Brothers
Grigori Rasputin

save the life of her sickly son. She would not allow the czar to expel the evil-minded and unprincipled monk from the court; and gradually Rasputin gained a strong influence over government appointments and other important matters. Rasputin's influence was eliminated only by his murder by members of the nobility.

But by this time, December, 1916, it would have taken much more than the elimination of Rasputin to save the czar's throne. The Duma, the Russian congress, which before the war had had little power, gradually felt itself being called upon to perform more and more of the tasks that the czar's government could not handle. France and Great Britain, who were allied with Russia in the war against Germany and Austria, found that they could rely on the Duma to get things done. The leaders of the Duma urged the czar to give them greater responsibility in the government; but the czar refused to do so.

In March, 1917, strikes and demonstrations for food increased in number. Riots broke out in Petrograd.* The czar called upon the

* Because St. Petersburg was a German name, the name of the capital was changed to Petrograd in 1914. The name was changed to Leningrad in 1924.

Petrograd garrison of the army to suppress the riots, as they had done many times before. But this time the soldiers refused, and stood by as the rioters broke into bakery shops. By March 12, many of the regiments stationed in Petrograd had mutinied and joined with the rioters.

The Duma met that day; and at the end of the day, March 12, 1917, the Duma announced that it had taken over the government. The czar was without army support and could do nothing; three days later he abdicated. The hated autocracy of Russia had at last been overthrown.*

The Provisional Government and the October Revolution

Russia had had a revolution, but it certainly was not *the* revolution that Lenin dreamed of. The new government was headed by members of the nobility and the middle class; it was scarcely "proletarian" in nature. And, most important of all to Lenin, neither he nor his faction controlled it.

The Provisional Government

As soon as the czar had abdicated, the Duma set itself up as a *provisional* government; that is, a temporary government that would govern Russia until a permanent one could be established. Although there were great differences among the members of the provisional government, most of them looked forward to a constitutional convention that would establish a republic. Most of the members, too, were firm believers in democracy.

From the beginning the provisional government was faced with overwhelming problems. By far the greatest was the war. The great majority of the Russian people were sick of the war and wanted peace at almost any price. But Russia had allies—France, Great Britain, and, after April, 1917, the United States—who urged that Russia stay in the war. They knew that if Russia left the war, tens of thousands of German troops could be moved to the western front, in France; and they appealed to the provisional government on the basis of honor and with the hopeful promise that the war would soon be won. So the provisional government kept Russia in the war, and

* This revolution is called the "February Revolution" because the Julian calendar, which was then in use in Russia, was thirteen days behind the calendar used in the West and now in the Soviet Union as well. Thus March 12 was, according to the Julian calendar, February 27.

in July launched an attack. At first the attack succeeded; but when the enemy counterattacked, the demoralized Russian troops broke and ran. There could be no doubt that the army had lost its will to fight.

There was discontent among the workers and the peasants as well. They had hoped that the fall of the czar would bring an end to the war, and therefore an end to the food shortages that plagued Russia. As soon as the czar fell, the workers of Petrograd reorganized their soviets; and soon there were similar soviets in almost every city and town in Russia and throughout the army. The soviets became so powerful that they were like a second government, more powerful than the provisional government; but their leaders were timid men who lacked the will to seize complete control.

In the countryside there was hopeless disorder. In many places the peasants took over the land from the landowners, and there were many cases of livestock killed, houses burned, and landowners murdered. The chaos in the countryside meant that soon there was even less food available to the workers in the city.

Clearly, the provisional government was in trouble. At first the government itself was split into many factions, each hoping to move in a different direction. After several months one man, Alexander Kerensky, emerged as its leader. Kerensky was a well-meaning man, and the government that he headed was one of the freest in the world. But Kerensky was faced by many problems that he did not know what to do about—and all too often he did nothing.

The Return of Lenin

In March, 1917, Lenin was in Switzerland. He had been in exile for over ten years.

To get from Switzerland to Russia, one must cross Germany. The German government knew that the provisional government was unsteady, that Lenin would do his best to overthrow it—and that Lenin had been urging that Russia withdraw from the war. Accordingly, the German government arranged to have Lenin transported to Russia in a sealed railway car. Even if Lenin could not remove Russia from the war, the Germans reasoned, he would stir up trouble and thereby help keep Russia weak.

There have been many attempts to prove that Lenin accepted a large sum of money from the Germans as well. The accusation has never been proved. There is little doubt, however, that if Lenin had been offered German money, he would have accepted it. For he did not care who won the war; the war was only for the benefit of "capitalist exploiters." Lenin's one concern was making a revolution, and this seemed to be his opportunity.

Lenin arrived in Petrograd in April, 1917, and immediately began preparing for revolution. His first task was to convince the rest of the Bolsheviks that the revolution must be continued and the provisional government overthrown. Many of the Bolsheviks wanted to give the provisional government a chance to carry out its democratic reforms, and Lenin had to convince them that the time had come for a revolution. In a little more than a month, most of the Bolsheviks had been convinced.

But the Bolsheviks were still a tiny minority. Lenin's next task, therefore, was to increase their power. It seemed to him that the best way to do this was to work through the soviets.

"All Power to the Soviets"

The soviets, or workers' councils, had been suppressed after 1905, but sprang up again immediately after the February Revolution. In May Leon Trotsky returned from the United States, where he had been in exile, and immediately began working to regain the leadership of the soviets. Trotsky had been convinced of the need for a professional party of the kind demanded by Lenin. Therefore, Trotsky worked closely with Lenin, although he did not officially join the Bolsheviks for several months.

Lenin's policy was to attempt to bring the soviets under Bolshevik control. He reasoned that if the soviets could take over the government, and if the Bolsheviks controlled the soviets, the Bolsheviks would be in control of Russia. And so Lenin unfurled the slogan, "All power to the soviets."

In July, on the heels of the failure of the July offensive, the soviets attempted an uprising against the provisional government. The Bolshevik leaders, believing that the time for the seizure of power was not yet at hand, argued against the uprising. As they were unable to prevent the uprising, the Bolsheviks joined it. The attempt failed. Trotsky was arrested, and Lenin fled to Finland.

The failure of the July uprising convinced Lenin that the soviets could not be depended upon. He could not control them; they would not follow his commands. Now Lenin changed his slogan from "All power to the soviets" to one advocating that the Bolsheviks seize power and declare themselves the government.

Despite the fact that the top Bolshevik leadership was either in prison or in exile, the Bolshevik organization continued to function, and Bolshevik ranks continued to grow.

Alexander Kerensky (1881–),
prime minister of the Russian
provisional government from
July to November, 1917.

Brown Brothers

The Kornilov Uprising

Kerensky had become prime minister after the July uprising.
Soon after, General Kornilov was named commander-in-chief of the
army. Much as he feared the Bolsheviks, Kerensky feared a military
takeover of the government even more; and when General Kornilov
made certain demands, Kerensky became suspicious. As Kornilov
became more popular and powerful, Kerensky was increasingly
alarmed at the threat of an attempt to overthrow his government.
Finally in early September he ordered Kornilov's dismissal. The
general defied the command and prepared to march on Petrograd.

In the capital Kerensky sought to prepare all forces for the attack. The counterrevolution, which Kornilov was said to represent,
had to be stopped at all costs, said Kerensky. Trotsky, who was still
in prison, agreed. If Kornilov triumphed, he reasoned, the revolution was definitely finished. On the other hand, if the Kerensky
government remained in power, the Bolsheviks would still have an
excellent opportunity to seize power for themselves.

Accordingly, Trotsky ordered the Bolshevik-controlled forces in
the capital to fight on Kerensky's side. The scene was set for a
showdown—but the Kornilov forces did not even reach Petrograd,
and his attempt to take over the government collapsed completely.

The assistance of the Bolsheviks in the defense against Kornilov
made Kerensky believe that the Bolsheviks could be relied upon. As

he had few others upon whom he could depend, he soon convinced himself that he could cooperate with them. Trotsky and other Bolshevik leaders who had been arrested were released from prison.

It is doubtful that Kerensky's government, weak as it was, could have long remained in power. But by putting his trust in the Bolsheviks, Kerensky sealed his doom; for Lenin and Trotsky were both now convinced that the time for their own seizure of power was at hand.

"All Power to the Soviets" Again

Many factors led the Bolshevik leaders to the conclusion that it was time to act. One of the most important factors was the September elections in the Petrograd soviets, in which the Bolsheviks won the majority of the seats. Lenin could now use the soviets for his own purposes.

Once again Lenin changed the leading slogan; once again it became "All power to the soviets." In later years Lenin was accused of inconsistency (or perhaps even having been wrong) in adopting the slogan, dropping it, then picking it up again. But Lenin declared that such ideas were ridiculous. It was merely that in July the "situation" had changed. Now it had changed once again, requiring new "tactics." Said Lenin: It is ridiculous to be bound by dead words.

On September 28, 1917, the Central Committee of the party met and determined to plan the uprising. In Lenin's absence, Trotsky was clearly in command, even though he had only recently entered the ranks of the party. In the following weeks Trotsky worked hard at preparing the plan of the uprising.

On October 23 Lenin, in disguise, slipped back into Petrograd to attend a decisive meeting of the party's Central Committee. The majority of the Committee were convinced that the time was right for an uprising, and they set the date.

On October 26 the soviets established a Military Revolutionary Committee with Trotsky as its chairman. The committee was formed, said the Bolsheviks, to help protect the city from the Germans. Under the camouflage of this committee, the final touches were put on the military preparations for the seizure of power.

With each passing day the intentions of the Bolsheviks became more and more obvious. But those who opposed the Bolsheviks were divided, disheartened, and suspicious of one another. The Kerensky government could not decide what to do. Only at the last moment did Kerensky seek loyal forces to defend his position, and by then

The climax of the swift, almost bloodless seizure of the Russian government by the Bolsheviks was their capture of the Winter Palace in Petrograd on November 7, 1917. Above, the Bolshevik troops advance toward the Winter Palace. A few minutes later, most of the important members of the provisional government had been taken prisoner; Kerensky, however, escaped to western Europe.

it was too late. Earlier, a man of firm purpose and determination might have saved the situation.

But in the autumn of 1917 Lenin was the only leader of firm purpose and determination in all Russia. The Bolsheviks were far from able to count upon the support of the majority of the Russian people. But Russian political life was in a state of hopeless chaos; and in the midst of that chaos, the only order was to be found in the party led by Lenin. Thus it was to them that the authority fell.

The October Revolution

On the evening of November 6, and early in the morning of November 7,* strategic buildings in Petrograd were occupied by the Military Revolutionary Committee.

On the evening of November 7, the revolutionary forces began their assault on the Winter Palace, the seat of government. The

* October 25 by the Julian calendar. See the footnote on page 36.

building was only lightly held by a few cadets and a few members of the Women's Brigade. The victorious attack was soon over. The government surrendered. One person had lost his life in the fighting.

Thus on November 7, 1917, came to an end the only free government that Russia has ever known.

aids to learning

Check the facts

1. Why would Marx expect a revolution to occur in Great Britain rather than in Russia? In what ways was Russia unprepared for a Marxist revolution?

2. Name four groups of people in Russia that were dissatisfied with the czarist government at the end of the nineteenth century.

3. How did Lenin differ from Marx concerning the membership and purpose of the Communist party? What was Lenin's attitude toward the masses of the Russian people?

4. Name the functions Lenin thought the Communist party should perform for the people. How did Lenin change Marx's idea that the Communist party was to be the "vanguard of the working class"?

5. Give the name, date, place of meeting, and accomplishments of the first and second congresses of the Russian Social-Democratic Labor Party.

6. Why was the revolution in 1905 not a Bolshevik-led one? Name five reasons for the discontent of the Russian people in 1905. What classes of people were united by the events of "Bloody Sunday"? Name the reforms finally granted by the czar. What circumstances enabled the czar to regain control of the government?

7. What was the plan of organization and purpose of the soviets? What was the attitude of the Bolsheviks toward them?

8. Why was the Russian army largely unsuccessful in the war against Germany? What events led to the overthrow of the czar's government in March, 1917?

9. What was the purpose of the provisional government? What were the problems confronting it?

10. How and why did Germany aid Lenin to return to Russia in April, 1917? What part did the soviets play in enabling Lenin to bring about the Bolshevik October Revolution?

11. Why did Kerensky ally with the Bolsheviks? Why did the Bolsheviks aid Kerensky?

12. List the events from September 28, 1917—November 7, 1917 that brought the Bolsheviks into power. Why is the Revolution of March 12, 1917 called the "February Revolution" and the one of November 7 the "October Revolution"?

Know word meanings

Be able to define and use correctly the following terms:

autocracy	revisionist	soviet
czar	vanguard	Duma
serf	totalitarianism	provisional government
intelligentsia	democratic centralism	

Identify names

These names are significant in the Russian revolutions of 1917. What connection did each have with the revolutionary events?

Lenin	Trotsky	Bolsheviks	Mensheviks
Rasputin	Kerensky	Kornilov	

Use the map

1. On a map of Russia indicate, by coloring or shading, these divisions:

"Great" Russia	Ukraine	Byelorussia	Estonia	Latvia
Lithuania	Georgia	Armenia	Azerbaijan	

2. Locate, by writing the name on the map, these places:
Seas: Baltic, Black, Caspian; *Rivers:* Dnieper (Dnepr), Don, Volga; *Mountains:* Ural, Caucasus; *Cities:* Moscow, St. Petersburg (Petrograd, Leningrad), Minsk.

Do something extra

1. On an outline map of the Soviet Union show, by using different colors, the extent of Russian territory at approximately these dates: (1) 1000 (2) 1500 (3) 1725 (4) 1800 (5) 1900 (6) 1960.

2. Read and report on Lenin's *What Is to Be Done?* This book clearly sets forth Lenin's ideas of the role of the party, and its principles are still the basis of Communist action everywhere.

3. Read and report on the experiences of Lenin or Trotsky while political exiles in Siberia.

4. Make a study of some of the events of the Russo-Japanese War.

5. Report on the extent of Rasputin's control over the czar's government. Find out more about the character and personality of Czar Nicholas II.

6. Find the answers to these questions: (1) Where did Trotsky live while in the United States and what did he do to earn a living? (2) What happened to Kerensky after the downfall of his government? (3) What were the immediate circumstances of the czar's abdication? What became of the royal family?

7. Write a report on Lenin's return to Petrograd in October, 1917, and his part in the events of October 23–November 7.

8. Are there any similarities in the events of the first year of the French Revolution and the first year of the Russian Revolution?

9. Read and report on one of the following books:
   (a) Moorehead, Alan, *The Russian Revolution*
   (b) Wolfe, Bertram, *Three Who Made a Revolution*
   (c) Shub, David, *Lenin*

*A Bolshevik propaganda photo, taken soon after
the October Revolution, shows "bourgeoisie at work."
Lenin soon discovered, however, that there was more
to establishing a new society than simply forcing
former businessmen to work with picks and shovels.*

André de Saint-Rat

3

THE SOVIET UNION UNDER LENIN

In November, 1917, Lenin took over a country that was backward, devastated, hungry, and demoralized. There were many jobs to be tackled. Bolshevik rule had to be consolidated. A new system of government had to be devised. Able men had to be found to operate the government. Industry and agriculture had to be put to work again. The transportation system had to be reorganized. The promises to provide "bread, land, and peace" had to be carried out.

These were the tasks that Lenin faced in the first years after the revolution. In facing them, he discovered that many of his notions of what life would be like after the revolution were not coming true.

Lenin, however, was not the kind of man to give up. He was determined that Communism would work. Even more, he was determined that the Bolsheviks would remain in power, and he dedicated himself to that goal as earlier he had dedicated himself to the revolution. But in order to keep his party in power, Lenin was forced to take many emergency measures that conflicted with Marxist doctrine. Gradually these emergency measures established themselves; they became permanent features of Communism. Thus Communism moved several steps farther from the society predicted by Marx—and several steps closer to the totalitarianism that it was soon to become.

The Russian Civil War

The Bolsheviks seized control of the Russian government in Petrograd on November 7, 1917. Within a few days the Bolsheviks had seized control in most of the cities and towns of Russia.

45

The Bolsheviks, however, were far from controlling all of the vast Russian empire. In several areas movements arose that were controlled by people loyal to the czar; other groups were simply anti-Bolshevik. There were pockets of resistance everywhere in the country. Several of the national minorities on the border of the empire took advantage of the chaos in Russia to declare themselves independent. And a part of western Russia—soon to be much enlarged—was occupied by the German armies.

The Treaty of Brest-Litovsk

Almost immediately after their seizure of power, the Bolsheviks began negotiating a peace treaty with Germany. Trotsky was the principal negotiator. The negotiations took place at Brest-Litovsk in Byelorussia.

Russia was in no position to bargain. At first Trotsky tried to get a few concessions from the Germans in return for Russia's leaving the war. But the Germans knew that what was left of the Russian army could not back up Trotsky's demands; and they also knew that conditions within Russia made it important that the Bolsheviks sign a peace treaty at almost any price.

Still Trotsky hesitated. He refused to sign a treaty, but he announced that the war was nonetheless over. His slogan was "Neither war nor peace." But the Germans would not play Trotsky's game, and began to advance again. In February and early March, 1918, the Germans completed the occupation of the Baltic area, pushed far into the Ukraine, and advanced into the Crimea. No one in Petrograd was certain how far they would go. Lenin convinced his colleagues on the party Central Committee that they had no alternative but to submit to the German terms. On March 3, 1918, the Treaty of Brest-Litovsk was signed. Under the terms of the treaty, Russia lost 26 per cent of her population and 27 per cent of her farmland.

Independence Movements

As was noted earlier, Russia contains many national minorities. In 1917 and 1918 a number of these minorities on the Russian border took the opportunity presented by Russia's weakness to declare independence. The first was Finland. Soon Estonia, Latvia, Lithuania, Byelorussia, the Ukraine, Georgia, Armenia, and Azerbaijan had also set themselves up as independent republics.

The Whites and the Reds

Although the Bolsheviks controlled the government in a large part of Russia, they were still troubled by many opponents. Among

During the hectic years from 1914 to 1921, boundaries in eastern Europe changed many times. This map indicates the boundaries of the Russian Empire before the outbreak of World War I; the line of the farthest advance of the German armies into Russia; the areas that set up independent governments after World War I; and the boundary established at the end of the Civil War.

the most dangerous of these were the so-called "White" armies. The White armies were led by officers of the czarist army, and gradually came to include many others who were opposed to the Bolsheviks. Throughout the Civil War the Bolsheviks, who held the center of Russia, were attacked by White armies, who held most of the surrounding areas.

The Bolsheviks were not particularly strong, and they had made many enemies. But the Whites were not very smart. The Whites often antagonized the peasants by threatening to return the land that they had seized after the revolution to its pre-revolutionary owners. Furthermore, the anti-Bolshevik movements that existed in most of the border areas were unable to agree with one another on policies or on who was to lead. They could not even co-ordinate their attacks. The Bolshevik, or "Red," army, which was brilliantly organized and led by Leon Trotsky, therefore had the advantage of having to fight on only one front at a time. Eventually the Red army succeeded in wiping out the White armies; but the Civil War lasted three years, and it left Russia devastated.

The Bolsheviks also had to cope with small forces of foreign troops from Great Britain, France, Japan, and the United States. The original reason for sending these troops was to prevent Russian military supplies from falling into the hands of the Germans. After Germany had surrendered, the troops remained in Russia, although no one seemed to have a very clear idea of what they were there for.

The Allies had just completed a major war with Germany and were in no mood for further war. France and Britain, in particular, were exhausted. Although their governments had no sympathy for the Bolsheviks and would like to have seen Lenin overthrown, they were not prepared to enter a full-scale war in Russia. Thus, their troops in Russia did almost nothing and eventually were withdrawn. The principal result of the allied intervention was that it gave Lenin an opportunity to make loud and sometimes effective propaganda noises: "capitalist imperialists" were making wicked attempts to overthrow the Bolshevik "proletarian government." Even today, Communists continue to cite the intervention of 1918 in their propaganda as an indication of the capitalist desire to destroy Communism.

During the Civil War, Russia had also to deal with a Polish invasion. The Polish government felt that this moment of Russian weakness provided an excellent opportunity to settle old scores with Russia. The Polish troops struck deep into Russian territory; but Trotsky's army was able to launch a successful counterattack, and the Poles were driven back into their own territory.

The Formation of the U.S.S.R.

The Bolsheviks gradually consolidated their power in Russia. They also were able to bring most of the border areas that had declared independence under their control. Only Finland, Estonia, Latvia, and Lithuania were able to preserve their independence.*

In order to give the impression that the border areas had rejoined Russia of their own free will, "treaties" were signed with the Communist puppet governments of those areas. According to these trea-

* The independence of Estonia, Latvia, and Lithuania lasted only until 1940.

André de Saint-Rat

The Bolshevik success in the Civil War, like the October Revolution, could never have been brought about without the unceasing efforts of Lenin. Above, Lenin addresses Red Army troops about to be sent to the Polish front in 1920.

ties, the border areas remained independent republics but were joined to Russia in a very close alliance. In theory, each of these republics remains free to withdraw from the alliance at any time; in practice, they are part of Russia, completely controlled by the Kremlin.*

To indicate that the country had become a "union" of free and independent states, the name of Russia was changed to *Union of Soviet Socialist Republics*. The name is often shortened to *Soviet Union* or referred to by its initials, *U.S.S.R.*

Note that the name *Union of Soviet Socialist Republics* nowhere mentions *Russia*. The Bolsheviks hoped that the new name would please the reconquered border areas, most of whose people hated the Russians. The change was also intended to give Russia a name that could be used when Russia expanded to include additional territories. Nevertheless, the U.S.S.R. is still Russia. The Russians rule the land, just as they did under the czars; and under the Communists there is in many ways even less toleration of non-Russian groups than there had been under the czars.

* The capital of Russia was moved from Petrograd to Moscow in 1918. In Moscow many of the major government and Communist party offices are located in an ancient fortified area at the center of the city called the "Kremlin."

In considering this name, it must be noted that the Communists use the words *socialist* and *socialism* in a way that is quite different from that of socialists in western Europe and the United States. In these countries, the socialists believe in government ownership of all or part of industry; most (but not all) of these parties have drawn many of their ideas from Karl Marx. But these parties— and this is most important—believe that socialism must be brought about by *democratic* means. In other words, they hope to put socialism into effect by being voted into office by the people, and they believe in preserving the freedom of the individual. In the Soviet Union, on the other hand, *socialism* has come to mean, above all else, the dictatorship of the Communist party. The often ruthless actions of the Soviet power are explained away by saying that they are temporary and will disappear when Communism is achieved. The Communists will admit that Communism, as predicted by Marx, does not yet exist in the Soviet Union or anywhere else; but they also maintain that what they call socialism is a preliminary step in that direction.

War Communism and the New Economic Policy

When the Bolsheviks first came to power, they thought that some of the characteristics of Communism could be put into practice immediately. They were soon to discover that Russia was not prepared for such radical changes. Their attempts to practice Communism failed. Certainly the Civil War that was raging across Russia did not help them.

The presence at all levels of opposition to the Bolsheviks, including in particular members of non-Bolshevik revolutionary parties, required strict measures. As early as November 9, 1917, only two days after the revolution, freedom of the press came to an end. Less than a month later all non-Bolshevik newspapers were outlawed. And on December 7, 1917, the Bolshevik secret police force, called the *Cheka,* was created. In the "Red Terror" that followed, the Cheka ruthlessly struck out at all the enemies of the Bolsheviks. It continued to operate throughout the Civil War.

The Bolsheviks recognized that the task of conquering and reorganizing Russia would be a difficult one. It required not only tough political measures but tough economic ones as well. The economic measures were incorporated into a policy called *War Communism,* which was a policy based more on experimentation and the needs of the moment than on Marxist doctrine. War Communism asked a great deal of the Russian people—more than most of them were willing to give for the sake of Bolshevism.

Agriculture under War Communism

As the Reds, Whites, and Interventionists advanced and re-treated across the Russian countryside, they destroyed everything in their paths. When there was enough time and enough seed grain, the peasants would replant their destroyed fields, only to see them devastated once again as the battle line returned to their section. Understandably the peasants became disheartened.

In 1917 one of Lenin's promises had been that the Bolsheviks would give land to the peasants. He had made this promise because it was the only way to gain peasant support; but after the revolution he would have ignored the promise if that had been possible. Marxist doctrine held that a land-owning peasantry was among the most conservative elements of society, stubbornly unwilling to surrender its own possessions in the name of a Communist ideal. But Lenin had no choice: he needed peasant support (or at least their neutrality), and so Lenin recognized the division of the land that had already taken place in many areas, and he authorized it elsewhere.

However, Lenin also needed the produce of the countryside to feed the soldiers and the city-dwellers. As far as the peasants were concerned, Lenin's money was no good to them unless it could be used to purchase cloth, thread, needles, tea, and other things that they themselves could not produce. But these things were not available in Russia in 1918–1920. The peasants, therefore, did not bother to raise food to be sold; they produced only enough for themselves.

The Bolsheviks obviously could not allow this state of affairs to continue. To obtain grain, they sent military detachments into the countryside. These detachments were ordered to take all grain that, in their opinion, the peasants did not need for themselves. Often they simply took all of it, leaving nothing for the peasants. Not surprisingly, the peasants did not like this policy; and the policy did not make them any more willing to grow more grain to help the Bolsheviks.

Industry under War Communism

In the cities, the situation was even worse. Rationing of food had been in force all through the Civil War, but only rarely was there enough food to fill even the small promised ration. Furthermore, the amount of food a worker received depended upon the importance of his work. Obviously those workers whose jobs were considered not important were unhappy. As a result, many city dwellers (many of whom had only recently moved to the cities) returned to their farm villages. By 1921 many of Russia's largest cities were almost abandoned. For example, the population of Petrograd dropped from 2,300,000 in 1917 to 700,000 in 1919.

The Russians left the cities not only because of a shortage of food but also because of a shortage of work. In many industries there were not enough supplies to keep the factories going. The industry that was still operating was horribly mismanaged by the Bolsheviks.

It was a favorite belief of Marxists that after their revolution the workers would be capable of managing their own factories. But the Marxian theory was for a highly developed country with a large number of skilled workmen, and Russia was not that kind of country. Nevertheless, almost immediately after the revolution the Bolsheviks seized control of the "commanding heights" of industry, such as the power plants, the steel mills, and the railroads. These were placed in the hands of the workers. Lenin soon realized his mistake; but he refused to return the industries to the "bourgeois capitalists" who had formerly operated them, and there were few trained industrial experts among the Bolsheviks. Industry was forced to limp along as best it could. By 1920 Russia's industrial production was less than 14 per cent of what it had been in 1913.

The Kronstadt Uprising

In late 1920 and early 1921 discontent grew both in the cities and in the countryside throughout Russia. In almost half the provinces of Russia there were outbreaks of peasant resistance. In the cities the workers had become disillusioned; many of them had thought that taking the property of the capitalists and dividing it among themselves would make them all wealthy. The revolution had brought them neither peace nor plenty, but instead a continuation of war and shortages.

The growing unrest reached a climax in March, 1921, when the sailors of Kronstadt, a fortress in the harbor of Petrograd, rose up against the Bolsheviks. The uprising was particularly serious to the Kremlin leaders because the Kronstadt sailors had been considered the most loyal of the Bolshevik forces. But the men of Kronstadt had been peasants before they became sailors, and they remained peasants at heart; and their letters from home and the reports of comrades returning from leave told them of the hunger and the Bolshevik seizures of grain in the countryside.

The men of Kronstadt did not want to return to czarism or the provisional government; rather, they demanded, among other things, that the Bolsheviks carry out the promises of the revolution of freedom and equality. The call went out for a "third revolution" (February and October, 1917, were the first two) to get rid of the Bolsheviks and to establish "soviets without Bolsheviks." The men of Kronstadt felt, as many who have since become disillusioned with the international Communist movement have felt, that there was nothing wrong with the ideals of Communism, but that the movement itself and its leadership had wandered from the path.

On March 1, the sailors began their rebellion. On March 5 Leon Trotsky arrived in Petrograd and demanded the unconditional surrender of the rebels. The rebels refused, and Trotsky ordered the Red Army to march across the ice and attack the fortress. The men in the fortress fought fiercely, hoping that aid would come from outside or that all Russia would rise up against the Bolsheviks. The Reds fought with equal determination, for they knew that if this battle were lost Bolshevism would probably collapse. And on March 18 the Red army overcame the last resistance of the fortress. The defenders of Kronstadt had failed.

When the Kronstadt detachment had been defeated, the last substantial attempt to bring Communism under the control of the people was also defeated. From that time on, there would be no real challenge to the idea of the Communist party as the absolute ruler over the Russian people.

"Two Steps Forward, One Step Back"

After the Civil War had ended, Trotsky recommended that War Communism be carried over into the postwar period. According to his plan, the entire population of Russia would be made into a well-disciplined force ready to carry out the orders of the party leaders instantly and without question. Trotsky believed that using these methods would bring Communism more quickly.

Lenin, however, realized that Russia was exhausted, and the revolt at Kronstadt convinced him that a plan like Trotsky's would drive the Russian people past the breaking point. The Bolsheviks were not yet so strong that they could completely ignore the feelings of the people. Lenin therefore resorted to a tactic that he had used before: "Two steps forward, one step back." The time had come to back up a little. A small retreat now would make possible a greater advance later.

The Kronstadt uprising occurred at the same time as the Tenth Party Congress; and before the last gun had been silenced at Kronstadt, Lenin appeared before the congress to propose a new tactic.

Leon Trotsky (1877–1940) was Lenin's closest associate in organizing the October Revolution and consolidating Bolshevik rule in Russia. Trotsky negotiated the Treaty of Brest-Litovsk and organized and led the Red Army in the Russian Civil War.

André de Saint-Rat

Lenin told the congress that Russia faced economic collapse. The ability of the workers and peasants to produce had been so ruined and exhausted that, as Lenin put it, "all other considerations must be put aside in order to increase production." What Lenin actually meant was that concessions would have to be made to the peasants and to people who were experienced in industry and commerce. Making these concessions was the only way that Russia could be put back on her feet.

Lenin implied that the Russian people were no longer (or perhaps not yet) ready to put forth their best efforts simply because they believed in the revolution or because the Bolsheviks told them to. The people had to be offered something more than hard work and promises of a golden future. They had to be convinced that effort brought extra reward; that the one who gave more, got more. Too many Russians, said Lenin, were not working hard because they believed that under Communism all received equally, regardless of effort.

The members of the congress were not happy with Lenin's message. They were Marxist revolutionaries, full of revolutionary fervor. They had driven themselves hard and they had, they thought, accomplished much. There was still much to do, however. They were frustrated and disappointed because the people were not as inspired and were not willing to be endlessly pushed. With great reluctance, but unanimously, the party leaders accepted Lenin's analysis and his new approach. N.E.P., the *New Economic Policy,* was born.

The New Economic Policy

Under War Communism, the state had taken from the peasants everything beyond *what the state thought* the peasants needed to stay alive. In contrast, under the New Economic Policy the peasants were promised that the state would take only a fixed percentage of their crops, no matter how much they grew. The peasants were also promised that any left-over produce could be sold on the open market; it would not be confiscated, as it had been in the past.

In the cities and towns, small shops and factories were allowed to reopen under partial private ownership. Members of the middle class, whose businesses had been confiscated, were now encouraged to take the lead in operating them.

The word went out that Russia was returning to "normalcy" because capitalism had returned on a small scale. But Lenin and his followers knew that the New Economic Policy was only temporary; as soon as the economy was working again, the next steps toward Communism could be taken.

As the New Economic Policy was beginning, Russia suffered another great misfortune. Drought, sandstorms, and pestilence struck along the Volga River, in the heart of Russia. Crops were ruined, and there were no stockpiles. As a result, Russia suffered one of the worst famines in its history. It has been estimated that nine million people died in 1921–1922 as a direct or indirect result of lack of food. In some parts of Russia the starving peasants resorted to cannibalism.

The situation became so desperate that the Bolsheviks had to ask the hated American capitalists to extend relief aid. That more Russians did not starve was due to the help provided by the American Relief Administration directed by Herbert Hoover (later to become President of the United States). It is possible that the Hoover Mission saved the Bolshevik regime. The Communists, however, have seldom expressed gratitude for the help given by the United States at that time. To admit that the United States is capable of an act of kindness would contradict the image that the U.S.S.R. seeks to spread of the United States as a cruel enslaver of free peoples.

In spite of this initial setback, the New Economic Policy soon became a success. Between 1920 and 1926 grain collections rose 400 per cent; coal production doubled; and the manufacture of cotton textiles tripled. Retail trade revived, and as much as three-fourths of the trade was carried on by private traders, who received the name "Nepmen." By 1927 Russia had surpassed the production figures of 1913 in many areas.

The New Economic Policy represented a retreat by the Bolsheviks; but it was, all things considered, a minor retreat. The Bolshevik leadership still held the "commanding heights" of industry, and it employed four fifths of the industrial workers. It controlled banking, transportation, and foreign trade. Most important, it still held the government—and that, if anything, more tightly than before.

Two things about the New Economic Policy should be remembered. First, slight though its concessions may have been, they were enough to get Russian agriculture and industry rolling again. Second, successful as the New Economic Policy may have been, the Bolsheviks were never happy about the "reforms" that they had been forced to put into effect. They hated using capitalism to get started on the road to Communism, and they promised themselves that at the first possible moment they would throw out the New Economic Policy and all its changes.

The Elimination of Political Parties

The Kronstadt uprising had another effect in addition to the New Economic Policy. It ended all non-Bolshevik activity in Russia. Looking back, it seems that this was inevitable, because one of the basic Bolshevik beliefs was that all outside groups must be either controlled or destroyed. But Kronstadt was the event that finally brought it about.

During the Civil War the weakened remnants of other parties had continued to function, although they played no role in the government. By 1921 the Bolsheviks had come to regard the continuing existence of these parties as a threat.

The war with Germany, the revolutions, and the Civil War had resulted in the almost complete disappearance of the working class, from which the Bolsheviks had drawn their support. Most of the Russian workers had not been in the cities for very long, and in the chaos of the Civil War many returned to their homes in the country. As a result, the Bolsheviks were left virtually without support. The Bolsheviks still claimed to represent the working class and to act on its behalf—but there was no working class left. Actually the Bolsheviks acted only for themselves and represented only themselves.

Under these circumstances, the Bolshevik leadership feared that opposition to them might become organized, and therefore dangerous. They determined to get rid of anyone who might be able to lead the opposition to them. Many of the leaders of the Mensheviks and other parties were arrested and shot. Others survived—for a few years. Others fled to other countries. Still others, when they were allowed to do so, changed their coats and became Bolsheviks.

Socialism in One Country

By 1921 the Bolsheviks had successfully defeated the Whites, the Poles, and the other political parties. They found themselves in control of a weakened and somewhat shrunken but still gigantic Russia. But they stood alone. They were at the head of the only Communist power in the world. This was not at all the kind of situation that they had expected would develop.

The International Revolution

When the Bolsheviks seized control in November, 1917, Lenin asked only that his revolutionary government be able to last for a few months. He believed that the revolution would be crushed unless it quickly spread to other, more highly industrialized countries. It was impossible for Lenin to believe that the leading capitalist states could or would permit the Bolsheviks to exist for very long.

During the period of the Civil War (1918–1920) Lenin continually hoped for a revolution abroad. Whenever news arrived of a Communist uprising in Germany or Italy or Hungary, his hopes rose. This was it; the international proletariat was at last arising. But the revolutions always collapsed and Lenin's hopes were dashed.

Gradually, almost without realizing his own change of outlook, Lenin realized that two things that Marxist theory had led him to expect were not going to occur after all. First, the capitalist powers were not going to interfere in force. Second, the international proletariat was not going to arise. This meant that the Communists had Russia, but only Russia, in their control. No one was going to take Russia away from them, but at the same time no one was going to help them rebuild and develop Russia. Neither Marx nor Lenin had believed that socialism could develop in isolation. But there seemed almost no chance that a revolution would occur anywhere else. Therefore, Lenin had no choice; he had to develop socialism in one country.*

The Significance of Socialism in One Country

"Socialism in One Country" soon came to mean that whatever was good for the Soviet Union was good for international Communism. It means that if the Soviet Union were to be destroyed, the cause of Communism would be set back for generations; therefore,

---

* Although Lenin undoubtedly arrived at this conclusion and set the policy of "socialism in one country," the term is usually identified with Joseph Stalin, Lenin's successor, who announced it to the world in 1924.

As part of their effort to destroy any loyalty to czarism that might have remained in Russia, the Bolsheviks ordered that all monuments that did not have "historic" or "artistic" interest should be destroyed. Above, two small boys view the toppled head of a statue of Czar Alexander III in Moscow.

the welfare of the Soviet state always has to come first. It means that Communists in other countries must always look to the Soviet Union for leadership, because the only true Communism is Russian Communism.

In short, "Socialism in One Country" eventually changed Communism from a genuinely international movement to an instrument for promoting the well-being of the Russian Soviet state and the Russian Communists who control that state.

The Comintern

The Russian leaders had decided to concentrate on the development of their own country, but they had not abandoned the belief that an international revolution would eventually occur. All that they had given up was the idea that the revolution would probably occur in the near future.

In 1919 Lenin founded the *Communist International,* or *Comintern.* The purpose of the Comintern was to unite Communist movements throughout the world under a single leadership that would direct the world revolution. Not surprisingly, the so-called "International" was Russian-controlled from the very outset.

The Comintern shaped the Communist parties in the rest of the world according to the Bolshevik image. In other words, world Communism became the same thing as Russian Communism: a tightly-

André de Saint-Rat

In some parts of Russia, World War 1 and the Russian Civil War caused the slaughter of so many horses that men were pressed into service to pull the plow. Under "War Communism" everyone in Russia was expected to work in whatever way was necessary to help the Bolshevik cause in the Civil War.

organized, well-disciplined conspiracy, operating largely in secret and outside the law. And, because of "Socialism in One Country," the international Communist conspiracy soon became simply an agent of the Russian Soviet government. Although the Comintern occasionally went through the motions of holding congresses, it (and its member parties throughout the world) took no steps that did not originate in the Kremlin.

In order to make the United States and Great Britain think that Communists were nice people and no longer in the business of encouraging revolutions, the Russian Communists dissolved the Comintern during World War II. But only the name and the sham congresses disappeared; the various departments of the Comintern continued to function. They still are functioning today, and their purpose has not changed.

The Death of Lenin

Lenin had many qualities that made him a great leader: his determination, his iron will, his confidence in his own judgments, his flexibility, his ability to charm people, his ability to get men who despised one another to work together. Under him the Soviet Union survived revolution, Civil War, counterrevolution, and famine.

The First Illnesses

In 1921 Lenin was fifty-one years old. He had always enjoyed moderately good health. There was every reason to believe that he would be around for many years to guide the Soviet state that he had brought into being.

But such was not to be the case. Late in 1921 he informed the members of the Politburo (the power center of the party and thus of all Russia) that because of his health he found it necessary to be away from the Kremlin. In the following March he returned to the capital and to work, but more and more frequently he was bothered by headaches. Then, on May 22, 1922, while resting at his estate at Gorki, a village on the Volga, Lenin suffered the first of the four strokes that eventually would kill him.

In that first stroke Lenin lost the power to move and to speak. But by the fall of the year he was sufficiently recovered to be able to return to work. At first he tired easily, but with each week he seemed to gain strength. But in December, 1922, he suffered a second stroke.

Lenin's Testament

When he suffered his second stroke, Lenin was already concerned over what would happen to the party after his death. Now, in the first days after his second attack, Lenin turned rather desperately to dictating his "Testament." He warned the party that it could remain in power only if it continued to make common cause with the peasantry and only if it remained united. Then he turned to a consideration of his possible successors.

Although Lenin mentioned the names of all the prominent party leaders, it was apparent that he believed his successor would be either Trotsky or Joseph Stalin. "The relation between them," he wrote, "constitutes, in my opinion, a big half of the danger of a split in the party." Stalin, he warned, "has concentrated enormous power in his hands; and I am not sure that he always knows how to use that power with sufficient caution." As for Trotsky, "he is, to be sure, the most able man in the present Central Committee." But he is guilty of "too far-reaching self-confidence and a disposition to be too much attracted by the purely administrative side of affairs."

Lenin could recommend neither of the candidates whole-heartedly, but he appeared to favor Stalin over Trotsky. However, he warned that a struggle between the two could destroy the party. The struggle that followed Lenin's death did indeed ruin the party—but not in the sense that Lenin had foreseen.

About ten days after Lenin had dictated the "Testament," he made an amendment to it. The amendment indicated that he had had some serious second thoughts about Stalin. He now proposed to the party leadership, in terms that could not be misunderstood, that they "find a way to remove Stalin" from his position of power and replace him with a man "more tolerant, more loyal, more polite and more considerate of comrades, less capricious, etc."

No one can be certain what had happened to make Lenin turn so decisively against Stalin; however, an educated guess can be made. It is known that in December, 1922, Lenin had become greatly concerned about the so-called "Georgian Affair." Lenin had relied upon Stalin (who was a native of Georgia) to handle party affairs in his own native area. About this time, Lenin learned that Stalin had administered Georgia with horrible brutality, bringing it under his control by threats and by all kinds of violence, including murder. It is also possible that Lenin was infuriated by Stalin's behavior towards Krupskaya, Lenin's wife. After Lenin's second stroke, Stalin apparently considered him as good as dead, and therefore felt that he could treat his wife as insolently as he chose. Such behavior would understandably have infuriated Lenin.

Whatever the reason, Lenin became firmly determined to oust Stalin from his responsibility in the party. He was hard at work laying the groundwork for such action at the next Party Congress when —possibly because he was so aroused—Lenin suffered his third stroke in March, 1923.

The Death of Lenin

Lenin hung on to life for ten more months, but his capacity for work had been destroyed. Trotsky (and almost all the rest of the party) continued to hope, against all reason, that Lenin would recover and return to his leading role. Stalin hoped otherwise; he knew well that his own career would be at an end if Lenin should regain strength. But Stalin counted on Lenin's not recovering. He made plans for what he would do after Lenin's death, which finally came on January 21, 1924.

In looking back, Lenin's death clearly spelled the end of any expectation—if there could still have been any—that the revolution would not be transformed into pure barbarism. It is true that under Lenin all opposition was silenced, and even "fractions" within the party were outlawed. But Lenin expected that free debate would always occur within the party itself according to the rule of democratic centralism that debate continues until a decision is made.

To an outside observer, it seems obvious that freedom of debate cannot be limited to party leaders, for the followers will soon begin to debate as well. The Bolsheviks could not permit such a development; for free debate implies opposition, and the party was dedicated to stamping out all opposition. Yet while Lenin still lived, he could insure that at least some exchange of opinion would occur. After he had passed from the scene, however, there was no one who had enough strength of personality to guarantee that more than a single voice would be heard.

With Lenin's death, Russia's age of totalitarianism—the system of government in which every phase of life is planned, directed, and controlled by government—began in earnest.

aids to learning

Check the facts

1. Name five tasks that faced Lenin in the first years after the October Revolution.

2. Why were the Bolsheviks forced to make peace with Germany in March, 1918? What were the terms of the Treaty of Brest-Litovsk?

3. Name the various groups that opposed the Bolsheviks. Why were the anti-Bolsheviks unsuccessful in their attacks against the Bolsheviks?

4. Why did Russia change its name to *Union of Soviet Socialist Republics?* What city became the capital of the U.S.S.R.? What was the old capital?

5. What is the meaning of the term *socialism* as used in western Europe and the United States? What is its meaning in the U.S.S.R.?

6. To what extent did the success of Lenin's program depend upon the Russian peasants? Why did the peasants refuse to coöperate with the Bolsheviks? Give three reasons why industrial production had dropped sharply by 1920.

7. What were the causes of the Kronstadt uprising? What were the demands of the rebels? What were the results of their defeat? Why did the Kronstadt uprising lead to the destruction, by the Bolsheviks, of all opposition political parties?

8. What was the New Economic Policy? Why was it adopted? How successful was it? Why may the New Economic Policy be considered a "minor retreat" of Bolshevik leadership?

9. Why did Lenin decide to develop socialism only in Russia? Why did he and his successor emphasize that the welfare of the Soviet state must come first? Why do Communists in other countries look to the U.S.S.R. for leadership?

10. What was the purpose of the Communist International? How did it influence Communist parties in other countries? Why was it discontinued during World War II?

11. What advice did Lenin give to the party in his "Testament"? Why did he finally decide against Stalin as his successor?

12. Why did Lenin's death usher in an age of totalitarianism in Russia?

Know word meanings

Be able to define and use correctly these terms.

socialism (meaning in the West)	Interventionists
socialism (meaning in the U.S.S.R.)	Comintern
Reds	Politburo
Whites	Kremlin
Cheka	totalitarianism

Identify names

What contributions did each of these make to Russia in the period 1917–1924?

Trotsky   Lenin   Stalin

Use the map

On an outline map of Russia locate the following:

Byelorussia	Ukraine	Crimea	Georgia	Armenia
Azerbaijan	Finland	Latvia	Lithuania	Estonia

Do something extra

1. Give several examples of Lenin's policy of. "Two Steps Forward, One Step Back." Show why this phrase is an accurate name for the policy.

2. Make a list of the ways in which the events following Russian Revolution departed from Karl Marx's theory.

3. Read and report on the negotiations between Trotsky and the Germans at Brest-Litovsk.

4. Give an account of Trotsky's organization of the Red Army and its part in the Civil War of 1918–1919.

5. Read and report on the famine of 1921–1922 and the work of the Hoover Mission in relieving it.

6. Read and report on the relations between the United States and Russia during the period of Lenin's control. 1917–1924.

7. Two novels that give a vivid picture of the first years of the Russian revolution are (1) Sholokhov. Mikhail. *The Don Flows Home To The Sea*. (2) Pasternak, Boris, *Doctor Zhivago*. Read and report on one of these novels.

Joseph Vissarionovich Stalin (1879–1953), dictator
for almost 30 years, raised the Soviet Union from
weakness to great strength, but at a horrible price:
the disappearance of the last trace of freedom,
millions reduced to slavery, and millions murdered.

4

THE SOVIET UNION UNDER STALIN

When Lenin died, the Bolshevik leaders of the U.S.S.R. were faced with a problem that Communism even today has not solved: the problem of succession. Who was to be the new leader of the Soviet government?

In the United States the problem is solved by law. Presidential elections are held every four years. Whichever candidate receives the majority of the electoral votes becomes President. Should the President die during his term of office, the Vice-President becomes President. Should he, too, die, the office goes to the Speaker of the House of Representatives. The method and order of succession are clearly established by law, and we take it for granted that the law will be followed.

By contrast, the Soviet system contains no such laws for succession. The people have no voice in choosing their leaders, and there are no effective laws or party rules that might guarantee any orderly kind of succession to power. Thus far in the history of the Soviet Union, the only way to gain the position of top power has been to fight for it. As a result, the death of Lenin brought about a tremendous struggle for power among the leading members of the Communist party.

The eventual winner of that struggle was Joseph Stalin. Stalin won because he was the most ruthless of all the Bolsheviks; and he remained in power for the rest of his life by ruthlessly getting rid of anyone whom he thought might threaten his power. As a result of Stalin's victory, the Soviet Union became a totalitarian system that was—and still is—efficient, aggressive, and brutal.

The Struggle for Power

There were five serious contenders for Lenin's position: Stalin, Trotsky, Kamenev, Zinoviev and Bukharin.

The Contenders

Of the five contenders, Leon Trotsky was unquestionably the most prominent. To all appearances, he was the most likely successor to Lenin. Trotsky had been the engineer of the October Revolution. He had organized and led the Red Army to victory in the Civil War. His name was almost always linked with that of Lenin. And Trotsky was a man of undoubted genius. He both spoke and wrote with great eloquence. He was a brilliant organizer and a skilled politician. His greatest interest, however, was neither organization nor politics, but ideas. Of all Lenin's survivors among the Bolsheviks, Trotsky was unquestionably the most original thinker.

Despite his very great abilities, however, Trotsky was hampered by some mistaken beliefs. For example, he believed that he could cause the people to follow him by the power of his persuasiveness alone. He failed to see that the key to power is not only intellectual ability and exciting speeches, but also careful, detailed, patient organization. A second of Trotsky's faults was that he never hesitated to express his opinions—and he made it clear that he thought his opinions were always correct. He also left no doubt that he held his less brilliant comrades in contempt, and he never hesitated to say, "I told·you so." Trotsky's ability, his constant arguing, and his attitude of contempt caused him to be hated by many of the other Soviet leaders, and by Stalin in particular.

The other three contenders were Lev Kamenev, Grigori Zinoviev, and Nikolai Bukharin. Although none of these was as powerful as Stalin or Trotsky, each nonetheless held a great deal of power, and each was highly regarded in Bolshevik circles. Kamenev and Zinoviev were friends and allies; Bukharin was a lone wolf.

These five men, with two others, constituted the Political Bureau of the Communist party, or *Politburo*. Power in the U.S.S.R. rested in the Politburo, and it was there that the major part of the struggle for power after Lenin's death took place.

At the time of the Revolution in 1917, the Bolshevik party had been run by the Central Committee of the party. Just before the Revolution the Politburo, a small group of the party's most important members, had been organized to deal with the day-to-day problems of running the party and the government. All important

ПОЛИТБЮРО ЦК. РКП/Б/.
– С ИЮНЯ 1924г.
ЧЛЕНЫ
ПОЛИТБЮРО
И В СТАЛИН
Л Б КАМЕНЕВ
Г О ЗИНОВЬЕВ –
Н.И.БУХАРИН.
Л Д ТРОЦКИЙ
ТОМСКИЙ
А И РЫКОВ

André de Saint-Rat

The arrangement of this official Communist party composite portrait of the Politburo clearly shows the position of each contestant in June, 1924, early in the struggle for power. Stalin is at the top, with Kamenev (left) and Zinoviev on either side. The less powerful Bukharin is alone in the center. At the bottom are Trotsky (left), already relegated to a position at the end of the line, and the noncontenders Rykov (center) and Tomsky (right).

decisions of the Politburo were subject to approval by the Central Committee. But by 1924, the year of Lenin's death, the Central Committee had grown greatly in size, and it met only five or six times each year. When it did meet, it usually approved the decisions of the Politburo without questioning them. Thus in 1924 the real power in the Soviet Union belonged to the members of the Politburo.

For a few years after Lenin's death, however, there were occasions on which the Central Committee once again became important.

With Lenin gone, there was an open contest for power. None of the contenders was strong enough to seize power for himself. Each had his own group of supporters in the Central Committee, but none had a clear majority.

Stalin as Secretary General

In April, 1922, Stalin was appointed Secretary General of the Bolshevik party. The Secretary General's job was to run the party Secretariat. The Secretariat consisted of the full-time party workers, called *secretaries,* who operated at every level of the party. Because the secretaries had more knowledge, more time, and more interest in party affairs than other members of the party, the Secretariat was gradually becoming the most important influence in party affairs. In theory, however, the secretaries did nothing more than carry out the orders of the party's Central Committee.

Stalin probably was named Secretary General for two reasons. The first reason was that none of the other top leaders of the party wanted the job; they considered it confining and boring. It dealt with files and reports and paperwork—the kind of occupation that most people hate, but that seemed particularly suited to Stalin's talents.

The second reason was that Lenin wanted a tough administrator in the post. Stalin appeared to be such a man. After Kronstadt, Lenin insisted upon increased party discipline; he wanted a man who could control the party efficiently and keep it united. "Keeping the party united" often required getting rid of members who disagreed with the party leadership. Lenin thought he could depend on Stalin to see that that was done. And he could—to a greater extent than he had intended.

Stalin immediately began to convert the party Secretariat into his own personal machine. As Secretary General, Stalin took charge of appointing the party secretaries. These secretaries knew that their responsibility was to Stalin; and they knew that if they wanted to keep their jobs, and perhaps their lives, they had better carry out his orders. Stalin also increased the number of secretaries, and thereby again increased the scope of his control. He convinced the other party leaders that the membership of the higher party organizations should be increased, and then he had his own men appointed to these new posts.

An important part of Stalin's job was "suppressing intra-party fractions"; that is, purging the party of opponents to the party leadership. He therefore began to build a card index containing information about anyone that the party (or Stalin himself) might later want to get rid of. Painstakingly he developed a huge file of such information. In the years ahead he would make exhaustive use of it.

The Isolation of Trotsky

Stalin's rise to power followed a consistent pattern. He sought to eliminate his opponents in the Politburo one by one. To do so, he would form alliances within the Politburo against a particular opponent or group of opponents. Stalin and his allies would then have enough strength to destroy the influence of that opponent—and to remove his supporters from the Central Committee. Later, when Stalin found himself in a position to do so, he would turn against his former allies and destroy them in the same way.

The first object of Stalin's attack was Trotsky. In moving against Trotsky, Stalin's principal allies were Kamenev and Zinoviev. Stalin allowed his allies to take the lead; he remained quietly in the background, waiting to take advantage of the mistakes of others.

Early in the conflict, Trotsky could have destroyed Stalin: in his "Testament" and elsewhere, Lenin had provided all the evidence that was necessary. But Trotsky was too proud to fight for what he wanted. He felt that his own superiority would allow him to triumph whenever he wished. In his overconfidence, he stood by as Zinoviev convinced the Central Committee that Lenin's fears about Stalin were groundless and that Lenin's "Testament" should therefore be suppressed. Trotsky thus allowed an opportunity to destroy Stalin to pass by, and he ignored several other similar opportunities.

Gradually the Kamenev-Zinoviev-Stalin alliance deprived Trotsky one by one of his posts and honors. By the time Trotsky finally realized what was happening to him, it was too late for him to do anything. Trotsky was isolated, and he was almost powerless.

The Downfall of Kamenev and Zinoviev

As soon as the alliance had isolated Trotsky and taken away most of his power, Stalin turned against Kamenev and Zinoviev.

While Kamenev and Zinoviev had been busy attacking Trotsky, Stalin had quietly built up his power within the party. How successful he had been became evident in December, 1925, at the Fourteenth Party Congress. Stalin had completely infiltrated the party with his own men, who voted as he told them to. Whenever a vote was necessary, Kamenev and Zinoviev found themselves being voted down. Their arguments were of no avail among the delegates, who realized that their future well-being depended entirely upon Stalin.

Too late, Kamenev and Zinoviev realized what was being done to them. Stalin, with his new ally Bukharin, was doing the same thing to them that they themselves had done to Trotsky. By early 1926 they, too were virtually powerless.

In desperation, Kamenev and Zinoviev attempted to form a new alliance, this time *with* Trotsky *against* Stalin. But they had delayed too long; their cause was already lost. Stalin controlled the instruments of power, and he knew how to use them. When the new alliance sent its representatives to awaken the party to the danger of Stalin, Stalin sent his thugs to assault the messengers. Those who supported the alliance were threatened with physical and economic reprisals, and their families were threatened as well. Eventually the opposition found itself forced to meet in the woods, in basements and attics, just as they had before 1917. But now the enemy was not the czar, but Stalin, a fellow Bolshevik.

Trotsky, Kamenev, and Zinoviev made a desperate attempt to overthrow Stalin on November 7, 1927, the tenth anniversary of the October Revolution. They attempted to organize a series of street demonstrations, which they hoped would bring the opposition to Stalin to the surface. The attempt failed miserably. Five days later they were ousted from the party, the same party that only ten years earlier they had done so much to help bring to power.

Kamenev and Zinoviev humbled themselves before Stalin and asked to be readmitted to the party. To further humiliate them, Stalin ordered that they be allowed to return only after a period of probation. Their surrender allowed them to keep their comfortable apartments and most of their privileges as party members, but they had lost all power in the party. Ten years later, when Stalin no longer had any use for their services as puppets, he would order them executed.

Trotsky was sent into exile in Soviet Central Asia. A year later he was shipped across Russia by train, loaded onto an icebreaker, and sent to Turkey. Stalin probably hoped that in Turkey Trotsky would be shot by a follower of the late czar. Trotsky, however, survived for another decade, eventually finding a refuge in Mexico. There, in 1940, an agent of Stalin's Secret Police sought out Trotsky and murdered him.

The Last Challenger

Stalin's victory was now all but complete. The only man who could possibly threaten him now was Bukharin. In the struggle against Kamenev and Zinoviev, Stalin had allied himself with

Bukharin. As before, Stalin had remained in the background and let Bukharin do much of the fighting for him. But even before he sent Trotsky into exile, Stalin prepared to attack Bukharin, his last challenger.

Like the others, Bukharin did not realize what was happening to him until it was too late to do anything. He, too, now made an attempt to form an alliance with Trotsky, but the powerless alliance soon collapsed.

As Kamenev and Zinoviev had done before him, Bukharin humbled himself before the victorious Stalin. Like Kamenev and Zinoviev, he was allowed the privileges of party membership, but had no power. And he, too, would be executed in the late 1930's.

Thus in 1929 Stalin had completed the destruction of those who could have blocked his assumption of absolute power. From then until his death, Stalin's word would be the only law in the Soviet Union. He would determine who would be appointed to the Politburo, to the Central Committee, to the Secretariat. He would decide who would live and who would die. He would imprison millions of innocent people in the Soviet Union, and he would execute thousands upon thousands. Stalin had attained absolute power, and he would retain it for the rest of his life.

Joseph Stalin

Until Stalin was well on his way to stealing Lenin's power, he was never given serious attention by the other Bolsheviks, who considered him a dull plodder. Stalin had always been considered a follower, not a leader; one to receive orders, not to give them. Only too late was it discovered that the silent, dull Georgian possessed a huge ambition and an overpowering desire to dominate. He also had an unequalled ability to hide his feelings, not only from outsiders but from his Bolshevik comrades as well. And he was one of the most skilled schemers that ever lived.

The name *Stalin* means *man of steel*. It was an assumed name, the last of several to be adopted by the future Soviet dictator.

Stalin's Background

Stalin's real name was Joseph Vissarionovich Djugashvili. He was born in a small town in the Caucasus mountain region known as Georgia, and he was the son of an impoverished shoemaker. Thus, unlike most of the Bolshevik leaders, his origins were more nearly proletarian.

Stalin first became involved in Marxist revolutionary activities in the late 1890's, when he was a divinity student. He joined the Bolshevik party soon after Lenin had organized it in 1903, and for the next fourteen years he served the party in a variety of ways, including editing a newspaper and robbing banks to obtain funds. He attended the party congresses when he could, but often he could not attend because the czar's police had thrown him in jail for his revolutionary activities. Stalin gradually became known in the party; but he was not particularly respected, and he certainly was not among the top leaders of the Bolsheviks.

Before the 1917 revolution, Stalin's chief contribution to Bolshevism was a book called *Marxism and the Nationality Question*, which presented the Bolshevik position on national minorities. Lenin thought it desirable to have a member of a national minority speak for the party on this subject; and because Stalin was a Georgian, he was selected for the task. There are few historians who think that Stalin wrote the book all by himself. Some have suggested that Lenin provided the information and Stalin wrote it up. It has been suggested, on the basis of a study of the writing style, that Stalin did not even write the book. But Stalin always presented the work as his own; and, on the basis of his "research" and "writing," he became the Bolsheviks' leading expert on minority problems.

After the revolution of 1917, Stalin became Commissar of Nationalities in the first Bolshevik government. Stalin was therefore a member of the Council of People's Commissars, the cabinet of the Bolshevik government. Of the fifteen men on the council, Stalin was probably one of the less important.

The Personality of Stalin

Stalin's feelings toward the world were dominated by a boundless suspicion. He himself was always prepared to stab anyone in the back; therefore, he took for granted that the rest of the world was trying to do the same to him. To Stalin, everyone was an enemy poised to attack, and any means of defeating the enemy were permissible. He considered guile and trickery to be definite assets.

Stalin's only real goal in life was *power*—his *own* power. This does not mean that Stalin had no attachment to Communism; he was probably sometimes moved by Communism's promises for the future, and his thinking undoubtedly was shaped by the Communist world view. But to Stalin, the doctrines, plans, and hopes of Communism were all less important than gaining, maintaining, and increasing his own power. He probably saw his own goals and those of Communism as being identical.

An understanding of Stalin's personality is important in understanding Communism, because his attitudes were often the same attitudes that Lenin desired in all Bolsheviks. In a sense, Stalin was the kind of revolutionary that Lenin sought to mold. But Stalin carried Lenin's attitudes a step further. Whereas Lenin adopted these attitudes only toward the enemies of Bolshevism, Stalin adopted them toward *everyone,* Bolshevik comrades included. To Lenin, all non-Bolsheviks were enemies; to Stalin, *everyone* was an enemy.

Stalin in Power

After Stalin had eliminated his Bolshevik rivals for control of the Soviet government, he still found it necessary to develop a way of insuring that the great masses of the Russian people would do as he wished at all times. Stalin's ultimate goal was nothing less than to become the absolute, unquestioned ruler not only of the Communist party and the Soviet government, but also of every aspect of the life of every person in the Soviet Union.

To achieve this goal, Stalin relied principally on propaganda and on terror.

Soviet Propaganda

Freedom of speech and of the press had ceased to exist in Russia only a few days after the October Revolution. Under Stalin, the efforts to influence men's minds by controlling the information that reached them were greatly intensified. To serve his ends, Stalin created one of the most thorough propaganda machines ever known.

Stalin operated on the theory that people will believe any lie if it is repeated often enough. Soviet newspapers, books, radio, and even paintings repeated and repeated whatever Stalin wanted people to think. The people were told that they were happy, that the Soviet Union was the only country in the world where men were genuinely free and "equal," that if only they would work harder for Stalin everyone would be even happier, that the capitalist countries were on the verge of collapse, that Stalin and Lenin were the greatest men that had ever lived.

One of the chief goals of Stalin's propaganda machine became to convince the Russian people that Stalin was the greatest, kindest benefactor of the human race. Stalin thought that such a portrayal of himself made it easier for him to rule. In order to make the portrayal convincing, it became necessary to rewrite history.

Lenin's tomb, the massive granite structure halfway between the two towers, stands in Moscow's Red Square near the wall of the Kremlin. On the days that the tomb is open, a long line of Soviet tourists files slowly past Lenin's embalmed body, which is on display inside the tomb.

After Lenin's death, the Politburo began to deify Lenin. A huge tomb was built in Red Square, in the center of Moscow, where Lenin's embalmed body could be seen through the sides of its glass coffin. Pictures of Lenin were seen on almost every wall in the Soviet Union, and every word that Lenin had ever said was declared to be sacred. In short, the Bolsheviks did their best to turn Lenin into a Soviet kind of god.

As soon as Stalin had achieved absolute power, he began the process of turning himself into another god. He completely rewrote the history of his own life so that it would appear that he had always been Lenin's closest associate. On those occasions when Stalin had been in the background, he was now placed in the foreground. Where others had stood next to Lenin, Stalin now took their places. Where Trotsky had been in command during the Civil War, Stalin now took over. Where Stalin had disagreed with Lenin, he now agreed. Thousands of pictures showing Lenin and Stalin side by side were painted to look as much like photographs as possible, and all pictures of Stalin's former rivals in the presence of Lenin were either hidden or destroyed. In short, history was rewritten to show that a man who had never been in Lenin's closest circle had actually been Lenin's closest collaborator in all that he did. Stalin became the Lenin of the new age.

A typical Soviet propaganda photograph of the Stalin era shows a smiling, kindly-looking Stalin being hugged by a Moscow schoolgirl. The setting is the reviewing stand on top of Lenin's tomb; the onlookers are Nikolai Bulganin (left) and Georgi Malenkov, high-ranking members of the Stalin regime.

As the years passed, Stalin increased his efforts at convincing the Russian people that he was a god. His smiling, mustachioed face was pasted on telephone poles, suspended from roofs and over assembly lines, and hung in every office and schoolroom. Stalin was everywhere; he knew everything; he controlled everything. And he always smiled. The climax of the glorification of Stalin came in 1949, when Stalin celebrated his 70th birthday. For more than a year the Soviet newspapers were filled with congratulatory telegrams from all over the world, and the story of Stalin's life was told and retold.

At the same time that Stalin was converted into a god, Trotsky was transformed into a kind of devil. He was pictured as the greatest of all the enemies of Communism. Whenever Stalin wanted to accuse someone whom he suspected of threatening his power, the victim was called a "Trotskyite." Russian schoolchildren were taught to hate Trotsky even more than capitalists or the czar. The name of the man who, next to Lenin, had done most to bring Communism to Russia was transformed into a swear word.

In order for the lies of the propaganda machine to be effective, it was necessary to keep the truth out of the Soviet Union. Stalin therefore cut Russia off from the rest of the world. Foreign books, newspapers, and magazines were banned. Radio broadcasts from outside the Soviet Union were "jammed"; that is, made impossible to understand by broadcasting loud noises on the same radio frequency. Soviet citizens were not allowed to travel outside the Soviet Union, and permission was required even for travel within the country. Few visitors from other countries were allowed into the Soviet Union, and those who were admitted were allowed to see only what the government wanted them to see. This was particularly true in the last years of Stalin's life.

Terror

Whenever propaganda failed to get him what he wanted, Stalin used the weapon on which he knew he could always rely: terror.

The basic idea of terror is simple: if someone disagrees with you, kill him. If someone acts as if someday he might disagree with you, kill him, too, or throw him into a slave-labor camp. Eventually everyone with the courage to oppose you will be dead; and the rest of the people will be so afraid that they will not dare even *think* against you, much less speak or act against you.

Terror was (and to a certain degree still is) a constant companion in the Soviet Union. It operates in several ways, most notably through the Secret Police system.

The Secret Police System

The Soviet Secret Police force was established in 1917, only a few weeks after the October Revolution. At first it was called the *Cheka,* or "Extraordinary Commission." Since then it has changed names several times. With each change of name, the Soviet government said that the Secret Police had been abolished; but everyone knew that its operations were being continued under a different name. Thus the Cheka became the G.P.U., then the O.G.P. U., then the N.K.V.D., then the M.V.D., then the M.G.B., and most recently the K.G.B. (Committee of State Security), the name under which it operates today.

The Secret Police have been more active at some times than at others, but they are ready at all times to crack down on the Russian people.

The Secret Police maintains a file of information on everyone in whom it is interested and in whom it thinks it may be interested in the future. Some of this information is supplied by the individuals themselves when they fill out applications for jobs or apartments. Most of the important information, however, is obtained from informers who report the activities of their friends and neighbors. There are informers in every Communist party group, in every of-

76

fice, in every factory, and in every school. Many of the informers are forced to spy on their friends against their will, but they know that refusing to coöperate with the Secret Police would place their own lives in danger.

When Stalin was in power, the Secret Police were at the peak of their power and ruthlessness. A typical Secret Police action was to make arrests quietly and in the middle of the night. In the Soviet Union, a knock on the door in the middle of the night was the most terrifying sound imaginable, for it usually meant that the Secret Police had come to take someone away. When the arrested person was led away, his family felt that they would never see him again. No one can tell how many millions of Soviet citizens have thus disappeared into the night.

Most persons arrested in this manner were sent either to a slave-labor camp or to be killed without a trial. Some, however, were put on "trial." At these so-called trials, it was taken for granted that the accused would be found guilty; indeed, he usually "confessed" to crimes that he had not committed. The Secret Police obtained confessions by using threats, torture, and drugs on its victims. The prisoner was questioned for hours at a time, for week after week, until finally his resistance was completely broken. Often the Secret Police were so effective in breaking a prisoner's resistance that an innocent prisoner came to believe his own "confession."

The Purges

The Secret Police organization, which has existed since a few weeks after the revolution that brought the Bolsheviks to power (and which still exists), reached its peak in both activity and brutality under Stalin. It was particularly active during the years 1935–1938, the years of Stalin's great purges.

By the middle of the 1930's Stalin had become convinced that the Soviet Union would sooner or later find itself at war with Nazi Germany. He therefore directed all his effort toward preparing for the war. Stalin wanted, of course, to make sure that if a war came, the Soviet Union would be able to defend itself. He wanted to make sure that anyone who might attempt to undermine the war effort (or who might take advantage of the confusion brought by the war to attempt overthrowing Stalin) would be eliminated before the war began. He therefore began to "purge" the party and the army of all enemies, real and imaginary, of the system and of himself.

Another purpose of the purges, perhaps more important than preparing for war, was ridding Russia of all those who knew the truth about Stalin. Since Stalin had taken power, history had been re-written to glorify Stalin. But many were still alive who remembered the details of his rise to power, who knew how comparatively un-important he had been in 1917, who knew his real relationship with Lenin. Stalin was haunted by the presence of these people who knew the truth about him; if he had rewritten history, he must get rid of those who knew the truth. This he proceeded to do.

The purges began in 1935 and continued, with only brief inter-ruptions, until 1938. During those three years, the Secret Police had little rest; they were constantly at work arresting people, forcing confessions from them, and executing them. The Soviet "fact fac-tory," in which "evidence" of treason was made to order, operated 24 hours a day. The newspapers told of former leading Bolsheviks having plotted with the Germans since 1922, of hidden supplies of weapons, of long-standing plans. Eventually the entire Soviet Un-ion became involved in the purges; everyone suspected everyone else. Russia found itself in the midst of a vicious witch-hunt, at the end of which more people at the top of the system were to be found in prison than out, and more were dead than were alive. During the three years of the purges, one out of every ten Soviet citizens was arrested, and more than 1,000,000 lost their lives. Thousands of those arrested were executed, and millions were sentenced to from eight to 25 years of forced labor.

Slave Labor

We do not know how many Soviet citizens were at one time or another sent to slave-labor camps in the northern forests of Russia, in the torrid southern desert, or in Siberia. Certainly the figure is higher than 7,000,000, and perhaps it is as high as 20,000,000. Very few of these people ever saw their homes again. Eyewitness accounts indicate that the fatality rate was very high; death, by starvation, disease, or suicide, was a constant companion in the slave-labor camps. Escape was rare, because the prisoners lacked the strength to run away and because there was no place to flee to. The slave-labor camps were set off in the middle of wastelands; there was no place of refuge to be found.

The plight of the political prisoners (those arrested by the Secret Police) was made even harsher by the fact that they were mixed in with common criminals, men who had been convicted of robbery, ex-tortion, and murder. In the Soviet system, these men were consid-ered less dangerous than the "politicals," because their crimes were against individuals, not against the Soviet state. In effect, the "politicals" were placed at the mercy of the common criminals. In addition to starvation, the political prisoners had to endure the oppression of the often sadistic criminals in their midst.

As the number of slave laborers increased, their contribution to the Soviet economy also increased. In the remote areas of Russia, often rich in national resources but not very inviting as places to live, slave labor became the means of carrying out the plans of the Soviet government. The prisoners built roads, canals, and railroads; felled timber; mined gold, diamonds, and coal; drilled for oil; and made bricks. In a very short period, the slave-labor camps came to be an industrial empire, but one whose workers died at an unusually high rate. But the camp directors had production quotas to be met. They needed more workers. They urged the Secret Police to send new prisoners. The men of the Secret Police were usually only too willing to oblige.

Undoubtedly, when the purges started their purpose did not include providing labor for projects in the far reaches of Russia. But once prisoners were used for such jobs and the carrying out of those jobs became part of the national plan, it became necessary to secure more prisoners who would be used to undertake still bigger jobs requiring still more people. At least one reason for the wide sweep of the later purges was to provide such labor.

Even after the purges had officially ended in 1938, the need to provide laborers for the far-flung projects of the Soviet economy persisted. The knock on the door in the middle of the night continued after 1938, to guarantee loyalty, to instill terror—and to provide workers. After World War II, those Russians who had been German prisoners were sent from the slave-labor camps of Germany directly to those of the Soviet Union. Hundreds of thousands of Soviet citizens, captives of the Nazis, were used to replenish the reduced personnel of the Russian camps. For these, liberation from the Germans meant not freedom, but more slavery—this time in their own country.

Building the Soviet Union

Stalin's ultimate goal, the ultimate goal of every Communist, was bringing about a completely Communist world. But in the 1920's Stalin realized that he could not reach that goal unless the Soviet Union became more powerful in relation to the rest of the world. In other words, it was necessary to transform the Soviet Union into a major industrial power.

When Stalin came to power, the N.E.P. (New Economic Policy —see pages 55–56) was still in effect. Under the N.E.P., Russian industry was recovering to the level of 1913 production, but it was not expanding. Russia was not opening new mines, constructing new blast furnaces, or building new machine tools—all of which were needed to produce the equipment to open still more mines, build still more blast furnaces, and so forth. In the meantime, the United States and other Western countries were steadily pulling ahead of the Soviet Union, both in total production and in production per capita.

Stalin knew well that the Soviet Union could not become a major world power until it had become a major industrial power. The problem was how to industrialize.

"Build on the Backs of the Peasants"

In order to industrialize, the funds or resources for industrialization must somewhere be found. Under capitalism, they are realized from savings. If a man with a small factory makes a profit of $20,000, but uses only $10,000 to live on, he can save the rest. If he continues to make profits, eventually he will have enough money to build a new, larger factory. But this kind of "primitive capital accumulation," as the Communists call it, could take place only over a long period—and Stalin was in a hurry.

But the savings were still required. Where, then, were they to come from? Russian industry could not supply it; and foreign investment was ruled out, because it would have placed Russia in the hands of foreign capitalists. There remained only one source: the peasants.

The peasants still made up the overwhelming majority of the Russian people. They were the primary source of income, and it was in them that the greatest potential for savings existed. The peasants must be made to produce as much as they possibly could. In return, the state would give them as little as possible. That difference would be considered "savings," and could be used for investment in industry. Thus, Russian industry was to be constructed "on the backs of the peasants." (This phrase, and most of the ideas as well, were Trotsky's; Stalin took them over after he had gotten rid of Trotsky.)

According to Marxist theory, it is better, more efficient, and more "progressive" to be big than to be small. Big countries, big factories,

Collectivization of agriculture gathered small, one-family farms, which Lenin had permitted, into larger and supposedly more efficient units, each with a great many workers. Above, women carrying rakes and scythes march off to work in the fields of a collective farm of the early 1930's.

and big farms are to be preferred to small ones. This meant that the maximum could be squeezed out of the peasant only if the small farms, privately owned and operated, were eliminated. In their place would be established giant mechanized farms, which would be completely under the control of the state and would fulfill the purposes of the state.

The peasants could not be expected to like this idea. In order to develop industry, they were to be asked to provide the state with as much grain as possible; to receive practically nothing in return; and on top of everything else, to give up control of their land. It was probably obvious to Stalin that force would have to be used to put these proposals into effect. The peasants would have to be forced onto the new farms, and their labor would have to be forcibly extracted from them.

The Collectivization of Agriculture

Sometime in late 1927, Stalin gave orders to begin the collectivization of agriculture—by force, if necessary. In February, 1928, the Communist party newspapers openly declared that the rich peasant had to be destroyed. By April, 1929, Stalin had begun to push the collectivization of agriculture in earnest.

During the balance of 1929 and into 1930, the peasants, rich and poor alike, were driven into the collectives. In thousands of instances they put up stubborn resistance against the idea of "sharing" their land, their buildings, their farm implements, and their animals with the other members of the collective. If the government insisted that they enter the collective farm, then, they protested, let the government provide for them! And, so saying, they burned their barns, broke their implements, and slaughtered their animals. If they could not have them, neither could the state.

Sometimes the fury of the peasants led to the murder of party officials sent out to oversee the collectivization. Stalin responded by sending Red Army detachments, which surrounded the peasants at gun point, stuffed them into cattle cars, and shipped them off to perform slave labor in Siberia—or shot them. In this manner nearly 5,000,000 peasants lost their lives or were deported (which in many instances was the same thing).

Total disorganization of agriculture followed Stalin's enforced collectivization. Between 1929 and 1933, the number of horses in Russia decreased from 34 to 16 million; the number of cattle, from 68 to 38 million; and the number of sheep and goats, from 147 to 50 million. Grain production decreased similarly. As a result, Russia suffered a famine even greater than that of ten years earlier. In the early 1930's more than 11,000,000 Soviet citizens starved.

By January, 1930, Stalin had accomplished a substantial part of his goal of collectivization and had violently incited the bulk of population in so doing. He therefore indicated that it was now time to slow the pace. He acknowledged that there had been abuses in carrying out the collectivization; but he said that this was due to "certain faults on the part of party workers," who forced "the pace of collectivization artificially without regard to the conditions of time and place, and heedless of the degree of readiness of the peasants to join the kolkhozes." In other words, Stalin said that if anything had gone wrong, it wasn't his fault. He really didn't know anything about those 5,000,000 people who were shot or exiled. It was really some over-eager subordinates who were responsible. Then, as if to make amends, Stalin announced that each peasant would be able to keep a cow, some pigs, his house, and a small acreage to till as his own, apart from the land of the collective.

But Stalin did not end collectivization. By 1933, nearly two thirds of all peasant households in the U.S.S.R. belonged to kolkhozes, as did more than four fifths of the farmland. Today virtually all of Russian agriculture is collectivized or directly operated by the state.

Building Soviet Industry

Stalin's collectivization policy did not basically improve Soviet agriculture; even today, agriculture remains the greatest problem of the leaders of the U.S.S.R. But the purpose of collectivization was *not* solely to improve agriculture; more important, it was to provide the Soviet economy with savings, so that it could industrialize as rapidly as possible. The peasant was to be exploited to the maximum in order to pay for a gigantic Soviet industry.

But even the ruthless methods of Stalin against his own people would provide only a limited amount of funds to be invested. The Soviet Union required all the essentials of a modern industrial economy. Where should it begin? What should it emphasize?

In order to deal with this problem, the Bolshevik economists used the techniques of a *planned economy.*

The Planned Economy

In the United States, what is produced or not produced is for the most part determined by "the market." If people want automobiles, automobiles are produced. If girls want green lipstick and purple stockings, green lipstick and purple stockings are manufactured. The market responds to consumer desires. Ideally, in this process there is no government interference. The two basic ingredients are the consumer, who demands, and the manufacturer, who seeks to satisfy the demand in order to make money.

In the planned economy of the Soviet system, consumer demand has no role whatsoever. It is not what you or I want that counts, *but what the Communist party thinks is necessary.* In the Soviet system, the consumer can desperately need more clothing and shelter; but if the party decides that a new blast furnace is more necessary, the new blast furnace will be built. The basic assumption of the planned economy, as practiced in the Soviet Union, is that the consumer comes last in importance.

Using the tools of economic planning, the Soviet economists seek to determine how much money there will be available to be invested during the coming year or years. After the amount available for investment is determined, the decision is made as to how to invest it. Priority must be decided. What should be done first? What next? What last? A gigantic planning system is devised to help in making the decisions. Usually plans are set up that cover a several-year period. The most famous of these plans were the five-year plans.

The first five-year plan was undertaken in 1928. It was to be the first step in developing Russia into a modern industrial giant. Not all of the early goals of that first five-year plan were achieved. Over the years, however, and particularly in recent time, the *industrial* goals set by the plans have been realized, except in one major area: consumer goods. The plans have not been successful here simply because the government has not cared enough to make them succeed. But the government has cared very much about heavy industry, and here Soviet industry has moved ahead.

Stakhanovism

In collectivization, Stalin had sought and found a method of exploiting the peasants in order to build up industry. He now sought a method of getting the most from factory workers while giving them as little as possible.

Stalin realized that if he used some of the factories that he was building to make clothes, shoes, furniture, and perhaps even automobiles, the people would have something worth working and saving for. But Stalin was not willing to use factories in this way; the goal was building more and more heavy industry.

Still, effort had to be extracted from the people. How could this be done at no cost? One idea that occurred to the Soviet leaders, and that they have used in great measure ever since, is that of bestowing "honor." Every worker who established a new record for mining coal or making steel or digging sugar beets was declared to be a "Hero of Soviet Labor" and had his picture plastered all over the Soviet Union. He would be sent on tour to teach his "methods"—working at a killing pace—to others. Within a few weeks some other worker would exceed the pace of the previous record holder, and he would become the new "Hero." In this way there was maintained a constant stream of examples for the Soviet labor force.

This technique of extracting more labor from the workers was called the Stakhanovite movement after a miner who on August 1, 1935, mined 102 tons of coal on a single shift, exceeding the fixed quota by 1300 per cent. New Stakhanovites sprang up all over the U.S.S.R. There were even Stakhanovite shock battalions that were to spur their comrades on to greater achievements. A new wage scale was introduced: the more produced, the more the worker was paid. It was the kind of piece-work wage that is violently opposed by labor unions all over the world. But in Soviet Russia, the "workers' state," the worker had nothing to say about his own fate. In one

United Press International

A portrait of Stalin gazes at the patrons of the Moscow subway from the front of a train. The Moscow subway, with its modern equipment and lavishly decorated stations, is a showpiece of Stalin's industrialization program.

way or another he was lashed on to greater and greater production, under circumstances that showed less and less concern for his welfare. Seldom has a crueler system for the exploitation of labor been devised than the one used in the Soviet Union since the 1930's.

The Results of Stalin's Policies

Unlike its agricultural policy, the Soviet Union's industrial program must be considered a success. Today Russia is one of the two mightiest nations of the world, second only to the United States.

But it must never be forgotten that Soviet gains have been achieved only at a tremendous human cost, not only in lives lost but also in lives lived out in suffering and privation. Industrialization was carried out on the backs of the peasants; but the workers were made to help, as well. They have been held at the bench for long hours, under miserable conditions, and with few safety devices; and they have been paid slave wages for their labor. They have lacked decent shoes, clothing, and housing. The system could spare nothing to make life easier for the worker who was building the future. Everything was tomorrow, tomorrow.

Stalin was a cruel despot, a murderous tyrant. He has been accurately characterized as one of the most thoroughly evil men that ever lived. But it must be recognized that he did make the U.S.S.R. one of the two greatest powers in the world. With collectivization, barbarously carried out, and industrialization, achieved at superhuman costs, this was achieved.

aids to learning

Check the facts

1. What method does the United States follow in acquiring a new head of the government? How is a new leader for the U.S.S.R. selected? In Russia, what organizations choose the leader? What are the major differences between the Soviet system and that of the United States?

2. Name the qualifications Trotsky had for leadership of the Soviet Union. What were his weaknesses?

3. What were the functions of the Politburo? How many members did it have? Name the five leading members. What was the Central Committee and what part did it play in the government of the U.S.S.R.?

4. Why did Lenin appoint Stalin as Secretary General of the Bolshevik party? How did Stalin use his position to build his political machine?

5. Describe the procedure by which Stalin brought about the downfall of his rivals for power. Name the chief characteristics of Stalin's personality.

6. What was the "technique of the lie" developed by Stalin's propaganda machine? Give examples of the falsifications this propaganda imposed on the Russian people.

7. Why did Stalin isolate the Soviet Union from the rest of the world? How did he bring about this isolation?

8. What were the functions of the Soviet Secret Police? How did they operate? What were the purposes of the purges? How were political prisoners used to develop the economy of Russia?

9. Why were foreign loans and the profits of Russian factories not used to expand Russian industry? How did Stalin use the Russian peasants to obtain the needed funds?

10. What was the purpose of collectivization? How was it carried out? What was the reaction of the peasants to this plan? What was the cost in lives and products?

11. Define the term "planned economy." What was the purpose of the first five-year plan? What methods do the Soviet leaders use to persuade the workers to exert every effort to increase production?

12. Summarize the achievements and failures of Stalin's policies.

Know word meanings

These terms are of especial significance in this period of Russian history. Understand not only their meaning but their operation and importance.

Central Committee	Secret Police	collectivization
Politburo	propaganda	kolkhoz
Secretary General	purge	Stakhanovites
Secretariat		

Identify names

What part did each of these play in the events after 1924?

Stalin　　　Trotsky　　　Kamenev　　　Zinoviev　　　Bukharin

Use the map

In an atlas or geography, locate a map of the Soviet Union. Study the area east of the Ob River and north of the 60th parallel. Make a list of ten cities in that area and the population of each. What conclusions would you make concerning the development of that area?

Do something extra

1. Make an outline or chart showing the steps by which Stalin rose to power, 1903–1929. Indicate at each step his contributions to the Bolshevik party.

2. Find the origin of the term "Iron Curtain." What does it mean? Is it a good metaphor? Why?

3. Compare and contrast the use of terror in the French revolution with its use in Russia (1) under Lenin and (2) under Stalin.

4. Are there any similarities in the treatment of political prisoners by Soviet Russia and czarist Russia? Are there any differences?

5. Describe the differences, in Russia, between a collectivized farm and a state farm.

6. Read and report on the use, by Russia in the 1930's, of skilled technicians from Germany, England and the United States.

7. Several novels are of value in giving one a picture and understanding of this period: (1) Sholokhov, Mikhail, *Seeds of Tomorrow;* describes the collectivization program of the 1930's. (2) Koestler, Arthur, *Darkness at Noon;* this novel's chief character is a composite of Trotsky and Bukharin caught in the purges of the 1930's. (3) Orwell, George, *Nineteen Eighty-Four;* an account of life in a collectivized society.

Nikita Sergeevich Khrushchev (1894–   ), dictator
of the Soviet Union and leader of world Communism,
has brought about important changes since Stalin's
death. Khrushchev is able, shrewd, and flexible,
and dedicated to increasing his own and Soviet power.

THE SOVIET UNION UNDER KHRUSHCHEV

Joseph Stalin died in 1953. After his death the surviving leaders of the Communist Party of the Soviet Union became involved in a struggle for power, which was similar in many respects to the struggle of the 1920's. The eventual winner of the new struggle was Nikita Sergeevich Khrushchev.

Even before Khrushchev had completed his takeover, the Soviet Union had changed slightly. Under Khrushchev, the pace of the change was speeded up. Changes are still being made.

Today the Soviet Union is a less unpleasant place than it was a few years ago. No one—probably not even Khrushchev—knows whether the changes that have occurred will be lasting, or whether further changes will occur, or whether conditions will return to what they were under Stalin. The last possibility seems unlikely; but the Communist party is still in complete control of the Soviet Union, and whenever it wishes it can take away the few benefits that it has recently bestowed upon the Soviet people.

The Second Struggle for Power

Stalin maintained his absolute power until the end of his life. Under him, a number of men rose to positions of considerable power in the Communist party and the Soviet government; but all were, in effect, servants of Stalin. None would ever seriously challenge his power.

While Stalin lived, there were many rumors as to which of his assistants he had chosen as his successor. Sometimes he appeared

89

to favor one man, sometimes another. But Stalin probably was not able to trust anyone in a favored position for very long; he would suspect that if he named a successor, the successor might become too powerful and threaten Stalin's absolute power. Moreover, Stalin probably refused to think about what would happen after he was dead, because he simply had no intention of dying.

But Stalin did die, on March 5, 1953. After his death, another struggle for power began. Although the names were different, the methods were the same as in the struggle of the 1920's.

The Positions and the Contenders

When Stalin died, he held two offices: Premier of the U.S.S.R. (the head of the Soviet government) and First Secretary of the Communist party (the dominant position in the party, the position that Stalin had used to gain his power in the 1920's).* Two days after Stalin's death, it was announced that both these positions would be taken by Georgi Malenkov.

In addition to Malenkov, the two most powerful men in the Party Presidium (the name of the Politburo since 1952) appeared to be Vyacheslav Molotov and Lavrenti Beria. Molotov had been a close associate of Stalin for more than thirty years, and had held many important party and government positions during that time. Beria was the head of the Secret Police, Stalin's chief instrument of terror, and was probably the most feared man in the U.S.S.R.

Two weeks after Stalin's death, a new name appeared among the Soviet leaders. It was announced that Nikita Khrushchev had replaced Malenkov as First Secretary of the Communist party. Unlike Malenkov, Molotov, and Beria, few people outside the inner circles of the Communist party were aware of Khrushchev. Under Stalin, Khrushchev had remained in the background, much as Stalin had remained in the background under Lenin.

No one outside the Presidium knows why Khrushchev replaced Malenkov in the all-important party post. It has been suggested that Khrushchev already had enough power to force Malenkov out; but this seems unlikely. Perhaps it was because the other members of the Presidium feared that Malenkov might turn against them if he were allowed to have too much power. Perhaps it was because other members of the Presidium gave Khrushchev the job temporarily, each member hoping that he himself would soon be able to

* In 1952 the title "Secretary General" was changed to "First Secretary." At the same time, the Politburo was renamed "Presidium of the Central Committee of the C.P.S.U."

replace Khrushchev. But we do not know the answer, and perhaps we never shall. What we do know is that after Khrushchev got the job, he held on to it.

Khrushchev, like Stalin, was familiar with the machinery of the Communist party. He knew how to run the party, and he knew how to use the party—and he did not hesitate to do either. As First Secretary, the same position that Stalin had held, Khrushchev began to build up his own following within the party. He filled the Secretariat and the Central Committee with his own followers, men who would be loyal to him and who realized that their fate depended on Khrushchev's remaining in power.

The Rise of Khrushchev

As Stalin had done before him, Khrushchev remained in the background whenever he could and used other people to fight his fights for him; then, when his allies were no longer useful to him, he removed them from their positions of power in the party and the government.

The first victim of the struggle for power was Beria. As head of the Secret Police, Beria was feared by most of his comrades on the Presidium, who were afraid that he might attempt to seize power for himself. In July, 1953, Beria was arrested and executed.

The next to go was Malenkov. By 1955 Khrushchev had gained sufficient power to force Malenkov to resign from his position as Premier of the U.S.S.R. Malenkov was replaced by Nikolai Bulganin, a man whom Khrushchev could more easily manipulate.

Khrushchev was aided in his rise to power by Georgi Zhukov, the Soviet Union's most popular war hero. Zhukov was too independent and self-assured to have been given any power under Stalin. Stalin went so far as to send him into political exile. After Stalin's death, however, Zhukov was admitted to the Presidium in order to gain the loyalty of the Red Army to the new regime. Zhukov's support as the army's representative was undoubtedly a great help to Khrushchev in the struggle that shortly occurred.

The Showdown

The last serious challenger to Khrushchev's increasing power was Molotov. In May, 1957, a desperate Molotov thought that he had sufficient power within the Presidium to get rid of Khrushchev. Molotov called for a vote in the Presidium, and by a vote of 7–4 Khrushchev was removed from his position as First Secretary.

Khrushchev then played his trump card. He contended that the

Khrushchev smiles and Georgi Zhukov grins as they attend a reception in Moscow in June, 1957. Three weeks earlier Zhukov had helped save Khrushchev from being expelled from the Presidium; three months later Zhukov was himself expelled from the Presidium—by Khrushchev.

power to dismiss him belonged not to the Presidium but to the Central Committee of the Communist party. The Central Committee is much larger than the Presidium; and, more important, it had been filled with Khrushchev's followers. Khrushchev sent messages to the members of the Central Committee indicating that, if they valued their positions, they had better get to the Kremlin as speedily as they could. All the time Khrushchev used a number of devices to keep the meeting of the Presidium going.

Molotov gave orders that the members of the Central Committee were not to be admitted to the Kremlin, where the meeting of the Presidium was taking place. According to one report, the members had to sneak past the Kremlin guards. But sneak they did. Khrushchev's men arrived at the meeting and demanded to be heard. Molotov and his collaborators had to give way, and Khrushchev was saved. Molotov, the third challenger was defeated.

The Consolidation of Khrushchev's Power

After the defeat of Molotov, Zhukov was the only man in the Soviet Union who might have had enough power to seriously chal-

Nikolai Bulganin throws his arm around the shoulder of his friend Khrushchev in 1955. Within three years Bulganin was to be sent into oblivion by Khrushchev. (For another photograph of Bulganin, and of Georgi Malenkov, see page 75; for a photograph of Vyacheslav Molotov, page 181.)

lenge Khrushchev. The fact that Zhukov had helped him defeat Molotov did not prevent Khrushchev's turning against his former ally. Only three months after the crucial meeting of the Central Committee, Zhukov was expelled from the Presidium.

A year later, in 1958, Bulganin was removed from his position as the figurehead Premier of the Soviet government. Khrushchev took the job for himself. By holding the positions of both the head of the Communist party and the head of the Soviet government, Khrushchev tried to indicate that he was in control as firmly as Stalin had been. Thus Khrushchev, like Stalin before him, had overcome all of his challengers one by one—and he had done so with the help of his future victims. He stood alone at the top of the pyramid of power.

There is nothing to indicate that anything has been done to solve the problem of the transfer of power following Khrushchev's death. Khrushchev is over 65, and not in the best of health; his years of active life are numbered. As matters now stand, however, there is every reason to believe that his death will be followed by yet another vicious struggle for power.

Nikita Khrushchev

Khrushchev belongs to the post-revolutionary generation of Bolsheviks; that is, he did not join the party until after the October Revolution. Khrushchev is therefore the first of the Soviet leaders who does not qualify as an "Old Bolshevik."

Khrushchev's Background

Nikita Sergeevich Khrushchev was born in a small village on the border between Russia and the Ukraine in 1894. His father was a miner, presumably of Russian ancestry (although perhaps of Ukrainian ancestry). As a youth Khrushchev worked in the fields, as a shepherd, as a locksmith, and in factories. He did not learn to read until he was 20. In 1918, when he was 24, he joined the Communist party, and by 1925 he had gained a position of importance in the party organization of his district.

In the late 1920's the party began a program to give industrial training to those of its members who had proletarian backgrounds. As a result of this program, in 1929 Khrushchev was sent to study at the Industrial Academy in Moscow; he was then 35. After arriving in Moscow, Khrushchev rose rapidly in the party. In 1934 he was made a member of the Central Committee, and five years later he was named to the Politburo, the most powerful body in the party organization. Thus from 1939 on, Khrushchev was among the two dozen most powerful men in the Soviet Union.

Yet when Khrushchev was made First Secretary of the Communist Party of the Soviet Union, the move came as a complete surprise to the outside world. Few outsiders had ever heard of Khrushchev, and almost nothing was known of his background. Even today, at a time when Khrushchev has for several years been recognized as one of the most important men in the world, very little is known about him. We do not know, for example, why Khrushchev was given the all-important job of Communist party First Secretary two weeks after Stalin's death.

We also do not know how Khrushchev managed to stay alive during the Stalin purges, when all around him were being executed. There are several possible explanations, each probably correct to some extent. Khrushchev was probably saved from some of Stalin's suspicion because he had not been involved in the struggle for power of the 1920's. He was not an intellectual, but a "man of the people"; this, too, made him less suspect to Stalin. In addition, there is evidence that from the very beginning of his career Khru-

shchev was an uncritical supporter of Stalin. Sheer luck, too, probably helped keep him alive. And so did his ability to play the role
of a clown, so that no one could consider him a threat.

The story is told that on one occasion Stalin ordered Khrushchev to dance a vigorous Ukrainian folk dance. Khrushchev began to dance. "Now, faster," yelled Stalin; then "Still faster . . .
faster, faster, faster." So Khrushchev danced and danced, faster and
faster, all the time smiling. In order to stay alive, Khrushchev
played the fool for Stalin. But Khrushchev was no fool: he did stay
alive.

The Personality of Khrushchev

From earliest encounters with Khrushchev, some people gained
the impression that he was a clown, a jester, a fool. On his first trip
outside the Iron Curtain, Khrushchev tumbled drunkenly down a
flight of stairs. Later on the same visit, Khrushchev, the leader of
one of the mighty nations of the world, Indian-wrestled with a fellow member of the Presidium while their chauffeur changed a flat
tire. To some, it appeared that the Soviet Union was governed by a
fool. Later in his career, when Khrushchev removed his shoe and
used it as a gavel at the United Nations, it appeared to some that he
was a madman.

Khrushchev is neither a fool nor a madman. He is a shrewd
politician, a skilled in-fighter, and a dangerous enemy. He is dedicated to extending his own and Soviet power; and he firmly believes
that the world of tomorrow will be a Communist world, and a better
one for it.

Since 1955 Khrushchev has probably been the most powerful
man in the U.S.S.R. He is not, however, the absolute ruler that
Stalin was. When Stalin was the chief, his every word was law, and
no one dared question him. Under Khrushchev, the other members
of the Presidium feel much more free to express their own opinions,
even though they may occasionally disagree with Khrushchev.
Khrushchev apparently is willing to admit, as Stalin was not, that
there is usually more than one side to a question.

Under Khrushchev, Russia has changed greatly in many respects. Largely this is because the times and the situation have
changed. To some degree, the reason is that Khrushchev is not so
powerful as was Stalin. But some of the change can also be attributed to the fact that Khrushchev is *different* from Stalin. He is
not so suspicious, so resentful, so full of hate. Russia, even under
a Khrushchev as strong as Stalin, would not be the same as Russia

under Stalin himself. Khrushchev is a determined Communist, and therefore dangerous; but he is much closer to being a normal human being than Stalin ever was.

Lenin has gone down in history as the man who brought about the revolution. Stalin will be remembered as the man under whom Russia became one of the mightiest nations in the world. Khrushchev hopes that he will be remembered as the man who raised the Soviet standard of living to the highest in the world. Khrushchev knows how the Soviet people have suffered, and he would like their lives to be less hard. Of course, Khrushchev is a dedicated Communist—dedicated to keeping the Communist party in full control of the Soviet Union, to strengthening the Soviet Union, and to bringing about a Communist world. But to Khrushchev the needs of the Russian people are of much greater importance than they were to Stalin, who had nothing but contempt for the masses.

The Soviet Union since 1953

Most of the changes that have occurred within the Soviet Union since 1953 have been for the better. Indeed, conditions were so bad at the time of Stalin's death that they could scarcely have become worse.

The Soviet Union at Stalin's Death

When Stalin died, the Soviet Union was a dreary land. The Russian people were tired, numb, disillusioned, cynical. Those who had been born before 1910 had lived through two world wars, the Revolution, the Civil War, collectivization and industrialization, the continuing purges, the unending demands of the government to produce more and more, and the ever-present terror of the Secret Police. They were exhausted. They had endured perhaps as much as any other generation in history.

The people had been told that they must work hard for the sake of tomorrow, but tomorrow seemed never to come. They had hoped that after they had rebuilt the industry destroyed by World War II, life would become easier. This, however, did not happen. By the end of the 1940's, pre-war production figures had been surpassed, but still Stalin was not satisfied. Production was plowed back into the economy to open new mines, build new steel plants, build new railroads. The satisfaction of the day-to-day needs of the people was kept to a minimum. Decent housing was almost im-

A boulevard in Moscow in March, 1953, the month that Stalin died. Note the dark, drab clothing of the people on the sidewalk and the almost complete absence of automobiles in the wide street.

possible to find: seven, eight and more people would live in the same room, and an entire floor would share the same badly-equipped kitchen. It was necessary to stand in long lines to buy even a few potatoes or a badly-made suit or pair of shoes.

The average worker was forced to work 48 hours a week, and he could not refuse overtime. If he were late to work or absent without a medical certificate, he could be severely penalized. He could not leave his job, and was subject to arrest if he quit without permission.

For the average peasant, conditions were even worse. The government took almost all the production of the collectives, and paid a miserably low price. To stay alive, the collective farmers were often forced to steal from the collectives. When they could, they neglected the collective fields and worked mostly on their own small plots of land; however, if they did not work a certain number of days on the collective land, they were subject to arrest and prosecution as criminals. In the last year of Stalin's life there was a small improvement in the situation, but the standard of peasant life remained terribly low.

Every Soviet citizen, no matter where he lived, had to be continually aware of the Secret Police. Its spies were everywhere, and they were prepared to report him for even the slightest criticism of the Soviet government or its leaders. The slave-labor camps continued to need laborers to fill the places of the many who had died and the few who had been released. No Soviet citizen dared talk to any of the few foreigners who were admitted to the U.S.S.R. unless he was officially ordered to do so. Even in his conversations with his fellow citizens he was very guarded in his remarks. An office or a home might be wired, or a telephone might be tapped. Soviet citizens were wary of one another; they could not trust even their friends.

It might seem that such a situation would have aroused great opposition on the part of the Soviet people. Such, however, was not the case. The lack of opposition was due in part to the fact that the Soviet people were proud of their country's achievements, such as its victory in World War II, its new position of power in the world, and its industrial accomplishments.

Probably a more important factor behind the lack of opposition was that the Soviet people were exhausted. After long hours at work, more hours standing in line, and sleepless nights brought on by their crowded living conditions, they had little energy left for resistance.

Moreover, the image of an all-powerful government, so powerful that no one could stand against it, was constantly impressed upon the people. No one could hope to change the system; no one would dare mutter complaints to his friends. With the agents of the Secret Police seemingly everywhere, complaining was dangerous, and resisting was about the same as suicide. The only thing to do seemed to be to adjust to the system and try to make the best of things. The people hoped that someday conditions would be better; in the meantime, there appeared to be nothing they could do.

Thus were the Soviet citizens of Stalin's time forced into accepting the Soviet system. In the great majority of cases, their acceptance was passive; the outstanding quality of Soviet citizens was *inertia*. They rarely did anything until they were ordered, and then they did only what they had to do. To take independent action of any kind might be dangerous.

Relaxation of Terror

Since the death of Stalin, there have been important changes within the Soviet Union. These changes have produced a new atmosphere in the country; however, the Soviet Union of today is still far more like the Soviet Union of Stalin's day than it is like America or any other free country. The Soviet Union remains a dictatorship under the control of the top leaders of the Communist party.

But the Soviet Union is no longer a terrorized society. The Secret Police have been severely cut back. Soviet citizens do not now live in constant fear. They feel much freer to speak what is on their minds, to complain when something displeases them, to make little jokes against the party or the government—so long as they do not go too far. Soviet citizens can now more seriously and openly than ever before comment on the shortcomings of Soviet life, though most people still hesitate to do so.

These changes do not mean that the Soviet Union has become a free society. Critics of the Communist party and the Soviet government must not become too active, or they will find themselves in trouble—although the punishment is likely to be far milder than it would have been under Stalin. Although the Secret Police are now much less a part of Soviet life than they were when Stalin lived, they still exist; they still act; and they could at any moment increase their activity. For the great majority of Russians, however, the fear of a midnight visit of the Secret Police has passed.

The slave-labor camps have also been greatly reduced in scope. Even before Stalin died, the number of those at forced labor had decreased from its high point of a few years earlier. With Stalin out of the way, slave labor was further reduced. Today slave labor camps still exist in Russia, but they are no longer an important part of the Soviet economy. Most of their inmates are common criminals; most of the political prisoners have been released.

Rise in the Standard of Living

Since Stalin's time, the Soviet system has also begun to give more to the people. Khrushchev has continued Stalin's policy of building the industry of the Soviet Union; the first goal of Soviet industry is to expand at a rate somewhere between six and nine per cent per year. But Khrushchev realizes that the Soviet people are no longer willing to work for medals and awards and publicity. They want material things as well; good housing, better food, more attractive clothes, and occasional luxury items, such as television sets.

Khrushchev and other top Communist party leaders have recognized the consumer demands of the Russian people, and they are attempting to satisfy them. But providing for the Soviet people remains of secondary importance; building heavy industry still comes first. As long as industry expands at the desired rate, however, anything that is left over will now be used for consumer industries.

United Press International

Although the quality and quantity of the goods available to Soviet consumers has improved somewhat, many items are still scarce, and in the stores the service is bad. Above, customers patiently wait their turn in Moscow's GUM (State Department Store), the largest store in the Soviet Union.

One of the more noticeable improvements in Soviet life is the improved quality of clothes. When Stalin was alive, a walk down the main thoroughfare of Moscow would have revealed the Soviet people to be miserably dressed. The colors and patterns of the material were dull and uninteresting, the cloth was bad, and the quality of workmanship was low. Because almost no one could afford new clothes, patched clothing was seen everywhere. A sense of style had been declared "bourgeois" by the party, and no one seemed to have the slightest awareness of what it meant to be well-dressed.

This situation has changed, particularly in the major cities. The Russians are not so drably dressed as they were, and the quality of the clothes has been improved. The younger people are copying American and western European clothing styles. Among the girls, nail polish, eye shadow, and American-style hairdos are becoming fashionable. The Soviet government is taking steps to meet the consumer demand for cosmetics and stylish clothes—but it has not moved quickly enough to satisfy the would-be consumers. As a result, an American shirt with a button-down collar can be sold in Moscow for several times its value, and there was at one time a flourishing market in illegal lipstick (until its leader, the "lipstick king," and his "crown prince" were executed for "economic crimes").

The major problem of most Soviet citizens is housing. The majority of the dwellings in the Soviet Union are slums, badly built and terribly over-crowded. Probably what the average working family in the Soviet Union desires more than anything else is a new apartment of his own.

To relieve the housing shortage, Khrushchev has undertaken a vast apartment building campaign. The new apartments are small: even the great figures of Soviet science and art consider themselves fortunate to have four-room apartments. The quality of Soviet construction is exceedingly poor. Complaints are often heard, even in the newspapers, of green lumber, imperfect bricks and tiles, and bad workmanship. However, the Soviets are experts in prefabricated reinforced concrete construction; and as they gain experience in building apartments, the quality of the construction is improving.

Khrushchev has promised that within ten years every newly married couple in the Soviet Union will have their own new apartment. It is doubtful that he can keep his promise, the majority of Soviet housing still being slum housing. But a notable effort is being made.

Soviet Agriculture

One of the major demands of the Soviet citizens today is for better food. There is enough food in Russia to keep the people from starving, even to make them fat—but it is mostly bread and cabbage and potatoes. The people would like more meat and vegetables and fruit. But until there is a notable improvement in the state of Soviet agriculture, the people will have to be satisfied with what they have; and there seems to be little reason to expect such improvement.

Agriculture is one of the greatest Soviet failures. It has never fully recovered from Stalin's enforced collectivization of the early 1930's. Farm goals set by Soviet economists are almost never realized. Every few years a new plan for agriculture is presented —and fails. The Communist leaders of the Soviet Union make all sorts of promises to exceed the United States in agricultural production, but there is little likelihood of such a development. If 1953 (the year of Stalin's death) is taken as a base and the agricultural output of that year is placed at 100, the current seven-year plan calls for production of 257 by 1965. However, Khrushchev openly admits that Soviet agriculture is lagging behind badly. He will probably have to be satisfied with an index of around 175 by 1965 —and this with almost half the Soviet population engaged in agriculture. In the United States, by contrast, we are deluged with farm surpluses. Yet we have only 3,500,000 farmers, and, of these, 1,500,000 produce 87 per cent of our total crops. Our problem is too much production; theirs is not enough.

Why is it that Soviet agriculture has failed despite all the concern that Russian leaders have given it? They have tried one scheme after another, yet nothing seems really to help. There are a number of difficulties, some natural and some man-made. One important factor certainly is the fact that most of Russia has a shorter growing season and less rainfall than the United States. But Soviet agriculture also suffers from a lack of trained and dedicated manpower and from a reluctance on the part of the government to make the required investments in fertilizer and agricultural machinery. The peasant has traditionally come last in Russia, and the same is true today.

In the Soviet Union, the collective farms are considered the least desirable places to live and work. The more able among the young people are usually eager to be off to the cities—even though their wages in the city are sometimes less than half what they would be on a collective farm. As a result, the older, less able, less energetic, and less coöperative portion of the population is left to operate the collective farms. And many of those who remain on the collective farms are discontented with their lives. For them, life has improved less in recent years than it has for the people in the cities. The collective farms offer few opportunities for excitement, for a higher standard of living, for the consumer goods that the cities are beginning to enjoy. Conditions on collective farms are simply not the kind that inspire people to hard work.

If Khrushchev were to raise the incentive for the peasants and give them more land, Soviet agricultural production would probably increase. But giving the peasants more land would be a step away from the collective system. In other words, it would be a step away from Communism and toward capitalism, and the Soviet leaders are not willing to take any such steps. On the other hand, if the peasants were deprived of the small plots of land that they now farm for their own profit, they would probably coöperate with the Soviet government to an even lesser extent than they do now. Thus, the Soviet leaders appear to be trapped; they try this and they try that, but the results are seldom satisfactory. As a result, the Russian people will probably continue to eat more bread and potatoes than meat and vegetables for many years to come.

The New Generation

Since the death of Stalin in 1953, a new generation has come to maturity in the Soviet Union, one that differs greatly from its parents. One of the principal reasons for the changed character of this new generation is the "de-Stalinization" of the Soviet Union.

Khrushchev's "De-Stalinization"

When Stalin was alive, every possible method was used to convince the Soviet people that he was a kind of god—all-wise, all-powerful, all-knowing. For a few years after his death, the Soviet leaders continued to present him to the people as an object for reverence. Stalin's embalmed corpse was placed on display beside Lenin's in the huge tomb in Red Square; his picture remained beside Lenin's on almost every wall in the Soviet Union; and Soviet textbooks continued to praise him in the same way that they praised Lenin.

At the same time, however, Stalin's successors were aware that they could not continue to rule as Stalin had ruled. They feared the possibility of opposition if they attempted to follow Stalin's methods, and they themselves knew what it was to have suffered at Stalin's hands. Furthermore, Stalin's successors were at that time fighting among themselves for power; therefore, it was almost impossible for them to rule as effectively and ruthlessly as Stalin. The result was a slightly changed atmosphere in Russia, sometimes called the "Thaw." No great changes took place overnight: but slowly, sometimes almost unnoticeably, life in the Soviet Union became less harsh. By American standards, Russia was still a prison; but by Soviet standards, conditions were much improved. It was at this time (1953–1956) that the Secret Police greatly reduced their activity and the first increases in the supply of consumer goods became noticeable.

The "Thaw" suggested that there would be further changes. But no one expected that the changes would take the form that they did.

In February, 1956, the Twentieth Congress of the Communist Party of the Soviet Union assembled in Moscow. At one of the sessions near the end of the congress, the delegates were told to leave pencil and paper in their hotel rooms. The representatives of foreign Communist parties, who had attended all other meetings, were excluded from this one. The doors of the assembly hall were locked. In an atmosphere of great tension and expectation, Khrushchev waddled to the speaker's stand.

Scarcely any of the delegates knew what Khrushchev was going to discuss. They received a tremendous shock, for on that day Khrushchev made a speech that for a while threatened to tear the Communist world apart. The results of the speech are still being felt. Communist leaders debate the wisdom of its having been made and indicate the speech as the source of many of their problems.

In his speech Khrushchev struck out at Stalin. The great Stalin, who had been elevated to the role of a demi-god, whose statue adorned every park in the Soviet Union, whose name was attached to every prominent Soviet development, was dragged through the dust. He was portrayed as a coward and a fool, a bully and a murderer. The delegates were told, for the first time in their lives, of Lenin's "Testament." They were told that 70 per cent of the members of the Central Committee had been arrested and shot, and that "thousands upon thousands" of other innocent men and women were executed at Stalin's command. They were told that the purges of the late 1930's had not been required in order to rid the country of spies and saboteurs, as Stalin had said, but that they were the result of Stalin's excessive suspicions and his mental sickness.

Probably the reason that Khrushchev made the so-called "Secret" speech was to strengthen his position in the struggle for power in which he was then engaged: some of the men with whom he was struggling were Stalin's disciples who favored Stalin's tough policies. In order to destroy them, Khrushchev found it necessary to destroy their idol. The speech was not intended for the Soviet public; it was supposed to be known only to members of the Communist Party of the Soviet Union. But within a few months the United States government obtained a copy of the speech and published it, so the "Secret" speech has become well-known in most of the world. But the speech was never mentioned in the Soviet newspapers; and, so far as most Soviet citizens knew, Stalin was still considered a great man. However, the leaders of the Soviet party praised Stalin much less often than they had; some of the statues were quietly removed; and some of the pictures came off the walls. But most remained, and Soviet tourists in Moscow continued to file reverently past Stalin's corpse.

The body of Joseph Stalin now rests in a simple burial plot beneath the plain stone marker in the foreground. Looming in the background is the tomb in which Stalin's body lay for eight years in a place of honor beside that of Lenin.

The process of "de-Stalinization" was carried even further at the Twenty-second Party Congress in October, 1961. At that congress, Khrushchev renewed his attacks on Stalin—but this time in public, and with full newspaper coverage. The statues and pictures suddenly came down all over the Soviet Union. Places that had been named for Stalin changed their names—including Stalingrad, the site of the greatest Soviet victory of World War II, which became Volgograd. And Stalin's body was removed from the Lenin-Stalin tomb and buried near the Kremlin wall. Lenin's tomb was once again occupied only by Lenin.

The Spirit of the New Generation

The "de-Stalinization" process has had a profound effect on the attitudes of the young people who have grown up since Stalin's death. Because they have grown up under conditions quite different from what their parents knew under Stalin, their outlook on life is somewhat different from that of the older generation. The older generation was shaped—and stifled—by the demands and persecutions of the Stalin era; the younger generation has only dim—if any—recollections of Stalin. The older generation was forced to accept everything and not to ask questions, and the habit is, in most cases, difficult to break; but the younger generation asks questions and makes demands. They are much less inclined than their parents to believe what the government tells them or to meekly accept whatever the government is willing to give them.

Khrushchev's attacks on Stalin have increased the questions asked by the younger generation. They had been told when they were in school that Stalin was wise and kind; now, suddenly, they are told that much of what they had been taught in school was a lie. This naturally raises more questions in their minds: Is the government still lying to us? How can we tell? Is Khrushchev really always right, as the newspapers say, or is he as big a liar as Stalin was? And why did he find it necessary to hide the truth about Stalin for so long? These young people have no desire to overthrow the Communist system; they have grown up in it, they are used to it, and to them it seems natural. But they would like to be told the truth; and more and more often they are letting it be known that they will not be satisfied with lies, with half-truths, or with "answers" that do not answer their questions.

And the members of the younger generation are less likely than their elders to be satisfied with other aspects of the Soviet system. The changes that have occurred since Stalin's death have been gratefully welcomed by the older generation; they tend to be pleased with whatever benefits they get. The younger generation, which cannot remember what life was like under Stalin, is not so easily satisfied; they know what it is like to have a little freedom of expression, a little taste of good living, a little opportunity to live their own lives. To many of the young people, the little that they now have is not enough. They want more—more and better housing and clothing, the right to travel, the right to state their own opinions without having to fear being condemned, or worse, by the government—the right, in short, to live their own lives.

In today's Russia, the new idols of the young are the new generation of poets. These poets represent the young people's yearning for freedom and truth and a private life. Poetry readings, which have always been popular in Russia, have now become mass experiences.

The poets express the indignation of the young at the bureaucracy and hypocrisy of the Soviet system. They write of the life

United Press International

They say that I am a brave man.
I am not. Courage was never my strong point.
It just seemed beneath my dignity
To fall to the level of the cowardice of others. . . .
The time will come when men will remember . . .
This strange era, these strange times, when
    Ordinary common honesty was called courage.

These lines—very outspoken, considering that they were written in the Soviet Union—are by Yevgeny Yevtushenko, the most popular of the young Soviet poets. Above, Yevtushenko recites his poetry before a gathering of more than 5,000 in Moscow. Note that most of his audience are young people.

and love of real people, not of the Spartan behavior of young Bolsheviks who are only interested in producing more pig iron or setting a new record for the number of cows milked in a day. The poets do not attack the Soviet system or the Communist party or its leaders. Many of them belong to the party, and they are proud of the accomplishments of the Soviet Union under Communism. But they want more, and they want a better life—and they want it soon, while they are still young enough to enjoy it.

The attitude of the new generation does not extend throughout Soviet society; in some circles a tougher, or more "Stalinist," line is preferred. There are even some young people who would prefer that a more tough, Stalinist line be followed. Certainly the leaders of the Soviet Communist party are still concerned, above all else, with building the Soviet Union and spreading Communism throughout the world. There are many in the Soviet Union who believe that the poets of the younger generation should be silenced, considering them to be an evil influence on Soviet life. These opponents of the new generation think that the new attitudes can only weaken the determination of Soviet youth; they fear that the Soviet youth will become "self-centered" and "soft," that they will be "corrupted" by listening to jazz and dancing American dances, and that they will no longer be concerned with building a Communist society. Even some young people share this attitude, and try to interfere when a young man and his date enter a place where jazz is being played or poetry is being read. But those who are opposed to the changes taking place in the Soviet Union today are in the minority—though they sometimes have powerful support at the top of the Communist party.

The Russians and Freedom

The Russians, particularly the younger Russians, have had a taste of freedom, and they would like more freedom. But we must understand that the average Russian's idea of freedom is rather different from the average American's idea of freedom.

Most Russians are willing to tolerate much more government interference in their lives than an American would accept. For example, the average Russian probably would not be happy with the American system where the worker must find his own job; he prefers his own system, in which he is assigned to a job by the government. Russians are also much less concerned than are Americans concerning freedom of the press. Whereas an American wants to know everything about his government, the good and the bad, a Russian would be likely to approve suppressing information that might embarrass the government. Furthermore, most Russians do not object to the one-party system; all that they ask is that the party be honest and act correctly. They do not seem to object that they do not have any direct control over their government; but they do demand that the government act wisely and for the good of the people.

On the other hand, there are certain areas in which the Russians would like less government interference. This is particularly true in their private lives. They are tired of being told that they must always think and act with the good of the Communist party and the Soviet state in mind. They want to be able to pursue private interests as well as Communist party interests. In short, *they want to be themselves*—and this is what the Soviet system has never permitted them to be. The rights of the individual have always been less important than the interests of the Communist party and the Soviet state. The party and the state have come first, the individual a weak second; where there was conflict, the individual always had to give way.

Every society has a certain number of such conflicts, and the United States is no exception. But in the United States there is a strong tradition of governmental restraint. There are, by custom and by law, large areas in which the government may not interfere. For example, police cannot enter a home at will and seize persons or property as they choose. A newspaper that criticizes the government may not be suppressed. Neither the President, nor the governor, nor the mayor, nor any other official may tell you what church to attend, or that you shall (or shall not) believe in God. If any public official wanted to close down a newspaper or interfere with church attendance, he would be kept from doing so by our laws and traditions. In the Soviet Union there are no such laws or traditions.

Today the people of the Soviet Union have more freedom than they have had for many years. But at any moment Khrushchev could change his mind and apply all of the old restrictions once again. He would probably find the people more difficult to control than in the past. But the tools of oppression are still under his control. He still has the propaganda machine, the Secret Police, the tear gas, the machine guns, and the tanks. The Soviet people can never be sure that what Khrushchev has given today, he will not take away tomorrow.

The leaders of the Communist party, with Khrushchev at their head, have no intention of surrendering any of their power. From time to time, the party may appear to be moving in that direction; but then suddenly something happens that makes it go into reverse. Why? Because the party is still concerned, above all else, with preserving its all-powerful position. Sometimes, when the party considers that its own good may be served by putting the cause of the individual first, it will do so. But still the decision—and the power —belong to the party and the state. There is no sign that Khrushchev, or any other Soviet leader, is willing to surrender that power.

109

As long as the people of the Soviet Union do not control their government, they can have no assurance that their newly-achieved freedoms will grow, or even that they will last. Such assurance can come only from a government controlled by the people. Such a government does not exist in the Soviet Union, and there is little likelihood that it will soon come into existence.

aids to learning

Check the facts

1. What was the most important post in the Communist party? Why was this position given to Khrushchev shortly after Stalin's death? Why was Khrushchev able to hang on to it?

2. Why was Beria the first victim of the struggle for power after Stalin's death? In what way did Zhukov aid Khrushchev to gain power? How did Khrushchev reward Zhukov?

3. How did Khrushchev outwit Molotov's efforts to remove him as First Secretary of the Communist party? How many years elapsed between the death of Stalin and the control of the Soviet government and the Communist party by Khrushchev?

4. Who were the "Old Bolsheviks"? Was Khrushchev one of them?

5. Why is Khrushchev considered a "man of the people"? What events between 1929–1939 brought him into a position of power in the Communist party? What explanations are given for his survival of Stalin's purges?

6. Why has Khrushchev sometimes been considered a madman and a fool? Why is it a mistake to consider him to be either?

7. In what ways is Khrushchev less powerful than Stalin? What is Khrushchev's aim as ruler of Russia? With what achievements does history credit Lenin and Stalin?

8. Describe the conditions under which the Russian people lived and worked during Stalin's rule. Why did they not openly oppose the Soviet system? Why, for many years, was the standard of living low?

9. Make a list of the changes that have taken place in the Soviet Union since the death of Stalin. In what ways has the standard of living improved? Explain why it was an "economic crime" to manufacture lipsticks.

10. What has been done to relieve the housing shortage? How successful has this program been?

11. Why has Russian agriculture failed to supply the people with a greater variety of food? Why has agriculture been unable to achieve the goals set for it by the Soviet economists?

12. What revelations did Khrushchev make to the delegates at the Twentieth Congress of the Communist party in the "Secret" speech of February, 1956? Why did he make this speech? What further acts of "de-Stalinization" were carried out in October, 1961?

13. Name the differences in Russia today between the young people and the older generation. What are some of the questions the young people are asking? What are some of the things they want?

14. Why are poets and poetry important to the younger generation of Russians? What are some of the objections to the new attitude of the Russian younger generation?

15. In what respects does the Russian idea of freedom differ from the American? What is the role of the individual in the Soviet system? Why do the people of the Soviet Union have no guarantee that they will keep whatever freedom they now have?

Know word meanings

Be able to define and use correctly the following terms:

Presidium	inertia	heavy industry
Politburo	slave-labor camps	de-Stalinization

Identify names

These names were important in the period following the death of Stalin. What part did each play in the events of that period?

Georgi Malenkov	Lavrenti Beria	Nikolai Bulganin
Vyacheslav Molotov	Nikita Khrushchev	Georgi Zhukov

Do something extra

1. Make a chart showing the parallel events in the rise of Stalin and the rise of Khrushchev.

2. Contrast the life of a Russian worker with that of an American worker; a Russian peasant's life with that of an American farmer.

3. Read and report on the operation of a collective farm and the conditions of life and work on it.

4. Read and report on the ideas and poetry of the Russian poets. Some references are: *Saturday Review,* vol. 45, May 5, 1962, pp. 8–11. *Newsweek,* vol. 59, June 4, 1962, p. 55. Special supplement, "The Mood of the Russian People," *Harper's,* vol. 222, May, 1961, pp. 105 ff. *The Reporter,* vol. 26, March 15, 1962, p. 23; April 12, 1962, p. 6.

*Officers of the Red Army pass in review before Lenin's
tomb in Moscow. The Red Army, the strongest arm
of the Soviet government, is fully controlled
by the Communist party—as is all else in the U.S.S.R.
All high-ranking Red Army officers are party members.*

6

SOVIET GOVERNMENT AND THE COMMUNIST PARTY

By the early 1930's the form of the Soviet government had been established. Since that time, the U.S.S.R. has undergone tremendous industrial development; it has survived World War II, in which over 20,000,000 Soviet citizens lost their lives; and since Stalin's death in 1953 it has been living through an upheaval that is not yet over. In spite of these tremendous changes, however, the Soviet government today is in most respects the same as it was 30 years ago.

The Soviet Constitution

The outlines of the Soviet government are to be found in the Soviet Constitution, the so-called "Stalin Constitution," which has been in effect since 1936.

The "Most Democratic" Constitution

The Soviets have referred to their constitution as the "most democratic" in the world. According to them, almost everyone in the Soviet Union participated in writing it. After the first draft had been presented, it was discussed (according to Soviet sources) by 36,500,-000 people in more than 1,000,000 meetings throughout the Soviet Union. Those who attended the meetings proposed more than 150,000 amendments, some of which were included in the final version of the constitution.

But none of the suggested changes were very significant ones. For example, no one seems to have suggested that more power should be given to the people to decide their own fate. Everyone knew that it would be very dangerous to make such a suggestion—especially in a country where, supposedly, the people already had all the power. Rather, there were suggestions that the constitution perhaps needed a preamble or that it should include a section on "Marriage and the Family." All of the suggestions were safe, and many were designed to indicate that Stalin was kind and generous.

The Soviet "Bill of Rights"

One of the most noteworthy parts of the Soviet Constitution is Chapter Ten, the Soviet "Bill of Rights." Chapter Ten contains all the rights that were ever included in all the other constitutions of the world, including our own. To these the Communists added a few contributions of their own, and they produced a document that reads magnificently. Freedom of speech, freedom of assembly, freedom of the press, and dozens of other freedoms are "guaranteed" to the Soviet citizen.

But Stalin never intended that these promises of freedom should be fulfilled. Words are worth nothing unless there is the intent of living up to them. One can have the best-sounding document in the world and the longest list of promises; but if there is no wish to live up to those promises, they remain promises and nothing more.

The Russian people have waited for years to see the promises of their constitution realized, and they are still waiting. It is true that conditions in the U.S.S.R. are now slightly better than they were under Stalin—but only slightly. Freedom of speech is severely limited. The printing presses are controlled by the state, and only what the state approves may be printed. Criticism of top government officials is unheard of.

In recent years, however, a certain amount of criticism of the Soviet Union has been permitted. For the most part, however, the authors whose works are published are the authors who support the Soviet state. And it must be remembered that the Communist rulers may at any moment change their minds and stifle the small amount of criticism that they now permit.

The Law in the U.S.S.R.

In the Soviet Union, the idea of law as a permanent system has not taken root. What was legal yesterday may be illegal today. What was punished mildly yesterday may be punished by execution today.

The reason for the constant changes in Soviet law is that under Communism law serves the state. There is no understanding of the Western idea (which is particularly strong in the English-speaking countries) of law as an instrument, developed over a long period of time, whose function is protecting individual rights. In the Soviet Union, law is *whatever the good of the Soviet state demands.* Law protects the state and serves the state. The individual is left to get along as best he can.

Because of this idea of the law, it is not surprising that the law changes whenever the needs of the state change. The changes have led to difficulties in the U.S.S.R., as people have broken laws that they had not known even existed. The constant changes have also encouraged people to never do anything at all and thus be sure that they have done nothing wrong.

Since the death of Stalin, there have been some attempts to establish lasting laws in areas that are not closely connected to state interests. The law in these areas is developing, but very slowly. As a result, the profession of law has begun to receive greater respect in the U.S.S.R. Under Stalin, no one ever wanted to be a lawyer for a person accused of a crime. Anyone who seriously defended such a person might soon find himself on trial as well. In most instances, the defense lawyer limited himself to pleading for mercy for his client. Today, with certain areas of non-state concern beginning to be mapped out, Soviet law and lawyers are beginning to develop. Nevertheless, practicing law in the Soviet Union is far from the respected profession that it is in the United States.

The Structure of the Soviet Government

According to the Stalin Constitution, the basic unit of government in the U.S.S.R. is the *soviet,* or council. These organizations take their name from the workers' soviets that the Bolsheviks used to gain power in 1917. But today's soviets resemble the revolutionary soviets in little more than name.

The Soviets

There are more than 50,000 soviets in Russia today. The city council in Russia is called a soviet. The highest legislative body in the U.S.S.R. is called the *Supreme Soviet.* But the soviets in Russia today are almost powerless.

A city council in the United States usually has the responsibility of running the city. In Russia, the function of the city soviets is very limited. It is likely to concern itself with problems no more serious than at what time the children should have their mid-morning snacks or whether the town needs more newspaper stands. Important decisions are made not by the soviets but by the Communist party. Anything that the local soviet does is directed by the party.

In addition to the local soviets, there are soviets at four other levels of government: (1) *raion,* or district; (2) *oblast,* or province; (3) republic (of which there are now fifteen in the U.S.S.R.); and the *Supreme Soviet.*

Because they have little to do, the various soviets do not meet often. Republic constitutions call for three to six meetings a year, but there have been many local soviets that do not meet even once during a year. The Supreme Soviet meets twice a year for a few days each time.

116

The Supreme Soviet

The Supreme Soviet has two houses: the Soviet of the Union, in which representation is based on population, and the Soviet of Nationalities, in which representation is based on the various nationalities of the U.S.S.R. The Supreme Soviet has about 1,400 members.

The Russians would like people to believe that their Supreme Soviet is a body similar to our Congress. The Soviet Constitution states that "the highest organ of state power in the U.S.S.R. is the Supreme Soviet" and that "legislative power in the U.S.S.R. is exercised exclusively by the Supreme Soviet." In practice, however, the Supreme Soviet (like all the other soviets) is merely a "rubber stamp"; that is, it automatically approves what someone else has already done. Its members discuss what they are told to discuss, and they approve what they are told to approve; then they go home, where they stay until summoned to gather again.

At its meetings the Supreme Soviet elects the *Presidium* of the Soviet Union. The Presidium is a committee of members of the Supreme Soviet. In theory, the Presidium governs the U.S.S.R. when the Supreme Soviet is not in session; in practice, the Presidium follows the orders of the party just as the Supreme Soviet does.

The presiding officer of the Presidium is called the Chairman. Sometimes the Chairman of the Presidium is mistakenly referred to as the "President of the Soviet Union," thereby giving the impression that the U.S.S.R. has a president whose position is about the same as the President of the United States. However, the two are not the same at all. Our President exercises real power; the Soviet "President," on the other hand, is for the most part a figurehead. His principal function is to be present at boat launchings and cornerstone layings and to make a lot of speeches.

From the preceding paragraphs it should be evident that the "President" and the "Congress" of the U.S.S.R. have little real power. They are there because the leaders of the Communist party believe that they look good and that they help keep the people satisfied. It must always be remembered that they are almost completely powerless.

The Council of Ministers
The Soviet system also has a *Council of Ministers,* or *Sovmin.* The Council of Ministers is in some ways like the Cabinet in the United States. It is composed of the heads of the various departments of the Soviet state, such as the Ministry for Foreign Affairs or the Ministry of Defense. According to the Soviet Constitution, the Council of Ministers is "responsible and accountable to the Supreme Soviet of the U.S.S.R."

117

Because the Supreme Soviet is powerless, it might be expected that the Council of Ministers is also powerless. Such, however, is not the case. The Council of Ministers has the responsibility of carrying out the orders and decisions of the rulers of the Soviet Union. In so doing, it exercises very great power indeed. But the orders and decisions do not come from the "President" or the "Congress"; they come, rather, from the leaders of the Communist party, some of whom are members of the Council of Ministers.

Soviet Elections
Elections to the higher-level soviets occur every four years; elections to the lower soviets are more frequent. According to the Soviet Constitution, the members of the soviets are elected by the people. In practice, however, the people have almost no voice in choosing the members of the soviets.

Whatever the Communists may say, the chief purpose of Soviet "political" campaigns is *not* to elect candidates. Elections are held for several other reasons, the most important of which are (1) to convince the Soviet people and the rest of the world that Russia is a "free" country; (2) to preach the advantages of the Soviet system and to declare how much progress Russia has made (and will continue to make) under that system; and (3) to tell the people that because they are so grateful to the Soviet system they are going to produce more than had originally been scheduled. The struggle to increase production is an important part of every election campaign.

According to the Soviet Constitution, candidates may be nominated by almost any organization. In practice, however, the nominations are made at places of work, such as factories, collective farms, or army units. The suggestions of names almost always come from party members. Sometimes it happens that a person distrusted by the party is nominated; but when the final list of candidates appears, he will find that his name has been mysteriously left off.

Among the list of candidates for the Supreme Soviet will appear the names of the most important political, cultural, and scientific leaders of the Soviet Union. Khrushchev's name appears, as do the names of the leading party officials. Some of the U.S.S.R.'s leading scientists are honored by being nominated. Yuri Gagarin, Russia's first man in space, sits in the Supreme Soviet, as do leading artists, actors, musicians, writers, miners, steelworkers, and farmers.

A candidate who has been nominated is almost sure to be elected, because there is no one running against him. There is only one candidate for each seat. The candidate who is nominated, therefore, is the person that the Communist party wants in office. Not all candidates are party members. But more than 70 per cent of the candidates for the Supreme Soviet are party members. At the lower levels of the soviets, the percentage of party men is somewhat smaller.

Election day is always on Sunday (so that no one need lose any time from his job). It is a gala event, celebrating not only the election but also the production campaign undertaken in its name. The streets are decorated with banners advertising the Soviet state. Special displays of Soviet achievements are put in shop windows. Vendors are stationed at street corners with special supplies of flowers, ice cream, and pastries.

In the United States, election day is an important occasion with a great deal of tension. Who is going to win? Who is going to be at the head of our city, our state, our country? Who will lead us in the coming years? And who will sit on the sidelines, out of office? In Soviet elections there is no such tension. There is only one list of candidates, the slate of "Communists and Non-Party People," and the winners are known long before election day.

The Soviet ballot, too, is quite different from ours. It contains only the name of the one chosen candidate. There are no choices to be made, although in theory another name may be written in. All that the Soviet voter can do is vote *against* the candidate by crossing out his name. If the voter approves of the candidate, he simply puts the ballot into the ballot box without making any marks on it at all.

Supposedly, every Soviet polling place has a booth in which the voter may mark his ballot in secret. But if the voter does not vote

November 7, the anniversary of the October Revolution, is one of the two great Soviet holidays. Above, a flag-carrying crowd, waiting on a Moscow street to enter a parade, is entertained by an accordionist and a pair of dancers. The same festive spirit is a major part of election day in the Soviet Union.

against anyone, he does not need to mark his ballot; therefore, he does not need to use the booth. As a result, the overwhelming majority of Soviet voters simply receive their ballots, walk across the room, and deposit the ballots in the ballot box.

In every election, the official list of candidates receives an overwhelming majority—usually about 99 per cent—of the votes. Why? Simply because the voter is afraid to walk into the booth. The voter knows that the election officials are watching him. He knows that the officials will make a note of his name if he enters the booth, because entering the booth automatically indicates that the voter intends to vote against the Communist-approved candidates. Such voting may cost the voter his apartment, his job, or even (in extreme cases) his life. Thus it can be seen that there is no such thing as a free and secret vote in the U.S.S.R.

Despite the fact that Soviet elections are not free, they are well patronized by the voters. In the Soviet Union more than 99 per cent of the voters cast their ballots in every election. By contrast, in the United States it is unusual if more than 60 per cent of the voters turn out. Why the difference? There are several reasons. First, in the U.S.S.R. election day has been turned into a celebration, with music and ice cream and flowers—and voting is made part of that celebration. Second, in the United States the great emphasis is on which of the candidates will win the election. If the voter does not care who wins, there is no need for him to vote. It is unfortunate that so many Americans do not care who wins; but Americans are as free to not vote as they are to vote for anyone they choose. Third, and most important, in the United States a voter may stay away from the polls and no one will ever know (unless he tells on himself). In the Soviet Union, however, questions will be asked about anyone who does not vote. His boss will be alerted, and his name will be noted as a possible opponent of the Soviet system. Therefore almost everyone in the U.S.S.R. votes, and almost every voter votes for the official list of candidates.

The Communist Party of the Soviet Union

Political power in the Soviet Union rests neither with the soviets nor with the people. It is the Communist party that runs the U.S.S.R.; and the party, in turn, is run by a few people at the top of its organization.

Since 1952 the official name of the party has been *Communist Party of the Soviet Union (C.P.S.U.)*.

The All-Powerful Party

Every aspect of life in the Soviet Union is dominated by the Communist party. The party seeks to control everyone and everything. Its final goal is that there should be not even a single thought that the party has not inspired and encouraged. Because the Soviet newspapers often attack the ideas of some of the Soviet young people, we know that the party has not yet reached its goal, even after more than 40 years of trying; but the party has no intention of giving up.

The party is suspicious of anything that it does not originate, sponsor, and control. To the party there is always the danger that what is *outside* the party may be *against* the party. Something that the party does not control may be perfectly harmless; but it should not be allowed to become firmly established, because it may later turn into something harmful. Moreover, the Communists believe that everyone should devote himself to helping the party destroy its enemies and achieve Communism; therefore, they reason that anyone who is not clearly working *for* the party is shirking his duty. To not work for the party is almost as bad as working against it.

It is the *total* domination of life by the C.P.S.U. that gives the Soviet Union a *totalitarian* society. Because of its insistence on complete domination, the party must be involved in all activity. Any activities carried out without party participation are condemned.

The party therefore opposes the existence of any organizations not sponsored by the party itself. In the Soviet Union there are no such groups as the American Legion or Kiwanis, which are organized by individual citizens to represent their own interests. The members, meeting on their own, might develop ideas contrary to those of the *party line,* which is whatever the party wants the Soviet citizens to think at any given time. There are, of course, many organizations of Soviet citizens; indeed, the Soviet Union is super-organized. But all the organizations are sponsored and dominated by the party. Whether it is a steelworkers' club, an amateur symphony orchestra, or the Young Communist League, all were created by the C.P.S.U., and all have a core of party members to tell the others what the party wants them to read, to do, and to think.

Because the Communist party insists on its complete control of society, there is clearly no room for any other political party in the Soviet Union. The C.P.S.U. is not willing to allow its position to be threatened. In the United States, if the voters are dissatisfied with the job that one party is doing, they can "turn the rascals out" and give the other party a chance to do a better job. In the Soviet Union, there is nothing that the people can do.

It is true that the party is sometimes criticized—but only by itself. Such criticism usually points out inefficiency somewhere in the party; it never questions the basic ideas or policies. And the criticism is always directed at underlings in the party, never at the top men. The leaders are always pointed out as men who can do no wrong.

The Organization of the C.P.S.U.

A glance at the table of organization of the C.P.S.U. (see page 122) indicates that the party's organization is in many ways similar to the organization of the government. There is a reason: such system of organization makes it possible for the party to control the government at every level. Every soviet contains Communist party members who direct its affairs. The party determines who will run for office, what business the soviets will discuss, and (to a great degree) what decisions they will reach. It is therefore necessary that the party have men acting at every level of government.

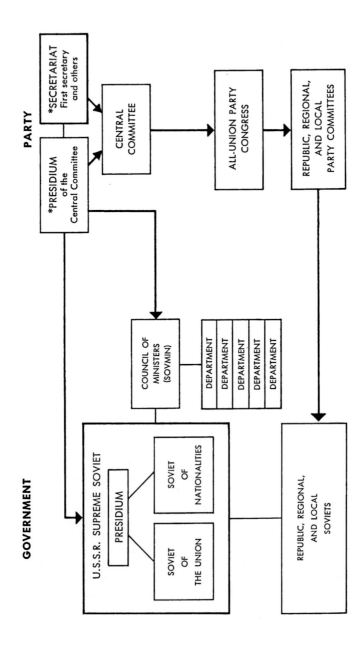

PARTY

*SECRETARIAT
First secretary
and others

*PRESIDIUM
of the
Central Committee

CENTRAL
COMMITTEE

ALL-UNION PARTY
CONGRESS

REPUBLIC, REGIONAL,
AND LOCAL
PARTY COMMITTEES

GOVERNMENT

COUNCIL OF
MINISTERS
(SOVMIN)

DEPARTMENT
DEPARTMENT
DEPARTMENT
DEPARTMENT
DEPARTMENT

U.S.S.R. SUPREME SOVIET

PRESIDIUM

SOVIET
OF
NATIONALITIES

SOVIET
OF
THE UNION

REPUBLIC, REGIONAL,
AND LOCAL
SOVIETS

*Members are often Chief Officers of the Government as well as of the Party

According to the party rules, the party Congress is at the top of the party organization; it is supposedly "the highest organ of the Communist Party of the Soviet Union." In practice, however, the Congress is only slightly less of a rubber-stamp body than the Supreme Soviet. It is summoned at least once every four years to listen to the party leaders and to approve decisions that the leaders have already made.

According to the party rules, the Congress elects the *Central Committee* to act when the Congress is not in session. Early in Soviet history the Central Committee was the actual ruling body of the party, but it soon lost its power. Today it occasionally is called upon to help in making important decisions. It is true that the approximately 300 members of the Central Committee are among the most powerful men in the Soviet Union. Nevertheless, for the most part the Central Committee is a group that the party leaders control for their own purposes. One of the first acts of a new party leader is to fill the Central Committee with his own men so that he will always have a majority in any vote. In effect, the Central Committee is selected not by the party Congress, but by the top party leadership.

The Central Committee meets at least once every six months. Its sessions are brief. It supposedly elects the party Presidium, a group of about 20 men (the number varies), to "direct" the work of the Central Committee between sessions. *It is the twenty or so members of the party Presidium who actually govern the U.S.S.R.* Even so, not all of the members of the Presidium are equally powerful.

The party Presidium must not be confused with the Presidium of the U.S.S.R. (see page 116), which is a quite different body.

The Party Secretariat

Besides the Presidium, the Central Committee also (in theory) is responsible for setting up the party *Secretariat*. The Secretariat is composed of the party secretaries. They are the political professionals of the Communist party, the men who have no other job than the party. Their job is to make sure that party orders are carried out and that the right people are chosen for the soviets and other organizations. The party secretaries operate at every level of government and party activity. They are the most important men in every town. They know everyone, and they keep files on all the important people. The files often contain the kind of information that the party could use against people that it wants out of the way.

The party secretaries honeycomb the entire Soviet political system, and they are its strongest organization. Therefore, the man who controls the Secretariat has an organization of trained professionals working for him in every part of the Soviet Union. The man at the head of the Secretariat is called the *First Secretary of the Central Committee of the C.P.S.U.* Because of the large and efficient organization that he commands, the First Secretary is *the most powerful man* in the U.S.S.R. It was by holding this position that both Stalin and Khrushchev gained and held their power.

The Soviet Power Structure

To determine who holds power in the Soviet Union, it is necessary to examine three small groups of men: (1) the top eight or ten men of the party Secretariat; (2) the party Presidium; and (3) the Council of Ministers of the U.S.S.R.

After he had eliminated all his opposition, Nikita Khrushchev clearly emerged as the single most powerful man in the U.S.S.R. He holds the position of First Secretary, and so controls the Secretariat; he is a full member of the party Presidium; and he is Chairman of the Council of Ministers (Premier). Khrushchev is the only person in the U.S.S.R. who is a member of all three of these groups.

Ordinarily, the most powerful among the other party leaders are full members of the Presidium and hold high posts in the Secretariat. Those who are members of the Presidium and the Council of Ministers (but not the Secretariat) are less powerful. Those who belong to only one of the three ruling groups are less powerful still.

These are good rules to observe in trying to determine the relative strength of the various top men of the Communist party. However, the rules are not foolproof. Sometimes a man who belongs only to the Presidium is near the top of the party in influence, perhaps because he has been involved in party affairs for many years or perhaps because he possesses some particular ability or friendship.

The Membership of the Communist Party

The men at the top of the Communist Party of the Soviet Union are a peculiar kind of person. Those who have long held power have had to survive the years of Stalin's madness, when the chief problem was simply staying alive. Later, in the struggle for power that followed Stalin's death, they had to have the foresight to bet on the right man, Khrushchev. They have to be agile and tough and determined and energetic, or they will not last long. In recent years, many have fallen by the wayside. Getting to and remaining at the top is not a game for weaklings. On the other hand, for those who desire power the rewards are great.

Even for those who are not at the top of Communist party power, the rewards of party membership are considerable. The best jobs, the best apartments and country houses, the best automobiles, the best seats at the theater and sporting events, and the best vacation spots all go to party members. A party member (or the son of a party official) has the best chance of gaining admission to one of the crowded universities, and he will probably get a better job after graduation than will a non-party member. In the Soviet Union, joining the Communist party is the key to success.

Not everyone in the Soviet Union is eager to join the party, and the newspapers sometimes complain about the lack of interest in "political matters" shown by some of the youth. But almost anyone who is ambitious seeks to join the party as soon as he can. Some of the young people join the party because of idealistic motives: they have become convinced that Communism represents the salvation of mankind. It seems very likely, however, that many others join simply to get ahead. The party leadership is opposed to those who join the party for this reason; it calls them "opportunists" and seeks to filter them from the ranks of the party. But it is largely unsuccessful; such opportunism is one of the most widespread facts of Soviet life.

The party does not attempt to enroll everyone, but only the "leaders" of the Soviet people. Today the C.P.S.U. has almost 10,-000,000 members; however, these are less than five per cent of the total Soviet population. Constant attempts are made to enroll the "best" people: the best scientists, the best workers, the best writers, the best collective farmers, the best musicians, the best milkmaids.

On the other hand, the party has established high barriers to keep out the incapable and the insincere. To become a member, an applicant must be recommended by at least three party members in good standing. Those who make recommendations must be careful; if they make bad recommendations, they may be deprived of their own party membership. After the necessary recommendations have been made, an applicant must pass through a period of probation, usually one year, during which he is on trial. During this time he will probably be given boring, distasteful, and time-consuming tasks. He must perform these tasks well to prove that he takes the responsibilities of party membership seriously.

Despite the high qualifications for Communist party membership, the party continues to grow. The rewards of party membership are great; to most people in the Soviet Union, the effort of gaining party membership is quite worthwhile.

Those who belong to the Communist party are the "elite" group of the U.S.S.R. They are the men and women who have brains and determination—and power and its rewards. Many people outside the U.S.S.R. have pointed out that the so-called "classless" society of the Soviet Union has developed a "new class," a new nobility. The Bolsheviks overthrew the czarist system in order to destroy the old nobility, but all that they have succeeded in doing is substituting a new nobility in its place. The new nobility is more powerful, more efficient, and in many ways more autocratic and oppressive. And it tends to reproduce itself as well: the sons and daughters of party members have less trouble than others in becoming party members, and do so much more frequently than do outsiders. Less than fifty years after the revolution, the "workers' paradise" has developed its own well-established group of bluebloods and snobs.

aids to learning

Check the facts

1. Why does the Soviet government call its constitution the "most democratic" in the world? Why would Americans consider the Soviet method of drafting its constitution lacking in democratic procedure?

2. Name some of the items included in the Soviet "Bill of Rights." To what extent have the freedoms listed in the "Bill of Rights" been realized?

3. What is the major difference between the Soviet Union's idea of law and the English-speaking countries' concept of law? How and why has the Soviet type of law discouraged the people from taking any initiative in developing organizations or activities?

4. Name the five classes of soviets and indicate the level of government at which each operates. How often does each meet? How much power does each have?

5. How many members does the Supreme Soviet have? Give the names of its two houses, and explain how the membership of each is determined. How much power does the Supreme Soviet have (1) in theory, (2) in fact?

6. How is the Presidium of the Soviet Union chosen? What are its duties? What is the title of its presiding officer? What are his duties? How much authority do the Presidium and its chief official have?

7. What is the make-up of the Council of Ministers? Why is the Council of Ministers, although technically responsible to the Supreme Soviet, more powerful than the Supreme Soviet?

8. How often are elections to the Supreme Soviet held? How are candidates nominated? How many candidates are there for each seat? Besides the election of candidates, what other reasons are there for holding elections?

9. Describe a Soviet election day. In what ways does a Soviet election differ from one in the United States? How does the Soviet ballot differ from those used in the United States? Why do the Soviet candidates usually receive 99 per cent of the votes cast? Why do a larger percentage of the voters in the U.S.S.R. vote than do the voters in the United States?

10. In what body does the real power in the Soviet Union reside? Name some of the organizations that the Communist party dominates. Why does the party refuse to let any organizations, other than those it sponsors, exist? What is the *party line?* Why is the Soviet Union a totalitarian society? Why is there no other political party in the Soviet Union than the Communist party? What is the nature and extent of criticism in the Communist party?

11. Describe the means by which the Communist party manages to control the soviets at every level of government. How often does the party Congress meet and what are its duties?

12. How many members are there on the Central Committee? How may a party leader manage to control this committee? How is the party Presidium chosen? What do its members do?

13. What is the party Secretariat? Who are its members and what are their duties? Who is the head of the Secretariat? Why does his position make its holder the most powerful man in the U.S.S.R.?

14. In general, what rule can one follow to determine the strength of each of the leading men in the Communist party? Give examples.

15. What are some of the qualities and characteristics of the men at the top of the Communist party? What are some of the rewards of membership in the Communist party? What percentage of the Soviet people belong to the Communist party? What are the requirements for membership?

Know word meanings

Be able to define and use correctly the following terms:

C.P.S.U.	raion	Sovmin	Presidium of the U.S.S.R.
soviet	oblast	Supreme Soviet	Presidium of the C.P.S.U.

Do something extra

1. Compare the qualifications for membership in the Communist party in Russia with those for membership in a political party in the United States.

2. Make a chart showing, in parallel columns, (1) the similarities in organization of the United States government and the government of the U.S.S.R.; (2) the differences in operation.

3. Read and report on the organization and operation of (1) the party Presidium, (2) the party Secretariat.

4. Read and report on elections and election day in the Soviet Union.

Women in the Soviet Union do almost every kind of work,
including the hardest. These women are marking lines
on the pavement of Moscow's Red Square. Behind them
rises the 16th-century Church of St. Vasily the Blessed,
which the Soviet government has made into a museum.

7

LIFE IN THE SOVIET UNION

According to Communist propaganda, the Soviet Union is a "workers' paradise" in which "class exploitation" has been completely eliminated. The leadership of the Soviet government "belongs to the workers as the advanced class of society." The "highest law," the Communists say, is the "raising of the well-being of the Soviet people, the complete satisfaction of its constantly growing material and cultural demands."

As the *Great Soviet Encyclopedia* describes it, the Soviet Union is the freest country in the world: "The citizens of the U.S.S.R. are guaranteed freedom of conscience, of speech, of the press, of assembly, of street processions and demonstrations; the right to join in public organizations; inviolability of the individual; inviolability of the home; and privacy of correspondence. . . . In the Soviet state, for the first time in the history of mankind, there has been realized the equality of citizens, independent of their nationality, race, sex."

This is what the Soviet Union says about its own system. These statements are, of course, bald lies. They are part of the myth that Soviet propagandists have attempted to build up in order to hide the sad truth of what life is really like in the Soviet Union.

The Soviet Union is a totalitarian state; that is, it is a state in which the government attempts to control every aspect of the life of every individual. Furthermore, it is probably the most thoroughly totalitarian state that the world has known. The Communist party and Soviet government interfere in almost anything that anyone may wish to do. Workers, peasants, and intellectuals are all told what to do by the government. Children's minds are formed, to as great an extent as possible, by the government. Religious beliefs and

129

minority interests are made, wherever possible, to serve the interests of the government; and if they cannot be made to serve the government, as is usually the case, the government tries to stamp them out. And the Soviet government even goes so far as to try to control the lives of tourists in the Soviet Union.

The Soviet Citizen as Worker

According to Marxist belief, Communism exists for the benefit of the working class. The supposed purpose of the Communist revolution is to bring the working class to power. In Russia, however, the effect of the revolution has been to put the workers at the mercy of the Communist party.

The Soviet worker enjoys few of the freedoms of the workers in the United States or other capitalist countries. For example, workers in the Soviet Union are not permitted to strike. According to the Communists, the workers own the factories of Russia themselves. How, they argue, can a worker strike against himself? Since 1953 there have been occasional rumors of strikes in the Soviet Union. But the strikes are never mentioned in the newspapers, because the government could scarcely admit that workers were unhappy in the "workers' paradise." If any strikes have occurred, they are certain to have been ruthlessly put down by the police or the army.

The workers do not consider that they own the factories. To them, the managers of the plants are still the bosses, even though they are Communist party officials rather than capitalists. The workers do not consider the factory to be theirs any more than they did under capitalism.

The Soviet labor unions are not workers' organizations, but a part of the state. The chief function of the Soviet labor unions is to keep the working class under control and to increase production. Instead of being the worker's friend, the union has often been his enemy. But the unions do perform some services for the Soviet workers. For example, they have been given the job of enforcing safety rules, and they administer the Soviet system of social security for disabled workers. If a workman becomes injured on the job, his benefits are distributed by the union. If his physician orders him to a resort to recover, the union arranges the trip for him.

To arouse the workers' enthusiasm for greater production, the Communists make believe that the unions are important in determining wage rates and working hours. In practice, however, these

In every Soviet factory, slogans urging hard work cover the walls, and the record of each worker in fulfilling his work quota is posted for all to see. The carpenter shop of a Soviet prison, above, is typical. The large sign in the foreground says, "Shame on loafers!"

decisions are made almost entirely according to instructions and demands from the government.

The workers of Russia often have reason to complain. They dislike the pay cuts that the government forces on them from time to time —often side by side with demands for increased production. They dislike the pressure to fulfill work quotas that the government is always placing upon them. They dislike the unsafe working conditions that they are often forced to put up with. In the United States, they could complain to their labor union officers. In the Soviet Union, however, the union officers are representatives not of the workers but of the government—the same government that caused the complaints in the first place. In the past few years, workers have been encouraged to write their complaints to newspapers, which have set up special investigation departments. Some workers' grievances are settled through these departments. But the only complaints that are listened to are those that do not conflict with government policy; complaints of low wages or of unreasonable work demands would be ignored. And even though some complaints are brought to light by this method, the workers still are not acting on their own behalf.

There is simply another government agency (the newspapers) acting for them.

In spite of their many reasons for complaint, it must not be thought that the Soviet workers are notably unhappy or that they are ripe for revolution against the Soviet system. The living standard of the average Russian worker has improved greatly in recent years, even though it is still less than half that of the average American worker. The lowest paid Russian workers have had their wages raised. The government has promised a shorter working day, and in some cases has already fulfilled its promise. But the six-day week is still observed.

The Soviet government has relaxed its restrictions on the workers' freedom of movement. At one time, workers were assigned to jobs which they could not leave. Absence from work, and even tardiness, were punishable by prison sentences or worse. Today, however, the Soviet worker is relatively free to transfer from one job to another, although much red tape may be involved. Some factories even compete with others for workers, offering such rewards as better apartments to those willing to change jobs.

The condition of Russian workers is probably better now than it has ever before been under Communism. They still suffer greatly by comparison to American workers; but their lives are greatly improved over what they were when Stalin was alive. The improvement is largely the result of decisions by Khrushchev and other Communist leaders, who realize that more can be obtained from workers by making them happy than by standing over them with whips. But the workers have no guarantee that the government will not change its mind and return to the old policy of force. And if the government should change its mind, there would be little the workers could do about it.

The Soviet Citizen as Peasant

Both Marx and Lenin considered the peasants to be the most conservative element in the population. Most peasants demand little more than a plot of land that they can farm in peace. To Lenin, the peasants were not a revolutionary group, and they were not to be relied upon. It was the workers who were to be the strength of the revolution.

But Lenin's revolution took place in a country where four fifths of the population was agricultural. Lenin could not ignore the peasants. He purchased their support by allowing them to keep the land that they had already taken away from the czarist nobility. But he remained suspicious of the land-loving peasants, as does the Soviet government to this day.

In the collectivization of agriculture in the late 1920's and early 1930's, the peasants were deprived of their property in a most brutal fashion and forced into collective farms, or *kolkhozes*. (See pages 81–82.) But after the beginning of collectivization, Stalin found it necessary to make some concessions to the peasants. He allowed them to keep a few barnyard animals and a small plot of land, on which they could raise what they pleased. They could keep the crops from these small plots of land for themselves, or they could sell them on the open market.

The peasants are supposed to spend most of their time working on the kolkhoz land, the land that is farmed by all the members of the collective. For every day of ordinary labor that a peasant works, he receives one *trudoden,* or "labor day," of credit, which is recorded by the kolkhoz bookkeeper. If he has a particular skill, he may receive more than one *trudoden* for each day of work. For example, a tractor driver may receive five *trudodens* for a day's work.

At the end of the year, the number of *trudodens* worked by everyone on the collective is divided into the profit of the kolkhoz. The resulting figure is the value of one *trudoden*. This figure is then multiplied by the number of *trudodens* worked by any single peasant to determine the share of the total profits to which he is entitled.

On most collective farms, the value of a *trudoden* is very low. As a result, most peasants find it more profitable to concentrate on working on their own tiny plots of land than to contribute to the collective. They must work a minimum number of days on the collective land, but they do so unwillingly and without enthusiasm. On their own land, however, they work with great care and energy. As a result, the output of these small, private plots makes up a large percentage of Soviet agricultural production in several important areas. In a recent year, private farming provided 82 per cent of all Soviet egg production, almost 70 per cent of all potatoes, 50 per cent of all meat and milk, and 45 per cent of all vegetables.

Figures of this kind are infuriating to dedicated Communists like Khrushchev, because they indicate how much Soviet agriculture depends on capitalistic private enterprise. The Communists would much prefer that this private-enterprise agriculture be completely eliminated. But they know that if the small, privately-held plots were taken away, even less food would be produced.

A peasant woman on a Byelo-russian collective draws water from an open well in the yard of her straw-roofed house. Note the similarity between present conditions in rural Rus-sia, as here, and in Russia un-der the czars, as in the picture on page 26.

134

United Press International

Khrushchev has attempted to pull the peasants away from their private plots by offering them the advantages of city life. He has championed the *agrogorod*, or "farm-city," which would gather the people from a number of villages together in one town. The town would have new apartment buildings, well-supplied stores, theaters, good schools, a hospital, and other advantages of a city. The peasants would leave for work in the morning just as their city brothers do, ride to the fields in trucks and buses, and return to the city at night.

If the government were willing to spend enough money to build *agrogorods*, the peasants would probably like living in them—but not at the price of having to surrender their own land. The Soviet government would like to get the peasants away from their land—but not if it would have to use force, which would undoubtedly cause Soviet agriculture to produce even less than it does now. Thus the tug-of-war between the peasantry and the Soviet state continues. Neither side will give way; and as long as the struggle continues, there is probably little chance for real improvement in Soviet agricultural production.

Today almost half the people of the Soviet Union live in the countryside, by far the largest figure for any industrial nation. Besides being so numerous, the Russian peasantry is also the poorest part of the Soviet population. A few collective farmers do very well; but the majority live in conditions that are only slightly better than those of their pre-revolutionary grandfathers under the czars.

For many peasants the only noticeable improvement between czarist times and the present is that education is more widespread. But the benefits of education are seldom introduced into the collectives, because the smarter peasants leave the collectives as soon as they can. In the Soviet Union today, collective farms are generally considered the least desirable places to be; anyone who knows better seeks to leave them. Only the less able and energetic remain; therefore, most of the kolkhozes remain extremely backward places.

Peasant life in Russia is difficult and dull. The peasants would probably remain in the country and produce more if the Soviet government would give the peasants good reason to work harder. But because the government refuses to do this, the collective farmers suffer a low standard of living, and agricultural production does little better than limp along.

The Soviet Citizen as Intellectual

During the czarist days educated Russians were often prevented from living in a world of action. A man who wanted to change the system could do little, short of plotting a revolution. Those Russians who were not revolutionary were therefore forced to concentrate their efforts in thinking and writing, and the life of the mind is still important to Russians.

In terms of material rewards, the Russian intelligentsia—the painters, composers, writers, poets, and scientists—have fared well under the Soviet regime. They have been given the best things that the Soviet system has to offer: four-room apartments, country villas, vacations, automobiles, electrical appliances. But it has been expected that, in return, they will carry out the tasks assigned by the state. In the U.S.S.R., *everything*—art and science no less than industry and agriculture—must serve the purposes of the Soviet state.

"Socialist realism" has been the official style of Soviet art. "Socialist realism" demands that Soviet life be depicted not as it actually is, but as the Communists would like it to be. At the height of the era of "socialist realism" in novels, the heroine would fall in love with the hero not because he was kind or handsome, but because he could dig more coal in a day than could anyone else. And a boy would admire a girl not because of her beauty and character, but because she was the best milkmaid on the collective farm. It is little wonder that Soviet readers became bored by this propaganda and returned to reading the great Russian classics of the 19th century.

Boris Pasternak (1890–1960), the great poet and novelist who refused to follow the formulas of "socialist realism," and who risked his life by having his works published outside the U.S.S.R.

Pantheon Books

Almost all of Russia's writers ground out volumes according to the dictates of socialist realism. But many of the best also wrote "privately," for themselves and a few trusted friends, even though they knew that there was little hope of their work's being published. The most famous example is the case of Boris Pasternak, probably the greatest Russian poet of the 20th century, whose novel *Doctor Zhivago* is recognized as a major work and has been translated into most of the world's leading languages. Yet *Doctor Zhivago* has yet to be published in Pasternak's own country; and when Pasternak was awarded the Nobel Prize for Literature in 1958, he was viciously attacked in the Soviet newspapers for his "anti-Soviet" novel. According to the Soviet government's literary critics, Pasternak's most important work was his translations of Shakespeare into Russian. Although Pasternak was world famous when he died in 1960, his death was given hardly any notice in the Soviet press.

"Socialist realism" opposes most music that is not written in the style of the 18th or 19th centuries. Stalin once criticized a symphony by Dimitri Shostakovich, one of Russia's greatest composers, because there was nothing in it that he could whistle. To regain Stalin's favor, Shostakovich was compelled to write music to Stalin's taste. One theme he composed to please Stalin begins with Soviet soldiers attacking a German-held village. They drive the Germans out. They are greeted joyously by the populace. They leave the village in pur-

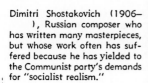

Dimitri Shostakovich (1906–
), Russian composer who
has written many masterpieces,
but whose work often has suffered because he has yielded to
the Communist party's demands
for "socialist realism."

137

suit of the retreating enemy. It was bad music, and Shostakovich
knew it; but it was something that Stalin could recognize as "patriotic," and it had a theme that Stalin could whistle.

During Stalin's heyday, "socialist realism" dictated that Stalin
himself be the principal subject of Soviet art. "Stalin Leading Revolutionary Demonstration in Batum," "Stalin with Lenin before October," "Stalin Addressing the Red Army," "Stalin Being Visited by
a Group of Young Pioneers"—these are typical titles at exhibitions
of paintings of the period. The other themes of Soviet painting were
the proletariat of Russia in idealized form, with bulging muscles,
extraordinarily healthy bodies, and happy faces, shown performing
the tasks of building the "Socialist Motherland." Modern or abstract
paintings were declared "bourgeois" and "decadent." Soviet architecture almost without exception followed old-fashioned styles, with
few of the innovations of modern American architecture.

Under Stalin, Soviet science was also stifled by the demands of
the Soviet state. Scientific ideas were accepted or rejected according
to whether they seemed to agree with something Marx had said;
whether or not they were correct often made little difference. For
example, the biologist Lysenko stated that environment could affect
heredity. This theory is in direct contradiction to the known laws of
genetics (the study of heredity). But it fitted in well with the Marxist notion that a man who is given food, clothing, and a good, whole-

some, Soviet atmosphere will develop into the "new Soviet man," who would thereafter not be able to act in a non-Soviet way. The theory was made a cornerstone of Soviet biology, and real advances in the biological sciences were prevented for many years.

The Soviets have killed, kidnapped, and imprisoned scientists and other intellectuals who have refused to do their bidding. The famous physicist Kapitza, who was invited to visit the Soviet Union, was not permitted to return to England, where he had lived for twelve years and where he had become a citizen. Later he was imprisoned for refusing to work on the hydrogen bomb. The economist Voznesensky was executed because he refused to prophecy that capitalism was dying, as Stalin insisted he should.

Today the intellectual atmosphere in Russia is somewhat more free than it was in Stalin's day. Scientists, in particular, are not bound by Marxist ideology in their research—although they must still be sure that their conclusions do not disagree too strongly with Marxist belief. And freedom of research does not include wide freedom of expression, either for scientists or for others. However, the poets, writers, artists, and musicians—particularly the poets—are now experimenting with methods and ideas long familiar in the West but until recently forbidden in Russia, and still regarded with suspicion by the Communists. Today the Russian intellectuals are far from being completely free to express themselves in any way that they may choose; but the freedom that they have has at least enabled them to struggle for still more freedom of expression.

Childhood and Youth in the Soviet Union

Almost from the very beginning, childhood in the Soviet Union is different from that in the United States. The reason is that far more Soviet than American mothers hold jobs: there is a continuing labor shortage in Russia, which is partly filled by women, and Russian families often need two incomes to make ends meet. As a result, many Russian babies spend large parts of the day separated from their mothers. There is an extensive system of day nurseries, where many of the children are looked after; but there are not enough of them to take care of all the children whose mothers must work. Grandmothers who are past their working years are therefore often called upon to raise the children—to the regret of the Soviet state, which feels that grandmothers are storehouses of old, un-Soviet ideas, which they spread among the young.

The Soviet educational system emphasizes physical fitness in a number of ways. Almost everyone participates in sports, of which soccer, basketball, and volleyball are the most popular. Above, girls march in a physical culture parade in Minsk, Byelorussia.

Soviet children do not start going to school until the age of seven, but once in school they work harder than schoolchildren in the United States. Sometimes Soviet teachers and parents complain that the children are forced to do too much homework. Great emphasis is placed on learning to read well and quickly. Soviet students are introduced to great writers like Tolstoy and Pushkin in their first reader; other reading lessons, however, contain much Soviet propaganda, such as "Mama Is a Stakhanovite."

In Soviet education, greater emphasis is placed on mathematics and science than in the United States, because the Communist party believes that the key to future Communist success lies in these areas. Foreign language training is also stressed. In the Soviet Union almost all students study a foreign language, usually for from four to six years. The quality of Soviet foreign-language instruction is poor, however, and the majority of students apparently never do learn to speak a foreign language.

Soviet schools are conducted six days a week. School begins at about 9:00 A.M. and lasts about five hours; there is a tendency, however, to extend the school hours and to do more homework in the school building. Soviet schools are more formal than American ones. The children wear uniforms: pinafores and collars for the girls, military-style tunics for the boys. The children stand when the teacher enters or leaves the room. But the Soviet children are full of high spirits, and they have been known to play tricks on their teachers as well as on their fellow students.

The Soviet system emphasizes physical fitness. Every day begins with exercises, and there are often game periods in the middle of the day. The official youth organizations do their best to develop athletic skills. Every district in the Soviet Union has its own "spartacade," an athletic competition for the students of the area. Those who win are sent to the all-republic "spartacade," and the victors of that competition go to the all-Union "spartacade." The winners of the all-Union contest usually go into training for the next Olympic games to compete for world championships. Because of the time and effort that its leaders have put into the development of athletic programs, the Soviet Union has had much success in international athletic competitions since World War II.

In the Soviet Union, a child belongs to a Communist political organization at every age. The youngest belong to the Little Octobrists, then they graduate to the Pioneers. At fifteen they become eligible to join the Young Communist League, or *Komsomol,* and great pressure is applied to them to do so. The next step would be to join the Communist party itself, for which a Komsomol member becomes eligible when he is eighteen.

The Soviet government sponsors each of these organizations. They are used to influence the child when he is not in school, lest his mind develop in ways dangerous to the party. The party has not succeeded in turning Soviet youth into perfect Communist robots, but its methods have had some success with all Soviet citizens.

In 1959, Khrushchev introduced a new educational policy. According to the new plan, there would be stronger emphasis on vocational education throughout all the grades of primary and secondary school. Almost all Soviet students would leave school after eleven years in order to obtain "experience in life." In other words, they would learn a skill or a trade. If they wished to continue going to school, they could study in night classes. If they did well in night school and at work for two years, they would be permitted to enroll in a higher school—if space could be found for them. The new policy is a warning to Soviet youth: if they want to go to a university, they had better work hard. For Soviet young people, as for their parents, life is fiercely competitive.

One of the objects of a Soviet education is to train young Marxist-Leninists. Thus, no child is ever away from the official Communist doctrine for very long. Special courses in "political indoctrination" are given in the secondary schools and in the universities. The students are usually bored by having propaganda repeated at each step of their education; but if they want to get ahead in Soviet life, they must attend and at least pretend to pay attention.

Few young Russians oppose Communism. As patriotic Russians, they are proud of the accomplishments of the country and of the party. Although they hope to have more contact with the West, more consumer goods, and more freedom, they expect to reach these goals within the Soviet system. And they expect that their lives will be better than the lives of their parents have been.

The Religious Soviet Citizen

Marxism denies God because his existence cannot be proved scientifically. Marx called religion "the opium of the people," because he believed that religion was a drug that made people content with their lot on earth, and thus postponed the inevitable revolution. Today Communism is opposed to organized religion for another reason: it fears that the people may feel a greater sense of loyalty to their church than to Communism, which has itself become the official religion in Russia.

During the 1930's the Communist party relaxed its fight against the Russian Orthodox Church in the interest of national unity. The Soviet constitution of 1936 recognized "freedom of religious worship" as well as "freedom of anti-religious propaganda." Nevertheless, the fight of Communism against God and religion has existed since the revolution. Sometimes it is pressed with determination, sometimes with less interest. The party has always attempted to forbid religious instruction to the youth, acting on the belief that if one does not learn to be religious as a child, he is unlikely to do so as an adult.

Most of the lovely churches of czarist Russia have been converted into apartments or storehouses or are covered with scaffolding. The visitor is told that the latter are being repaired, but some of them have been under "repair" since the revolution. The number of seminaries allowed to operate is set by the authorities at a low figure, and the number of prayer books and Bibles printed is strictly regulated.

A Russian may worship more or less freely in his church (if he can find one), but the paths to success will be closed to him if he does. He cannot become a party member; entrance to a university is denied him; and good jobs will be difficult to obtain, whatever

United Press International

Because most of the churches of Russia have been closed by the Communists, the few that remain open are usually overcrowded. Above, Russian women are forced to worship at the window of their church, which is not large enough to accommodate the number of worshipers who wish to attend its services.

his other qualifications may be. All of the pressures of the state apparatus are brought to bear to discourage the youth from following the way of God and religion.

The situation is particularly difficult for those who belong to the various religious minorities: the Catholics, the Baptists, the Jews, the Seventh-Day Adventists, and Jehovah's Witnesses. These groups were traditionally oppressed in Russia even under the czar. The Soviet regime oppresses them because they have no tradition of accepting a centralized Russian authority, as does the Russian Orthodox Church. This makes them difficult to control. Moreover, the Soviet authority is extremely suspicious of their foreign contacts. Members of these groups have been accused of being part of an international spy apparatus of world capitalism. The opposition to these groups is considered a matter of national security and is made to seem different from considerations of freedom of worship.

Yet religion continues in Russia. On Sundays and on holy days, the few churches and synagogs of Russia are filled to overflowing. While the congregations are mostly older people, those who have been in Russia in recent years report that the number of youth is increasing. Khrushchev says that this is due to the natural curiosity of youth. But there are indications that the youth of Russia, even the Communist youth, are more than simply curious. Many have found neither personal satisfaction, nor contentment, nor beauty in the Communist party. The church provides them with a sense of being a member of a group, thus overcoming the sense of isolation that is often felt in an industrial society. Youth sent to distant parts of Russia, away from homes and friends, find solace in religion. In the grandeur of a church wedding or baptism, they find a beauty denied them elsewhere. Young Communists rent cars and drive to villages outside the major cities where no one is likely to see them. There they are married or have their children baptized. Religion also forms an outlet for the natural rebelliousness of youth, which in the U.S.S.R. seems sometimes to take the form of going to church. Thus, although Soviet authorities make it difficult to be religious, they have not been able to wipe out religion. Future efforts toward its elimination will probably be no more effective.

Soviet Citizens of Minority Nationalities

Under the czars an effort was made to weld all of the nationality groups of the Russian Empire into one by forcing all to accept Russian Orthodoxy. These attempts only increased the desire of some of the non-Russian people of Russia to gain independence. Though Lenin did not approve of the division of big empires into little states, he realized that this drive towards independence could be used to strengthen his own movement. Therefore, for tactical reasons, he decided to favor what he called "self-determination" for minorities. But "self-determination" does not have the same meaning in the Communist dictionary that it has elsewhere. It does not mean the right to withdraw from the Soviet Union. It means little more today than the right to use national tongues as second languages and the right to practice some old national customs. It certainly does not mean the "autonomy" (self-government) that Soviet propagandists talk about.

Russia is divided into 15 republics. The largest is the Russian Soviet Federated Socialist Republic. The others are known by the names of their dominant national groups, such as the Ukrainian Soviet Socialist Republic, the Byelorussian S.S.R., the Kazakh S.S.R., and so forth. To further permit "self-determination" within the larger republics, there are Autonomous Republics, Autonomous

Regions and National Areas, each established for a minority group which is the dominant population group in the area.

The guiding principle of Soviet "self-determination" is that the activities of the nationalities must be "national in form, socialist in content." In other words, native stories may be written and native plays and dances may be produced, but their themes must conform to the Communist doctrine of "socialist realism." For example, an Armenian composer might write a folk opera about the life of his native area five hundred years ago. The characters would be dressed in Armenian costumes, and the tunes would be Armenian. But the poor would be presented as heroic workers, the wealthy as evil, grasping capitalists. Even though the Armenians of that time regarded the Russians as their greatest enemy, the opera would give no hint of this. Thus, Communist propaganda goals dictate the story of an opera, even though the style of music might be "national."

While non-Russian languages are tolerated, it is nevertheless apparent that the Communists hope that in the long run they will be abandoned. In the republics, those whose native language is not Russian must learn it; but those whose native language is Russian need not learn the local language. Moreover, anyone who wishes to advance in the Soviet system must be fluent in Russian.

One of Communism's strongest tendencies is to attempt to make everyone fit a common mold. National minorities make for differences; and differences, by Communist interpretation, are bad. If the Soviet citizen who belongs to a minority group is willing to abandon these differences that set him apart from the Great Russians, to forget the customs and language of his forefathers, he can advance far in the system. Stalin was not a Great Russian, nor was Beria, and some say that Khrushchev himself is Ukrainian.

Prejudice against some of the minorities in Russia is partly based on race. Almost without exception, the Russians look down upon the Asiatic peoples of the Soviet Union as being inferior, dirty, and lazy. The Asiatics, for their part, complain that all the good jobs and living quarters go to the Europeans who have moved into their midst. There is little they can do about this except complain.

The Soviets hope and expect that some day all national minorities will disappear and be replaced by a single "Soviet" or "Great Russian" culture. But for the moment they seem content to allow the national minorities to keep the so-called "autonomy" that they now possess. If the Communists were to attempt to eliminate the national differences by force, they would probably meet with resistance.

Force would also defeat another Soviet purpose. Many of the minority groups live along the Soviet frontier, and they have relatives just across the border in other countries. Often in the past the Soviet minorities have been used by the government in attempts to influence their relatives on the other side of the border to look favorably on the Soviet Union.

Tourists in the Soviet Union

Thus far in this chapter, we have considered various aspects of the lives of Soviet citizens. But what about foreigners? What might an American citizen expect if he were to visit the Soviet Union as a tourist? How would he be treated? What impressions might he gain of life in the Soviet Union?

During the Stalin years, hardly any foreigners were allowed to enter the U.S.S.R. for any reason. Since the late 1950's, however, the Soviet government has allowed tourists, including Americans, to visit Russia. In recent years, visiting the Soviet Union has become a rather fashionable thing to do.

Most Americans who visit the Soviet Union are at a disadvantage because they do not speak Russian. In France, Italy, or Germany, it is possible for a tourist to get by very well without speaking the language, because many of the people speak English; but in the Soviet Union, relatively few people speak English. As a result, tourists who cannot speak Russian are forced to depend on guides from Intourist, the Soviet travel agency. Intourist, like everything else in the Soviet Union, is a part of the government; therefore, a visitor who must rely on Intourist will receive a very one-sided view of Soviet life—the side that the Soviet government wants him to see.

It is difficult to obtain an accurate impression of the Soviet Union by visiting the country for a few brief days. Such an impression can be gained only by spending a long time in a country, by visiting every part of it, by walking its streets, by observing and talking with its people. It is difficult, and sometimes impossible, to fulfill these requirements in Russia.

One difficulty is that foreigners are seldom allowed to remain in the Soviet Union for more than 30 days. Another is that many areas of the country are closed to foreign visitors. Arrangements must be made far in advance—usually before leaving the United States—to visit many other parts of the Soviet Union. Even in the major tourist centers, such as Moscow, one cannot go beyond the city limits unless he has made arrangements to do so in advance. Another difficulty is the cost. Tours that visit the major cities—the Communist showplaces—are relatively inexpensive; but anyone who wishes to visit a place not on the tour, or to remain in a place a few days longer than the tour, must pay Intourist $35.00 a day for the privilege.

An American tourist may freely walk the streets in a Russian city, and he will probably not be followed. If he speaks Russian, he is often able to strike up a conversation with a friendly Soviet citizen. The latter may become silent or beat a quick retreat when he discovers that the person with whom he is speaking is an American. More often, however, curiosity will get the better of him. He is filled with all kinds of questions, some of which are quite straightforward. What do you do? How much do you make? How many hours a week do you work? How long is your vacation? Do you have an automobile? What kind? (The Russians know and admire American automobiles.) How old is it? Do you live in a house or in an apartment? How many rooms? How much rent do you pay? (This is a frequent question, because the average rent in the Soviet Union is much lower than in America.) How does it happen that you know Russian? And so on and on. Most Russians love to talk, and these conversations may last for hours. Other Russians will join in, asking questions and correcting one another. Sometimes the questions will touch on politics, on the merits of their system as opposed to ours; but usually their questions reflect a simple curiosity about our way of living. When the conversation breaks up, one may feel that he has made some Russian friends; but they seldom extend invitations to visit them in their homes. This is partly because they are not proud of where they live or do not have room to receive visitors. But also it is because they are aware that the Soviet government frowns on such close contacts between themselves and Americans. The Soviet government still suspects its own people.

Many Americans find the food in Russia more agreeable than that available in other parts of Europe. It is hearty, usually without frills. It is the kind of food that peasant populations in eastern Europe have eaten for centuries. The diet leans heavily in the direction of soups, potatoes, cabbage, boiled meat, and bread. The water in all the major cities is safe.

United Press International

Most Russians are intensely curious about the ways of life of the West. Above, a British sports car, probably the first sports car ever seen in the Soviet Union, is carefully examined by a group of Moscow pedestrians.

147

Even if there are several hotels in a town, the tourist must go to the one he is assigned to. In Moscow, Leningrad, or Kiev, it is possible to request a particular hotel; in all probability, however, the request will not be granted. Rooms in the hotels are large. Even in the newest hotels the furniture is, by American standards, huge and old-fashioned, but it is comfortable. Because Russian standards of workmanship in the building trades are extremely low, even the newest hotels often seem to be falling apart. But they are clean.

An American visitor to the Soviet Union can expect the Soviet government to put its best foot forward for him. It will try to keep him from seeing anything that the Communists consider unfavorable to their cause. If he has a chance to meet any of the Russian people, he will probably be impressed by their friendliness. But visitors to Moscow (unlike most visitors to London or Paris or Rome or New York) usually feel a sense of relief when the time comes to leave for home. The Soviet Union is a fascinating country, but it is not the most pleasant one to visit.

aids to learning

Check the facts

1. Name several of the contradictions between the description of the Soviet Union as given in the *Great Soviet Encyclopedia,* and the operation of the Soviet Union as a totalitarian state.

2. Why are workers in the Soviet Union unable to strike? Name some of the complaints they have. How may they bring their complaints to public notice? How effective are their efforts to improve working conditions?

3. What is the function of the Soviet labor unions? What services do they perform for the worker? Why is the Soviet worker unlikely to revolt against the Soviet system? What former restrictions have been relaxed?

4. How is a collective farm operated? How is each peasant's share of the profit of a kolkhoz determined? Why is each peasant permitted to own a little land of his own? How important are these private plots to agricultural production? Why is farming on the private plots more successful than on the collective farms?

5. What per cent of the Russian people were engaged in agriculture when Lenin came into power? What per cent of the Russian people are farmers today? What is the plan and purpose of the *agrogorod?*

6. What rewards are given to the Russian intellectual for his work? What requirements are made of him? Name some of the Russian writers, musicians, and scientists who refused to follow the Soviet requirements. What happened to them and their work?

7. At what age do Soviet children start school? Name the subjects that are emphasized in the schools. What are some of the differences between a Soviet school and one in the United States? What factors contribute to Russia's frequent successes in international athletic games?

8. Name the political organizations to which Soviet young people may belong. What is the purpose of these organizations?

9. What was Khrushchev's new educational policy of 1959? What is the object of Soviet education?

10. Why is the Communist party opposed to religious organizations? Why are they more opposed to religious minorities, such as Jews, Baptists, and Catholics, than to the Russian Orthodox Church? Name some of the pressures used by the Communists to discourage church membership or attendance. Why are many young people in Russia becoming increasingly interested in religion?

11. How does the Communist dictionary define "self-determination"? What is the meaning of this term in non-Communist countries? What restrictions are put on the study and use of non-Russian languages in the non-Russian republics of the Soviet Union? Why do the Russians refrain from using force to bring about the end of national minorities in the Soviet Union? Are Russians free from racial prejudice?

12. What are some of the difficulties an American visiting Russia would encounter in his efforts to obtain an accurate impression of the Soviet Union?

What opportunities would an American tourist have to talk with the Russian people? What would be some of the topics of conversation? What kind of food and accommodations would a tourist find in the large Russian cities? Why do visitors to Russia usually feel relieved when their Russian stay is ended?

Know word meanings

Be able to define and use correctly the following terms:

exploitation	totalitarian	kolkhoz	trudoden	Octobrists
agrogorod	spartacade	Komsomol	autonomy	Pioneers

Identify names

For what is each of these men renowned?

Lysenko   Kapitza   Pasternak   Shostakovich   Voznesensky

Use the map

Indicate on an outline map of the Soviet Union the fifteen republics into which it is divided. Write the name of each in its location on the map.

Do something extra

1. Consult the *Readers' Guide to Periodical Literature* since 1955 for accounts of visits to United States farms and the study of United States farming by Soviet officials and farm representatives.

2. Locate and read magazine articles concerning (1) the publication of Pasternak's novel *Dr. Zhivago;* (2) Russia's treatment of Pasternak when he was awarded the Nobel prize; (3) Pasternak's death.

3. Using the *Readers' Guide to Periodical Literature,* locate and read articles concerning Russian schools since 1955.

4. Report on the achievements of Russian scientists in atomic research, space exploration, biology, and medicine. Compare them with the achievements of United States scientists in the same fields.

5. What is the extent and purpose of the cultural exchange program carried on by Russia and the United States? Name some of the people and organizations from Russia that have performed in the United States. Name some of the American individuals and groups that have given programs in Russia.

6. The interest of Russian youth in jazz is shown in the success of Benny Goodman's concerts in the Soviet Union. Accounts of them are given in *Newsweek,* vol. 60, July 2, pp. 47–49, July 23, pp. 68–69, 1962 and *United States News,* vol. 52, July 11, 1962, p. 20.

7. Report on the observations and experiences of a tourist in the Soviet Union given in *Russian Journey* by Justice William O. Douglas.

8. Report on one or more of the articles in the paperback *The Many Faces of Communism,* edited by Harry Schwartz.

9. Read and report on *Kira Georgievna* by Victor Nekrasov, a novel that portrays the life of the intelligentsia in the Soviet Union in 1959.

Communist party members give the Communist salute,
a raised clenched fist, at the 1936 May Day parade
in New York. May 1, the "international day of labor,"
is observed by Communists everywhere. Communist party
membership in America reached its peak in the 1930's.

COMMUNIST TACTICS IN THE UNITED STATES

Marx believed that the world would inevitably become Communist. Lenin agreed that Communism would eventually take over, but Lenin wanted it to happen sooner rather than later. Lenin therefore turned Russian Communism into a conspiracy led by a few devoted revolutionaries. After the Russian Revolution, most of the nations of the world developed their own Communist movements. These soon fell under the control of the Russian Soviet regime.

Over the years many changes have been made in Marx's Communism. In spite of these basic changes in the nature of Communism, the end aim of Communism has not changed. At all times, in all periods of Communist history, *the end aim of Communism has been a Communist world*.

To bring this Communist world into being, the Communist activities in free countries have concentrated on one goal: gaining control of the masses. The goal is to *convert* the masses to Communism; but if it cannot do that, Communism is satisfied if it can *control* them, so that they will support (or at least not fight) the ideas that the Communists put forward.

To gain control, the Communists have developed a set of tactics that they use throughout the non-Communist world, including the United States.

The Tactics of Communism

The day-to-day plans of operation of the Communist party were established by Lenin. In fighting for the revolution in Russia, he established several principles that have become the rules for party

151

operation throughout the world. These are the tactics of Communism.

Of course, these tactics are not the exclusive property of the Communists. Other groups sometimes use one or more of them. But they are often referred to as "Bolshevik," because the Communists are particularly fond of them and use them frequently.

Communist tactics are often difficult for a non-Communist to understand. Because of their tactics, Communists often seem to be unprincipled. According to the principles that most Americans hold, Communists are indeed unprincipled. But the Communists do not look upon themselves in the same way; to them, there is only one principle, and that is success in achieving the revolution and Communism. In the Communist religion, this is the *only* principle; in its name almost any act may be justified.

A phrase sometimes used to explain this characteristic of Communism is "The end justifies the means." This means that to a dedicated Communist, nothing is wrong if it serves Communism. Even actions that most people would consider dishonest or destructive are accepted tactics to the dedicated Communist.

Consistency

In most societies, a person who argues for one thing one moment and for something completely different five minutes later is accused of being inconsistent. Most people object to being called inconsistent, and most people are rather embarrassed if someone proves that they have indeed been inconsistent.

But not the dedicated Communist. If it is pointed out that his arguments have suddenly changed, he is likely to shrug his shoulders and reply that "the situation has changed." Because the situation has changed, his arguments have been changed to meet it. He does not consider himself inconsistent, for he had been consistent to the one thing that, to him, really counts: the promotion of Communism. The dedicated Communist will do what seems best for Communism *at that moment;* at a different time and place he is likely to do something quite different.

The Party Line

The Communist party always has an official attitude toward every subject. This party position is called the *party line*. There is a party line on every aspect of life, including not only politics and economics but also education, relaxation, chess, and even baseball. The dedicated Communist is expected to know the party line, and he speaks and acts in strict accordance with it.

The party line changes often. For example, in 1934 Russian patriotism, which had been bad, suddenly became good; in 1939 the German Nazis, who had been enemies, suddenly became allies; and in 1956 Stalin, who had been good, suddenly became evil. Did these changes mean that the party line had been wrong and was now correcting its stand? No, said the Communists, the party had been correct all the time. But the "situation had changed," so a new position was required.

A loyal Communist must follow the party line. Being a loyal Communist therefore requires, among other things, the ability to quickly change opinions. The Communist, as Lenin put it, must be able "to tack, make agreements, zigzags, retreats, and so on."

Perseverance and Compromise

One of the favorite tactics of Communism is simple perseverance. Communists have found that constant pressure against their enemies often is effective. Keep pushing; keep fighting; be tough. They believe that Communists, who are prepared to struggle endlessly, can outlast any foe.

But when the situation requires, just the opposite tactic may be followed: back down, drop the issue, compromise. Perhaps Communist pressure is only causing the enemy to fight harder. If the Communists pretend that they have lost interest, the opposition will let down its guard—and then the Communists can more easily conquer.

Again, whichever tactic is used depends upon the "situation." If the "situation changes," the tactic changes. But the final goal—a Communist world—remains the same. No Communist may ever compromise that.

Coöperation

Particular situations may make it seem profitable for Communists to coöperate with other groups to achieve specific Communist objectives. The Communists may be too weak to secure these objectives by themselves. If they can find others moving in the same direction, the Communist task is simplified.

Communists always understand that such coöperation is temporary. Coöperation in achieving one objective does not make them lose sight of the unchanged final objective. The Communist group, therefore, must not become lost in some non-Communist organization. Communists must always maintain their ability to work toward the revolution, in their own way, without being limited by other commitments.

Unity

The purpose of Communists in working with other organizations is not only to receive help in reaching a limited goal. There is another purpose: to gain control of the larger organization.

For example, suppose there is a meeting at which an important decision must be made. The meeting is attended by 1,000 people, of whom 250 are disciplined Communists. Most of the other 750 will not have made up their minds in advance as to how to vote. But the Communists will have met in advance, and they will have been told how to vote. As soon as the decision is made, it is fixed; the Communists cannot be talked out of the party position. However, most of the other 750 members have come to the meeting with open minds; they will accept the most persuasive arguments. Therefore, all that the Communists need do is to convince 251—one third of the non-Communists, plus one—to vote with them, and they will win.

In such a situation, the unity of the Communists is the key to their success. The party members might be told to come to the meeting early and to seat themselves at various places around the room. When the meeting begins and comments are sought from the floor, the party members speak up. From all sides of the room the same argument is heard again and again; and since Communists look no different from anyone else, they are not identified as party members. Perhaps only a few of the non-Communists have anything to say, but all of the Communists want to speak. Soon it begins to appear that the overwhelming majority of those present agree with the Communist point of view. Those who have different opinions decide to keep quiet. Those who came with open minds hear only one argument, and are influenced to go along with it. In a vote, the Communists win.

Another Communist tactic that their unity allows them to use is staying late. If the Communists feel that they don't have enough votes to win, they drag the meeting out. They speak repeatedly, and thereby prevent a vote from being taken. Many of those attending must go to work the next day. By 10:30 some of the people will have left. By 11:30 still more will be gone. But none of the Communists leave. As the hours pass, more people leave, until the Communists and those supporting them are in the majority. *Then* they call for a vote to be taken—and they win.

The staying-late tactic is particularly successful among groups that have never before had to deal with Communists. Such tactics at one time helped Communists gain control of labor unions—until the unions began to understand what was happening.

Aggressiveness

The Marxian dialectic views all the world as being in a constant state of change. Communists believe that in this struggle of the dialectic, they (and they alone) represent the new that is in constant struggle with the old. They believe that even though the triumph of the new is certain, there is always a danger that the old may counterattack and prevail for a time. Should the counterattack succeed, it may postpone the achievement of Communism for many years. Therefore, they believe, Communism must be ever on guard against an attack; and the best way to prevent an attack from someone else is to keep Communism itself constantly on the attack. One of the Communists' favorite words is "struggle"; they talk about the "struggle to achieve," the "struggle to overcome," the "struggle to surpass." A dedicated Communist never rests.

While the Communists are always attempting to gain control of other groups, they are afraid that other groups are seeking to do the same to them. They believe that if they let down their guard, someone will surely attack them. It is the Communist intention that they always be the ones that act, not the ones that are acted against.

Retreat

Although aggressiveness is a basic Communist rule, a "changed situation" may sometimes call for a temporary retreat. If such a situation should arise, the idea of pushing forward must not blind the Communist to the need for a retreat. The retreat, however, should be ordered only as a last resort, and it should aim at keeping losses at a minimum. And even at the very moment of retreat, the idea of moving forward again at the earliest possible opportunity must be kept in mind.

Communist Tactics in Action

The Communists will seize any opportunity that presents itself to put their tactics into action. They will ally themselves with almost any cause that they think will help them gain their ends.

Communists in Labor Unions

It must be remembered that the Communist hope to achieve their goal of a Communist world by gaining leadership of the working class. To the Communists, their greatest enemy is *not* the middle class, which they consider to be doomed. The hated enemies, rather, are those groups that compete with the Communists for leadership of the working class. Thus, Communists consider labor unions to be one of their most bitter enemies.

The traditional Communist attitude toward non-Communist labor unions is that they are tools of the bourgeoisie. If the labor unions gain their aims, higher wages and better working conditions, the workers will be satisfied and will not care anything about revolutions. The Communists would prefer that the working class be as miserable as possible so that it will be eager to rise up in revolt.

Despite this attitude toward labor unions, the Communist tactic usually is not to destroy them, but rather to take them over. The party then uses the unions for its own purposes. One way that the Communists use unions is as a blackjack: they threaten to strike and disrupt the country's economy if Communist demands (often political and having nothing to do with higher wages or better working conditions) are not met. Another way is to use the unions to gain favor among the workers. The Communists reason that as long as a Communist union appears to serve the working-class interests, the workers will support the union, and thus the Communists as well.

Communism and Peace

Communist support of unionized labor, to whose independence they are in truth violently opposed, is just one example of the kind of cause that the Communists will support and even organize in order to gain popularity for themselves. Another example is the "peace" crusade that Communists all over the world have been leading since shortly after World War II.

The Communists do not care about peace. If they thought that a war would help them Communize the world (without destroying the part of the world that is already Communist), they would be for war. But the Communists have recognized that the people of the world yearn for peace. The twentieth century has seen two world wars, in which tens of millions of people were killed. Now there is the threat of yet another world war—a war that, if it should come, will be far more horrible than the first two. The Communists recognize that the peoples of the world are dismayed and fearful. They attempt to use this fear to serve their own causes: gaining popularity for themselves, and hiding the military plans of the Communist nations. The Communists hope that the man in the street will think that Communists could not possibly be preparing for war when they talk so much and so beautifully about peace.

Brown Brothers

Marchers in the 1936 May Day parade in New York carry a poster proclaiming one of the principal Communist propaganda themes.

Democracy and Personal Freedoms

Just as the Communists attempt to turn man's yearning for peace to their own advantage, so do they attempt to use other universal hopes of mankind. Today, almost all the world longs for democracy. Not everyone who wants democracy understands what it is, but it has become something that almost everyone favors. The Communists have therefore adopted "democracy" as one of their slogans. The U.S.S.R. is represented as the "most democratic" country in the world; and the Communist satellite states, such as Hungary, Bulgaria, and Rumania, are called "people's democracies."

The Communists do not deal in such terms as *peace* and *democracy* because they believe in them. They use them to gain support. They shout that they are in favor of peace and democracy and "freedom" and "free speech" because they think that such behavior will win them support. In truth, Communists are opposed to such things—unless they can be put to work to Communist advantage.

People who say one thing and believe another are called *hypocrites*. Communists are among the greatest hypocrites in history. The Communists advertise themselves as believers in all the freedoms, such as freedom of speech. But in the Soviet Union and other Communist countries there is no such thing as free speech—and anyone who complained aloud about not having free speech would be thrown in jail. Still, the Communists say they believe in free speech.

To a Communist, this hypocrisy is not immoral, because the Communists believe that anything is justifiable if it helps promote their revolution. But the Communists have another argument to prove that their system is the "most democratic" and the "most freedom-loving." They say that in the United States and other Western countries there may be freedom of speech, freedom of the press, freedom of assembly. But, they say, these freedoms are given only to the middle class, which is afraid to allow the workers to share these freedoms. The Communists therefore call these freedoms "bourgeois" and hold them up to ridicule.

The Communists also argue that if a worker and his family are starving and homeless, they do not care about "bourgeois freedoms." And because they have no money, they cannot afford to hire lawyers to defend their freedoms in court. Without a job, state the Communists, there is no freedom. To them, the basic freedom is the "right to work"; all other freedoms are based on it. And the Communists say that their system, and theirs alone, guarantees jobs for all.

Thus Communism makes light of the freedoms of the free world, calls them "bourgeois," and says that its own "freedom" is superior. Perhaps in theory the Communist argument for the "right to work" contains a certain amount of logic. But in Communist-controlled countries, the "right to work" has been interpreted as a *requirement* to work. Every person *must* work, and in many cases he does not even have the right to choose his own job. Until recently if a Soviet worker wanted a new job, he had to have official permission to change; and if he tried to quit without permission, he could be imprisoned or even shot. And the other freedoms that the "right to work" supposedly insures scarcely exist in Russia. The Soviet system has not led to greater freedom for the workers, but rather to no freedom for anyone.

The Communists are very skilled at using words like *freedom* and *democracy* to their own advantage. Their ability to use these words effectively is increased by the fact that both Marx and Lenin used them frequently in their writings. Marx often spoke of "freedom," and one of Lenin's basic principles is "democratic centralism." But both men looked on freedom and democracy as final results of Communism, to be achieved only in the very distant future. Lenin in particular placed the revolution before all other considerations: if freedom had to be curtailed, that was unfortunate, but it was necessary in order to establish "true" freedom at some future date.

In the United States, however, we already have a great amount of personal freedom, and we seek to preserve it. We are not willing to sacrifice our freedom for the sake of some vague reward in the distant future. To an American, his rights are basic and primary, and must not be bartered away. To a Communist, the same rights are not even important; they can be played with or disregarded, paraded or abused, in any way that will serve to bring about the Communist revolution.

159

Communists and Minority Groups

Still one other cause that Communists often seek to take over is that of minority groups.

In the Soviet Union minority groups are oppressed. They are not sponsored by the party, and therefore cannot be trusted to help promote Communism. If the U.S.S.R. were not concerned with reaction at home and abroad, it would probably eliminate all its minorities. Communist doctrine holds that sooner or later the minorities will disappear, because they represent the dying past.

It is interesting to note that in the United States we believe that the greatness of our country is, in part, the result of the great number of races and peoples that make up its population. Each group makes its own contributions and spurs the others on to greater efforts. The Soviet Union, on the other hand, considers its numerous nationalities to be nuisances and looks forward to their elimination. We believe in strength through diversity; they, in strength through uniformity.

Nevertheless, the Communist party has always championed minority groups in non-Communist lands. It supports them in order to stir up trouble in those countries and to gain support for itself —and *not* because it cares about minority rights, for which it has only contempt.

Communist Front Organizations

One of the most effective methods of Communist operation has been to form *front organizations*. A front organization is a group that seems to be fighting for a cause (such as peace or minority rights) but which is actually controlled by Communists and used for their own purposes. The organizations may be formed by the Communists, who then try to enlist a large non-Communist membership; or they may be organized by non-Communists and later fall under Communist influence or control.

Most members of front organizations are not Communists; they do, however, sincerely believe in the "cause" that the organization allegedly is fighting for. As they work closely with Communists in the front organization, some of these people become convinced that the Communists are fighting for the same good causes to which they themselves are devoted, though many of them never realize—until too late—that Communists have anything to do with the organization. The Communists are able to gain much wider support through the use of front organizations than they would ordinarily have. Moreover, the Communists are able to parade many respectable non-Communist names as their supporters and associates.

The non-Communists who are thus duped into working for and with the Communists are often referred to as "fellow travelers." Some fellow travelers are in basic agreement with the Communists, but for one reason or another do not wish to join the party. Other fellow travelers, however, are simply men of good will who are fooled by the Communists; and most of these sooner or later dissociate themselves from the Communist front organizations.

Revolutionary Morality

That the Communists support causes in which they do not believe is not difficult to understand. To achieve the revolution and Communism, anything is permitted. The goal is success. Nothing that contributes to that goal can be considered immoral; anything that helps reach the goal is right. This attitude is called *revolutionary morality*.

Using the tactics just described, and operating according to revolutionary morality, the Communists succeeded in gaining control in Russia. Because the Russian Communists were successful, and because the Soviet Union was for over a quarter of a century the only Communist country in the world, their tactics have become the tactics of world Communism. They represent the Communist method of action. No matter where one looks—in Italy or France, in Japan or India, in Vietnam or Brazil, in any of the more than eighty countries in which Communists now operate—these tactics may be observed.

The tactics may be observed in our own country as well.

William Z. Foster (1881–1961), chairman and unquestioned boss of the Communist party in the United States during most of three decades.

Communism in America: The First Years

The first Communist group in America was founded in September, 1919. In May, 1921, that group and another Communist group merged to form the Communist Party of the United States of America (C.P.U.S.A.)

Early Days

From the start, the American branch of the Communist party was dominated by the Communist International (Comintern) in Moscow. In 1921 the Bolsheviks still wanted to believe that the revolution was ready to spread throughout the world, and they believed that the methods that had worked in Russia would work elsewhere as well. Therefore, the Russians tried to insist that the Bolshevik doctrines be applied by the Communists in the United States. They demanded that the party call for the American workers to rise up and overthrow their capitalist bosses and for the peasants to seize the land from their masters. The only difficulties were that the American workers were in no mood for a revolution and that most of the American farmers already owned their own land (and would be insulted by being called "peasants"). In those hectic days of the Russian Civil War, however, Moscow could scarcely be concerned with such details.

At this time, in the early 1920's, Stalin had not yet cemented his control over international Communism. Although they respected and feared the Comintern, some members of the party in America still dared to speak out against the policies and decisions of the Comintern. A struggle over policies and power developed among the various factions of the party. As a result, the members of the Communist party in America spent more time and energy fighting among themselves than they did trying to spread Communism.

During this period of American history, there were many radical labor and socialist organizations. Ours was a rapidly growing country in which all the abuses of the Industrial Revolution had not yet been corrected. There was much dissension, and many ideas for improving the conditions of the workers and the farmers were being discussed. Communists did not stand alone in wanting to see far-reaching changes in the United States; and some of the other groups sought to work with them to achieve their goals.

The Communists were willing to coöperate, but only on their own terms. In other words, the Communists insisted on controlling whatever was done. This insistence was a typical Bolshevik tactic, but in the early 1920's few people knew about Bolshevik tactics. These socialist and labor groups soon learned, however. They came to despise the Communists, who insisted that they were always right, who were full of tricks, and who were eager to take advantage of those with whom they were coöperating. As a result, many of the labor leaders and socialists became the earliest and most persistent anti-Communists in the United States.

Stalinization

As Stalin took control of the party in the Soviet Union, he also took control of the Communist parties in the rest of the world. He intended to be ruler not only of the Soviet Union but also of the entire Communist movement. Communists everywhere would serve the cause of the man in the Kremlin.

In the late 1920's the Communist party in the United States had two important factions. One faction was led by Jay Lovestone, who was a friend and adherent of Bukharin; the other faction followed William Z. Foster, who was regarded as a Stalin man. Stalin had no difficulty choosing between the two factions; and as a result, Lovestone and his followers were expelled from the party. Foster, who always followed Stalin's instructions, became the top man in the American party.

From that time on, Stalin dominated the American party almost as completely as he did the Russian party. His commands

were to be carried out as unquestioningly in New York and Chicago as in Moscow and Leningrad—whether they made sense for
the American situation or not.

"Socialism in One Country" was the guiding principle of Stalin's
attitude toward non-Russian Communist parties. Their purpose was
to serve the interests of the U.S.S.R. After the late 1920's, the
American Communist party was always the obedient servant of
Moscow's policies, even though those policies often seemed designed to destroy the influence of the American party. But the success of the American party was not the main concern of the Kremlin.

The Heyday of Communism in America

In the 1930's and early 1940's a series of events made it possible for
the Communist Party of the U.S.A. to acquire more members and
sympathizers than it had ever had before—or would ever have again.

The Great Depression

The depression that spread over America and the world in the
early 1930's appeared to many to be the fulfillment of Marx's
prophecies. This seemed to be the latest and most severe in the series
of crises that Marx had predicted. Millions of Americans were
unemployed. "Bread lines"—lines of people waiting for free food
from government or charitable organizations—existed in every
community. Many workers could not find jobs no matter how hard
they looked, and many were hungry.

The theories of Karl Marx offered an explanation of what was
happening. And the Communists offered a solution: follow the path
of the Soviet Union. The Communists made much of the fact that
Russia was the only country in the world without unemployment.
When reports reached America of the brutality of the Soviet collectivization of agriculture, the Communists denied them. The
stories of peasants being loaded into boxcars at gunpoint were
"capitalist lies"; eyewitness reports were "exaggerations." Because
at this time few Americans understood the Communists and their
tactics, the Communists were able to raise doubts in most minds concerning the truthfulness of these accounts. At the same time, the
Communists said again and again that in Russia everything was
good; in America everything was bad and getting worse.

Despite the unemployment from which many workers were
suffering, the Communist party was never able to make much headway among the members of the working class. The unemployed
were interested in jobs, not politics. They wanted to find jobs so

Long lines of the unemployed and their families waiting to receive free food were a familiar sight during the Depression. Communists attempted to explain the Depression as a fulfillment of the predictions of Karl Marx.

that they could feed and clothe their families; they did not want to make a revolution. Belatedly, the Communists founded councils that attempted to find jobs for the unemployed; but other groups were already doing better jobs than the Communists in that field. The Communist efforts to win over the working class failed.

Although they could not attract the workers, the Communists were able to gain a foothold among the middle class and students. To some of these people, much of what Marx had said about America seemed to be coming true. American industry, capable of producing huge amounts of goods, stood idle, while millions were in need. There were surpluses of everything but jobs; millions had nothing. What was wrong? The Communists had an answer: it was the capitalist system. To end depressions, they said, it was necessary to change the economic—and political—system.

The complicated Marxist ideology, which held little of interest for the workers, particularly intrigued many students. Many had seen their fathers without work, bitter and frustrated; others had had the experience of having their families' businesses fail in the depression. All were worried about their own futures. They were ignorant of the lies and brutality that had accompanied the coming of Communism to Russia. They failed to see the fallacies in Marx's thinking, or they overlooked them in their desperation to believe in the beauties promised by the Communist Utopia. They joined such organizations as the Young Communist League by the thousands.

When 20,000 unemployed staged a protest march in Chicago in 1932, Communists tried to identify themselves with the cause of the demonstrators. Note the hammer and sickle, the emblem of Communism, in the foreground.

The Threat of Nazi Germany

In 1922 the Fascist dictatorship of Benito Mussolini had been established in Italy. In 1933 Adolf Hitler and his Nazi party seized control in Germany. Both Fascism and its close relative Naziism were totalitarian dictatorships. Of the two, Naziism was the more efficient, the more brutal, the more aggressive—and, because Hitler believed that the Germans were a "master race" who should rule the world—the more dangerous.

The Bolsheviks were among the first to recognize a threat in Hitler and his Nazi doctrines of German racial superiority. In the 1920's, several years before Hitler came to power, the Communists had placed themselves at the head of the anti-Nazi fight. By the time the rest of the world began to become alarmed, the Communists were already in the thick of the fight.

In many countries, including the United States, the Communists established anti-Nazi front organizations that attracted millions of people. Most of those who joined the anti-Nazi organizations were not interested in Communism, and many were anti-Communist. But in the 1930's the threat of powerful Nazi Germany was far greater than that of the then weaker Soviet Union; and many did not recognize that the Soviet government was just as totalitarian as the Nazi.

As a result, by 1937 the Communist-front American League against War and Fascism claimed a membership of 2,000,000. (The

Communists, not surprisingly, were lying; the actual membership was somewhat smaller.) Some of the people who joined this Communist-dominated organization were later attracted to the Communist party itself. The party thus gained both supporters and members, not because these people believed in Communism, but because they wanted to fight Nazis and Fascists—and the Communist front organizations were, at times, the only ones doing this with much determination.

The Popular Front

The Communist cause in America was aided by a sudden change in Soviet tactics that occurred in 1934. Stalin had earlier stopped expecting the world revolution. But the relations between the U.S.S.R. and the leading capitalist powers remained quite cool, as the party continued to urge the workers of the world to arise. But by 1934 Stalin feared that Nazi Germany would soon be strong enough to attack, and possibly destroy, the Soviet Union. It therefore seemed necessary for the Soviet Union to protect itself by signing treaties of assistance with other states. To further strengthen the chance for Soviet survival, Communists all over the world were ordered to be friendly and coöperative with anyone who was opposed to Fascism and Naziism. The alliances that the Communists formed with other groups and parties were called the "Popular Front."

In the United States, Communists suddenly changed their attitudes toward almost everything. The New Deal policies of the Roosevelt administration, which they had at first bitterly criticized, were now "accepted" and supported. Every popular cause suddenly became a Communist "cause," too. The Communists tried to enter the mainstream of American life. They even became "patriotic," announcing that "Communism is twentieth-century Americanism." Communists became friendly and willing to coöperate, sometimes almost on the other fellow's terms. They did their best to be liked by as many people as possible so that the Soviet Union would not be abandoned when the German attack came.

Shortly after the formation of the Popular Front, the Communists were given a chance to "prove" their new-found "devotion to democracy." The government of Spain, which was democratic but very weak, was attacked by a group of Spanish Fascists led by Francisco Franco. From the outset of the Spanish Civil War (July, 1936) Franco received aid from Hitler and Mussolini. Communists all over the world came to the support of Franco's opponents, the

In the late 1930's many idealistic young men joined the Communist-sponsored Abraham Lincoln Brigade, which fought the Fascists in the Spanish Civil War. Above, wounded veterans returning from Spain give the Communist salute.

government of the Spanish republic. Within a year the Communists were in virtual control of the Spanish republican government—and they sometimes ran their part of Spain with as much brutality as Stalin used in the Soviet Union. But the Communists had opposed Fascism while the democracies, in general, delayed or refused to help the republican forces. To many sincere anti-Fascists, the Communists became the heroes of the Spanish Civil War.

During the period of the Popular Front, Communist front organizations became particularly active. The largest of these groups was the American League against War and Fascism. In addition, there were Communist front organizations fighting for many other popular causes; and all these groups, such as the American Youth Congress, the American Student Union, and the National Negro Congress, followed the Popular Front party line.

Other aspects of Communist activity during the 1930's included a vigorous campaign to attract the support of American Negroes and an equally vigorous effort to gain the sympathy of the American Jewish community. In spite of the Communists' vigor, however, very few members of either group were fooled by the Communists.

During the 1930's, a period in which the labor-union movement was rapidly expanding, the Communists attempted to take over as many unions as possible. Using the tactics described earlier (see pages 154 and 155–56), they were able to gain control of a number of union locals and of several national organizations. Communist leadership of these unions lasted, in most cases, until shortly after World War II. The great majority of the American labor unions remained determinedly anti-Communist.

The High Point

The feverish activity of the Communist Party of the United States during the 1930's eventually brought the party some success.

Working among students, the unemployed, minorities, and labor unions—and, most important, leading the fight against Fascism—the party ranks began to swell. By 1939 the party claimed 100,000 members (but the Communists were, as usual, stretching a point; the true figure was probably about 80,000). It has been estimated by the Communists that as many as 7,000,000 Americans belonged to Communist front organizations; here again, however, the correct figure is probably somewhat smaller. Whatever the figures, they were the largest that the party and its front organizations had ever enrolled.

And they would never be as large again. For just as Communism was apparently making some headway, the Soviet government took a step that smashed the hopes of the party in America. In August, 1939, Stalin made an alliance with Hitler.

The Nazi-Soviet Pact

When Stalin signed a non-aggression treaty with Hitler, he in effect gave permission to Hitler to begin World War II. Russia stood by as Hitler conquered Poland—and Hitler allowed Russia to take a third of Poland for herself. And Russia continued to watch, and do nothing, as Hitler overran Denmark, Norway, the Netherlands, Luxembourg, Belgium, France, Yugoslavia, and Greece.

In coöperating with Fascism, Stalin—and with him, of course, the American Communist party—had made a complete about-face. The older members of the party, the hard core, were quite used to such shifts in the party line; they could fairly easily adjust from being anti-Hitler one day to being pro-Hitler the next.

But to many members of the party, and to a huge number of fellow travelers, the Nazi-Soviet Pact was a horrible shock. They had joined the party or its front organizations because of the party's strong anti-Fascist position. The swift change left them bewildered; they felt betrayed and alone. It suddenly dawned on many of them that the Soviet Union was as much an enemy of what they believed in as was Nazi Germany.

Because of the Nazi-Soviet Pact, many Americans left the Communist party. The party admitted that it lost 15 per cent of its membership in 1939–1940. The actual figure was probably much higher.

World War II

On June 21, 1941, Germany invaded the U.S.S.R. Suddenly Hitler was once again the arch-villain of Communists everywhere. In the United States, the party line now urged that the United States enter the war against Germany.

On December 7, 1941, the Japanese attacked Pearl Harbor, and America did enter World War II.

For the next three and one half years, the goals of the United States and of the Communist party were almost identical: both sought the speediest possible defeat of Hitler. Sometimes the Russians indicated that their allies were not fighting hard enough: they accused the United States and Great Britain of waiting too long to open a "second front" in western Europe. There was a suggestion that perhaps the United States wanted thousands more Russians to die so that the Soviet state would be weakened. These vague suspicions of the Russians were reflected from time to time in the party in America. But for the most part the Communists in America emphasized "national unity," the need for all elements of the population to coöperate against the common foe.

World War II made the Communist Party of the United States seem more respectable. The bravery and suffering of the Russian people created sympathy for the U.S.S.R. and for the party.

At the same time it was widely argued that since the Russian people were defending their land so courageously, the Soviet system could not be as bad as it had been pictured. Much later, after the war had ended, it was discovered that the Russian people had fought so well not *because* of the system but *in spite* of it. They did not love Communism; but they loved their native land, and they found that German brutality was often as great as or greater than that of their own leaders.

The American Communists also became more respectable because they sought to make themselves more acceptable to moderate people. They replaced their former militant party leaders with seemingly mild men who never mentioned "class struggle" or

From 1939 to 1941, when Nazi Germany and the Soviet Union were allies, Communists attacked American aid to Germany's enemies as "capitalist warmongering." Left, a Communist float in a New York parade on May Day, 1941.

United Press International

"revolution" or "dictatorship of the proletariat." The new leaders talked instead about the "non-partisan" character of the party and the achievement of something called "scientific socialism," which supposedly would come about rather painlessly.

The combination of Russian bravery and American "reasonableness" once again attracted people to the Communist party. Tens of thousands of other well-meaning Americans joined Communist front organizations. These people were somehow able to forget that only a few years earlier Stalin had coöperated with Hitler and had made possible Hitler's early successes in the war.

But in the early 1940's the Soviet goal was *not* to increase the number of Communists in the United States, but rather to increase the number of American soldiers in Europe. Therefore, in an effort to prove to the American and British governments that the Communists were no longer interested in world conquest, Stalin dissolved the Comintern in 1943. A year later it was announced that the Communist Party of the United States had been dissolved.

Of course, the mere announcement of the dissolution of the Comintern and the party meant nothing. Both continued to operate; all that changed was their names. The party was simply replaced by the so-called Communist Political Association, which was controlled by the same people who had headed the supposedly dead party. The party organization remained intact. The dissolution announcement was merely a collection of words with which the party attempted to deceive the gullible.

A few years after the war had ended, it was discovered that our Communist allies had not been all they had seemed. All the time that Stalin had been fighting Hitler, he had also been laying plans for expanding Communist power as soon as Hitler was defeated; and in the United States, the Communists had of course been working for the Soviet Union. Some Communists, including a few who held important positions in the American government, had been acting as spies for the U.S.S.R.

The Decline of Communism in America

Since World War II, the movement of the Communist Party of the United States has been in one direction: downhill.

The Cold War

Very soon after the end of World War II it became apparent that the Soviet Union was not so sweet and reasonable as it had seemed when it needed the United States' help. It could clearly be seen that the Communists intended to keep all the land that they had overrun in the closing phases of the war, and that they were attempting to take over other countries by using infiltration, subversion, and force. The United States and other free countries determined to halt the spread of Communism. The "Cold War" had begun.

In the Cold War, both sides have sought to avoid the outbreak of fighting. It is true that armed clashes have been part of the Cold War; but none of these clashes has directly involved both the United States and the Soviet Union. If both sides should become involved, the struggle would probably develop into nuclear war.

Despite the desire of both the United States and the U.S.S.R. to avoid shooting at each other, the years since World War II have given more than enough evidence of the determination of the Soviet Union to destroy the United States and all that it stands for.

In the earliest stages of the Cold War, the Communist Party of the United States was reëstablished. The new party line denounced the United States as an "imperialist aggressor." The United States was said to be on the road to Fascism. Before long it would be portrayed as the successor to Hitler.

As a result of the Cold War, many Americans realized for the first time just exactly what Communism is: a conspiracy dedicated to taking over the whole world. Thousands of those who had joined or closely coöperated during World War II now began to drift away. Americans gradually became more aware of Communist tactics and of Communist attempts to take over labor unions. The Communist Party of the United States was struck a hard blow in 1950 when the Communist-dominated unions were expelled from the Congress of Industrial Organizations (C.I.O.). In the early 1950's the Korean War, in which the United States fought Communist North Korea and Communist China, caused a sharp decline in party membership.

In the late 1940's the United States government intensified its activities against Communists. In Congress the House Un-American Activities Committee thoroughly investigated the Communist conspiracy in America. Several Communists were tried and sentenced to prison terms for having been spies for the U.S.S.R. In 1949 twelve leaders of the Communist party were tried and sentenced to prison terms for having violated the Smith Act. The Smith Act, which was passed in 1940 and whose original purpose was to curb the activities of Nazi-supported groups, makes it a crime to advocate or teach that the United States government should be overthrown by violence or to organize any group that has such a purpose. In 1950 Congress passed the Internal Security Act (McCarran Act), which, among other things, (1) strengthened the laws against peacetime subversion in the United States; (2) established the Subversive Activities Control Board, which prepares the Attorney General's List, a listing of all known Communists or Communist-controlled organizations in the United States; and (3) stated penalties for anyone who would substantially contribute to the establishment of a foreign-controlled dictatorship in the United States. And in 1954 Congress passed the Communist Control Act which withdrew from the Communist movement the right to pose as a legitimate political party.

As a result of the Korean War, legislation, prosecution and the intense anti-Communist feeling in the United States, membership in the Communist Party of the United States declined from almost 60,000 in 1950 to less than 25,000 three years later.

More recent developments, such as Khrushchev's 1956 exposure of the murders and other crimes of Stalin, have caused further drops in party membership. Thousands left the party after the ruthless suppression by the Soviets of the Hungarian revolt in November, 1956. Differences of opinion concerning the future have caused other long-time Communists to leave the party.

Communism in America Today

Today the membership of the Communist Party of the United States is reliably estimated to be between 8,000 and 10,000. This is the hard core of the party. These people have resisted all information concerning the treachery and brutality of the international Communist movement. They have also resisted the fear of being social outcasts and perhaps of being sentenced to prison terms. They have chosen to remain Communists.

Why have they taken this path? Obviously they have convinced themselves of the correctness of Marxism-Leninism; but why? There can be no simple answer—but in most cases the answers seem to be more psychological than political. Some continue to belong to the party because for some reason they enjoy being the attacked, the hunted; it satisfies a strange psychological need. There are others who are, by nature, against everything that exists; they seek, above all else, a radical change in the social order. For them, too, the party is an outlet. Others continue in the party for the same reason that they joined: their membership gives them a feeling of belonging, whereas previously they had always felt that they were on the outside. These people are actually afraid to leave the party out of fear that they will find themselves alone again. For many, the party with its routine and meetings and speeches and reports and duties has become a way of life. They have grown old following this routine, and are now unwilling or unable to get out of the rut. Still others have grown so accustomed over the years to accepting lies that it is now impossible for the truth to get through to them.

It seems unlikely that any future developments will further shrink the ranks of the party. There is the possibility that disputes within the party might split the party into various factions. For all practical purposes, however, the present party members should be considered hard-core cases, unlikely to leave the party unless ordered to do so by the party. It is likely that attacks on this hard core would only increase their determination to stay in the party.

The party still continues under Moscow's thumb and preaches the causes that Moscow wants it to. It advocates peace—on Moscow's terms. It is against nuclear testing—after Moscow has tested. It is for "civil rights," even though it knows that every time a Communist comes out for civil rights, the civil rights cause loses. But the Communists are not interested in the issue. What interests them is creating dissension and distrust—and serving Moscow's ends.

Communists continue to attempt to worm their way into govern-

In the late 1940's, investigations by the United States Congress of the activities of the Communist party were bitterly attacked by Communists. Left, a party speaker lashes out at a gathering of dock workers on the waterfront in San Francisco.

United Press International

ment. Their success in another free country, Great Britain, was clearly indicated by a report published there in April, 1962. It was discovered that Communists in Britain were making strong efforts to penetrate the British Civil Service, and that many had succeeded. We must assume that the Communists are making similar efforts in the United States. However, the American people and their government have long been awake to this danger; and there is little evidence that the Communists have been successful in recent years. But if we should let down our guard, the Communists' efforts to penetrate our government would succeed, and the danger that Communism presents to our democratic institutions would be increased.

What Should We Do about the Communists?

There is a Communist party in the United States. That party is controlled by the Communist Party of the Soviet Union. The Communist Party of the Soviet Union has sworn to destroy the United States. The question then arises: *What should we do about Communists in the United States?*

Some say that we should arrest them all and keep them in prison. But this would mean the establishment of political prisons, which have always been considered incompatible with the freedoms that Americans cherish. For if such prisons were to be established, it is possible that no one could prevent their being filled with many other people besides Communists.

Some people say that the party should be outlawed. Such action, however, would probably drive the present party members underground. As the party now exists, the government agencies charged with our protection are able to keep close watch on the Communists' activities. The Federal Bureau of Investigation (F.B.I.) knows who the Communists are and what they are doing. If they were driven underground, it would be far more difficult to keep track of them.

Though it is far from an ideal solution, it is generally agreed by the officials who are responsible for our national security that the best way to protect our nation is to allow the Communist party to continue to function—and to keep it under close watch at all times.

It should be recognized, of course, that the great danger from Communists in the United States does not come from those who openly belong to the party. Rather, the most dangerous Communists are those who long ago dropped from sight or perhaps were never even in the party's records. These (and probably others sent to this country by the U.S.S.R.) are awaiting the day when they will be given the order to destroy the dams and bridges and factories and military bases of the United States. In the meantime they will try to live as quietly as possible. They do not want to attract attention, which they would certainly get if they joined the party.

To say that there are Communists awaiting the signal to try to destroy this country does not mean that there are millions or even thousands of them. Consequently, it is seldom reasonable to suspect that people who seem to have some peculiar ideas are part of the Communist conspiracy. The Communist spy or saboteur hiding in our midst will display no "peculiar" characteristics. On the contrary, he will do his best to appear as normal as possible. His safety depends upon it.

J. Edgar Hoover, the director of the F.B.I., has warned, "Our fight against Communism must be a sane, rational understanding of the facts. . . . Emotional outbursts, extravagant namecalling, gross exaggerations hinder our efforts. . . . We must remember that many non-Communists may legitimately, on their own, oppose the same laws or take the same positions on issues of the day which are also held by the Communists.

"Their opinions, though temporarily coinciding with the party line, do not make them Communists. Not at all. We must be very careful with our facts and not brand as Communists any individual whose opinion may be different from our own.

"Freedom of dissent is a great heritage of America which we must treasure."

aids to learning

Check the facts

1. How did Marx and Lenin differ concerning the methods by which the world would become Communist? What is the final goal of all Communism? What is the goal of Communist activities in free countries?

2. Why do Americans consider Communists unprincipled? Explain the meaning of the phrase, "The end justifies the means," as applied to Communism. Why do Communists never consider that their arguments are inconsistent?

3. What is the Communist *party line?* Give examples of its use. Under what conditions do Communists use the tactic of perseverence; of compromise? When, why, and for how long do Communists sometimes coöperate with groups other than their own?

4. By what tactics may a minority of Communists gain control of an organization? Why is Communism aggressive? When do Communists use the tactic of retreat?

5. Why do Communists consider free labor unions their enemies? Why do Communists pretend to support peace and democracy? Why are Communists considered hypocrites?

6. What do Communists consider to be the basic freedom? Why do they consider American freedom of speech, press, and other civil rights "bourgeois"? What use do Communists make of minority groups in non-Communist lands? Give examples of Communist front organizations. How do Communists make use of them? What is "revolutionary morality"?

7. When was the first Communist group in the United States founded? When was the Communist Party of the United States organized? Why did some members of the American Communist party criticize the policies imposed on it by the Kremlin? Why did socialist and labor leaders in the United States become anti-Communists? Who were the leaders of the two major factions of the Communist Party of the United States? How did they differ? How and to what extent did Stalin control the Communist Party of the United States?

8. Why did the Communist Party of the United States fail to win over the unemployed workers during the depression? Why were they more successful in gaining support from the middle class and students? Why did these groups fail to see the fallacies in the Communist answers to the problems of the time?

9. Why did the Communists establish anti-Nazi organizations? Why did many non-Communists join these groups? What changes were made in Soviet tactics in 1934? Why?

10. What was the Popular Front? Why was it formed? Name several organizations that belonged to it. How did Russia make use of the Spanish Civil War to further her purposes?

11. Name the groups in the United States that were attracted to the Communist Party in the 1930's. In what year did the Communist Party and its

affiliates in the United States reach their largest membership? What was the approximate membership of the Communist party? Of the front organizations? What event in 1939 brought about a drop in Communist party membership in the United States?

12. Why did Communists and the Communist Party of the United States become more respectable during World War II? Why was the party dissolved in 1944? What organization replaced it?

13. What is the Cold War? Make a list of the events that brought about a decline of Communist Party membership in the United States from about 60,000 in 1950 to 8.000–10,000 today. Why do the people who still belong to the party choose to remain Communists? In what ways do they aid or attempt to aid the Kremlin?

14. Why has the United States not outlawed the Communist party? Which Communists are the most dangerous? Why is it difficult to detect them? Name the points, listed by J. Edgar Hoover, that should be kept in mind in dealing with suspected Communists.

Know word meanings

Be able to define and use correctly the following words:

inconsistent	party line	front organization	fallacy
perseverence	aggressive	fellow traveler	hypocrisy
bourgeois	Fascist	bread line	Nazi
Comintern	Cold War	infiltration	subversive

Identify names

What part did each of these men play in the period covered in this chapter?
Jay Lovestone   William Z. Foster   Benito Mussolini   Adolf Hitler

Do something extra

1. Name several of the national groups that make up the American people, and indicate the contribution each has made to the United States.

2. Read and report on the efforts made by the Communists to gain control of United States labor unions, 1935–1950. Show how the unions dealt with these attempts.

3. Compare the attitudes of Marx and Lenin toward freedom and democracy with those of Thomas Jefferson, Abraham Lincoln, and other American leaders.

4. Make a list of the steps taken by Hitler. 1933–1940, to gain control of Europe for Nazi Germany.

5. Read and report on the work of the Federal Bureau of Investigation in combatting Communism in the United States, as described by J. Edgar Hoover in *Masters of Deceit*.

The wall that cuts across the heart of Berlin,
built on orders from Moscow, stands as a symbol
of the Soviet enslavement of eastern Europe.
The wall was built to prevent the escape to freedom
of refugees from Communist-controlled East Germany.

THE SPREAD OE COMMUNISM

From 1917 until World War II, the Soviet Union was the only Communist country in the world. In 1940, the year after World War II began, three independent countries—Lithuania, Latvia, and Estonia —were invaded and made parts of the Soviet Union. Since World War II ended in 1945, Communist control has spread to twelve other countries. Eight of these Communist governments—Poland, Rumania, Czechoslovakia, Bulgaria, Hungary, Yugoslavia, Albania, and East Germany—are in Europe. Three of them—China, North Korea, and North Viet-Nam—are in Asia. One—Cuba—is in Latin America.

The methods used by the Communists to gain control of these countries have varied greatly. In none of them, however, was Communism voted into power in a free, democratic election. In almost every instance, Communism took over through the use of armed might, and not because the people were convinced of the superiority of Communism. Where Communism has spread it has been because of the superiority of Communist weapons, not because of the attractiveness of Communist doctrines.

World War II Makes Communist Expansion Possible

Communism would probably not have been able to spread beyond the Soviet Union had it not been for World War II. World War II created conditions in many countries that were similar to the conditions that had enabled the Bolsheviks to take over Russia in 1917. Furthermore, the end of World War II found the Red Army occupying most of eastern Europe.

179

Before these conditions were created by World War II, the Soviet government had had remarkably little success in its attempts to establish Communist governments in other countries.

Background: Soviet Policy to 1941

In the first years after the revolution of 1917, Lenin and the Bolsheviks believed that their regime in Russia could not last unless the proletariat rose up in other lands as well. To promote the international revolution, the Communist International, or *Comintern,* was established in 1919. (See page 58.) Even after it became evident that the Soviet regime would survive by itself, the Comintern continued its activities: directing the operations of Communist parties throughout the world, with the hope of bringing about Communist revolutions. Generally, the Communist parties everywhere operated in about the same way as the Communist Party of the U.S.A. (See pages 161–169.)

The rise of Nazi Germany brought a sharp change in Soviet policy. The very life of the Soviet Union was threatened: Hitler, the Nazi leader, made no secret of the fact that he intended to destroy the U.S.S.R. Stalin became thoroughly alarmed. After 1934, almost every important development in the Soviet Union can be interpreted as a reaction to the Nazi threat.

In the light of the German threat, the Soviet Union's lack of allies became of great concern to Stalin. He was frightened at the prospect of a German invasion that would find a weakened Soviet Union having to fight alone. Consequently, he began making efforts to form alliances with other countries. The U.S.S.R. tried to prove that it belonged to the "family of nations." For the time being, Communists throughout the world gave up their attempts to create unrest in their own countries. Their principal concern was to strengthen the governments of their own countries so that they could more effectively fight Fascism and Naziism.

Stalin gradually realized, however, that his efforts to make firm friends for the Soviet Union were not succeeding. The leaders of Britain and France, the most powerful of the western European countries, did not trust him. In the spring of 1939, the Soviet Union was still without any allies that Stalin thought he could count on.

Stalin hated Hitler. But he also greatly feared Hitler, and he wanted at all costs to avoid a war with Germany. Stalin reasoned that if he and Hitler could reach an agreement not to attack each other, Russia would be safe from Hitler. Hitler would then be able to wage war against France and Britain without having to fear an attack

Stalin gives a pat on the back to Joachim von Ribbentrop, foreign minister of Nazi Germany, as Soviet foreign minister Molotov signs the Nazi-Soviet agreement to the 1939 partition of Poland.

181

by Russia. Stalin undoubtedly hoped that such a war would be a long and bloody one and that Britain, France, and Germany would all become so weakened that Communists could take them over. Negotiations therefore were begun with Nazi Germany. On August 23, 1939, the world was dumbfounded by the announcement that a non-aggression treaty had been signed by Germany and the Soviet Union.

The pact was a guarantee to Hitler that he could attack Poland without having to fear that the Soviet Union would come to Poland's aid. A week later, on September 1, 1939, Hitler invaded Poland. Britain and France, who had a mutual assistance treaty with Poland, declared war on Germany two days later. Hitler—with a tremendous assist from Stalin—had begun World War II.

The Soviet Union in World War II

During the first year and ten months of World War II, the Soviet Union stood on the sidelines as Nazi Germany conquered most of Europe. At the same time, Stalin took advantage of the Nazi-Soviet pact to add territory to the Soviet Union. According to the terms of the pact, Stalin was allowed to take one third of Poland for himself. In 1940 the independent countries of Estonia, Latvia, and Lithuania were absorbed into the U.S.S.R., without a protest from Hitler. And in 1940 Stalin launched an attack against Finland. The Finns fought bravely and inflicted heavy damages on the Red Army, but eventually they were forced to ask for peace and to give up some of their land to the Soviet Union.

Hitler, meanwhile, overran almost all the rest of Europe. By 1941, only two powers blocked his complete domination of Europe: Britain and the U.S.S.R. Almost everyone expected that Hitler would next attack Britain. Instead, he turned on his ally. On June 21, 1941, Nazi Germany invaded the U.S.S.R.

The war began disastrously for the Russians. By the end of 1941, the Soviet Union had lost all of western Russia and more than one-third of her pre-war population. In the North, the Nazi forces were in the suburbs of Leningrad; in the central section, they stood just outside Moscow; in the South, they stood ready to conquer the Caucasus. In the first eight months of the war, 3,600,000 soldiers of the Red Army surrendered to the Germans.

It was evident that the Red Army was badly led: its most capable leaders had perished in the purges of a few years earlier. More important, it was evident that many of the Russian soldiers lacked the will to fight for Stalin and the Soviet Union. In many parts of the Soviet Union, and particularly in the Ukraine, the Germans were greeted not as hated invaders but as liberating heroes. Hundreds of thousands of captured Red Army men were willing to form their own anti-Soviet forces to fight with the Germans against the Soviets. If Hitler had taken advantage of this opportunity, he probably could have won the Russian campaign in a few months. But Hitler refused to use his advantage.

The reason that Hitler refused to make use of these captives had to do with his racial theories. According to Hitler, the Russians, Ukrainians, and other eastern Europeans were subhumans, inferior to the Germans. In the German empire that Hitler thought he was organizing, their place was as slave laborers. From the very beginning of the war, the Germans began acting according to these theories. Instead of trying to win the people over, the Germans treated them brutally. Entire communities were uprooted and sent to work in German factories. Children were separated from parents, and husbands from wives. Violence against a member of the German army was revenged by killing many innocent civilians; in the German-occupied territory, the sound of firing squads was heard more and more frequently. And among the prisoners-of-war, lack of food and medical care brought frequent deaths.

The tactics of the Germans in the occupied territories soon turned the people against the Germans. Anti-German activity among the civilians developed. Units of guerrillas, or *partisans,* were formed

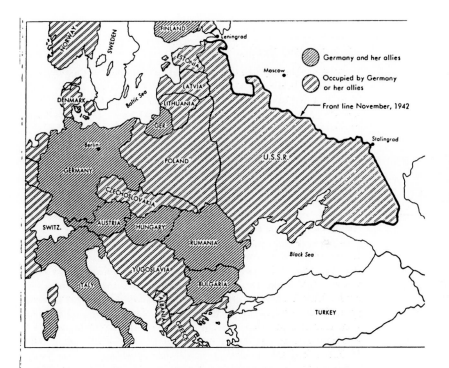

Germany and her allies

Occupied by Germany or her allies

Front line November, 1942

to operate behind the German lines. As the war progressed, these partisans were increasingly successful at spying and at sabotaging the German supply lines. At the same time, the resistance of the Red Army at the front stiffened. The Russians began to benefit from the assistance of the United States, which had entered the war against Germany in December, 1941. During the remaining years of the war, the United States delivered more than $11,000,-000 worth of supplies and equipment to the U.S.S.R. These included almost 500,000 trucks, 2,500,000 tons of aviation gasoline, 2,000 locomotives, and huge amounts of food, clothing, medical supplies, weapons, and ammunition.

The turning point of the war came in the winter of 1942–1943, when the Red Army turned back the Germans at Stalingrad. After Stalingrad, the Red Army began regaining Russian territory, and by 1945 was fighting in Germany. At the same time, American and British forces were driving the Germans from North Africa and western Europe. In March, 1945, American and Russian forces met on the River Elbe, in the heart of Germany. Two months later Germany surrendered.

Communist Expansion in Europe

Long before the war had ended, Stalin began to prepare for the post-war period. While his allies, particularly the United States, were thinking of little other than ending the war as soon as possible, Stalin was laying the groundwork for the extension of Communism into other countries.

The Wartime Agreements

During their wartime alliance, the leaders of the United States, Great Britain, and the Soviet Union came together in three major conferences at Teheran, Iran; Yalta, U.S.S.R.; and Potsdam, Germany. The purpose of these conferences was not only to plan the conduct of the war but also to make plans for the post-war world. The subjects included the post-war occupation of Germany by the allies; the establishment of democratic governments in countries that had been occupied by the Germans; and the formation of a world organization, the United Nations, to prevent future wars.

At the Yalta Conference, in February, 1945, the principal concern of the United States was getting Stalin to agree to entering the war against Japan. At that time, it was believed that without Soviet help the war against Japan might last as long as ten years. The United States therefore made a number of concessions to Stalin in return for his promise to enter the war in the Far East. These concessions included giving the Soviets what amounted to a free hand in the eastern European countries that the Russians had taken from the Germans. Stalin promised, in return, that democratic governments would be established in these countries.

Even before the war had ended, it became evident that Stalin would abide by agreements only when it was convenient for him to do so. Whenever it seemed that breaking an agreement would help the cause of Communism, he would break it. Later it became evident that Stalin's willingness to coöperate with the United States and Britain had ended with the end of the war. The U.S.S.R. was once again devoting itself to spreading Communism throughout the world.

Among the many agreements that Stalin ignored was his pledge that free governments would be established in eastern Europe.

The Establishment of the Satellites

Shortly before the end of World War II, Communist-dominated states began to appear. Whenever the Red Army marched into a state, it brought along local Communists who had spent the war years in Moscow. These "locals" would be reinforced by Russian

Photo from European

The "Big Three"—British Prime Minister Winston Churchill, President Franklin Roosevelt, and Stalin—smile for photographers in February, 1945, at the Yalta Conference. Many of the agreements made at Yalta were later broken by Stalin.

comrades who had been trained to help a Communist minority take over a country. These same men also served as Soviet agents, keeping Moscow informed as to the activities of the local Communists. In effect, one Communist party was spying upon another.

The Communist take-over of the eastern European governments took place largely in secret. First, middle-class parties were accused of having collaborated with the Nazis, the parties were suspended, and their leaders were either executed or imprisoned. At about the same time the Communists gained control of the Ministry of the Interior, which controlled the police. The Communists could then arrest whom they wanted and be immune from arrest themselves. Next the socialist and peasant parties, which had the majority of popular support, were forced to join with the Communists in a single "unity" party, which was dominated by the Communists. In this way, the possible rallying points of resistance against the Communists were eliminated. Finally, the socialist and other members of the "unity" party would be removed, and the government would be entirely in Communist hands.

One by one, all of the countries occupied by the Red Army were taken over by Communist governments. The early stages of the proc-

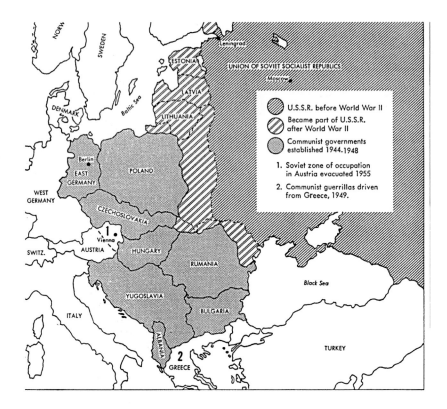

NORW.
SWEDEN
Leningrad
ESTONIA
UNION OF SOVIET SOCIALIST REPUBLICS
Moscow
DENMARK
Baltic Sea
LATVIA
LITHUANIA

U.S.S.R. before World War II

Became part of U.S.S.R. after World War II

Communist governments established 1944-1948

1. Soviet zone of occupation in Austria evacuated 1955

2. Communist guerrillas driven from Greece, 1949.

Berlin
EAST GERMANY
POLAND
WEST GERMANY
CZECHOSLOVAKIA
1
Vienna
SWITZ.
AUSTRIA
HUNGARY
RUMANIA
Black Sea
YUGOSLAVIA
ITALY
BULGARIA
ALBANIA
2
GREECE
TURKEY

ess were acted out in 1945 and 1946. The final steps were announced
to the world in 1947 and 1948. By that time Yugoslavia, Albania,
Poland, Rumania, Bulgaria, Hungary, Czechoslovakia and East Germany had completed the passage to becoming Communist states, the
so-called "people's democracies." Each was as exact a copy of the
Soviet regime as could be devised. Each was completely under the
control of Moscow.

These Communist governments, even more than the pre-war
Communist parties outside the Soviet Union, were completely dependent upon the Communist Party of the Soviet Union. Not only
did the Red Army occupy their territory, but Soviet spies were to be
found in every government office and in every section of the country.
A telephone call from Moscow could relieve any official of his office.

Stalin had succeeded in carving out a Russian empire in eastern Europe. Of course, he denied that he had acquired an empire; he said that the Soviet Union was simply extending friendly "advice" and "assistance" to other Communist states. In practice, however, Stalin had simply expanded the Russian empire, and he had done so largely by military conquest. If the Red Army had not been present, eastern Europe would not have fallen to Communism.

The Soviet colonies, or *satellites,* as they are called because of their complete dependence upon the Soviet Union, were more ruthlessly exploited than any Asian or African colony was exploited by a western European government. The Soviets took over the satellites not only politically, but economically as well. Stalin's aim was to control the production of the satellites for the benefit of the Soviet Union. The argument given for this policy was that the Soviet Union had suffered much in the war, and her economy had to be rebuilt as speedily as possible. The satellites had to aid in this rebuilding. As a result, many factories were dismantled and sent to the U.S.S.R., and those that were left were geared to fill the needs of the U.S.S.R.

In order to keep the satellites under control—and to prevent their inhabitants from fleeing to the free countries of the West—Stalin shut not only the Soviet Union but also the satellites off from the rest of the world. Travel, except for members of the diplomatic corps, was strictly prohibited. To keep people from leaving the satellites, Stalin went so far as to spread barbed wire and lay minefields along their borders. In the words of Winston Churchill, an "Iron Curtain" had descended across the middle of Europe.

Communist Threat in Other European Countries

The Communists were able to make satellites only of the countries that the Red Army occupied. For several years, however, they threatened to take over other European countries as well.

World War II had left most of Europe devastated. Cities were destroyed, people were out of work, and many were going hungry. It is conditions such as these upon which Communism feeds.

The most serious Communist threat was in Greece. There the Communists organized a guerrilla army which for a time controlled large parts of Greece. The guerrillas were supplied with weapons and food by the Soviet satellites bordering on Greece. During the late 1940's the guerrillas seriously threatened to make Greece another Communist state.

Italy, too, was threatened, but in a different way. The Italian Communist party had become the largest in Europe. It controlled many of the most important labor unions as well as several state and city governments. In elections the Italian Communist party always received a large percentage of the vote, though it never received a majority. It seemed for a time that the Italian Communists might take over the Italian government. But they were defeated in a crucial election in April, 1948. Today the Communist party remains stronger in Italy than in any other free country, but since 1948 there has been little chance that it will be able to gain control of the Italian government.

Communism in Europe Today

The spread of Communism in Europe appears to have been successfully halted, largely as the result of policies adopted by the United States in the late 1940's. These policies included (1) the Truman Doctrine (1947), a declaration that the United States would not allow Communist armies to overrun Greece and Turkey, coupled with military aid which enabled the Greeks to decisively defeat the Communist guerrillas; (2) The Marshall Plan (1948), a program of economic assistance that succeeded in repairing the wartime damage to the economies of the non-Communist European countries; and (3) the North Atlantic Treaty (1949), a military alliance of the United States, Canada, and most of the western European democracies against Soviet aggression.

Today the Communists are still attempting to win the working people of western Europe. In recent years, however, European prosperity has prevented the Communists from making any progress in Europe; in fact, they have actually lost ground.

In France, about one fourth of the people regularly vote for the Communist ticket in national elections. Many do this not because they are Communists, but because since 1789, the year of the beginning of the French Revolution, it has become traditional in their family or in their area to vote for the party that is the most "Left" or revolutionary. In France the Communists reap the benefit of this vote. There is a very strange situation in some parts of France: the peasantry, the most conservative part of the population, votes for the Communists, because to do so is traditional. Yet if the Communists were to take power, the peasants would be among the least likely to coöperate.

Italy has the largest Communist party outside the Iron Curtain. Yet here, too, the chances for a take-over appear rather dim. The Communists have made little progress in recruiting among the peasants of the South of Italy, whose conditions are miserable and who would appear most likely to be attracted by Communist promises. Communist successes are in the industrial North. Even so, Italy's present prosperity, the hope of the economic union of Europe, the fierce opposition of the Catholic Church, and internal strife in the Italian party seem to offer few prospects for Communist victory.

The spots in Europe where Communism would appear to have a chance are those countries which have a dictatorship which prevents political activity by a democratic opposition. Curtailment of freedom of speech and of the press, abolition of trade unions, suppression of civil liberties in countries like Spain and Portugal work to the advantage of the Communists. In these countries, the people who are opposed to the government cannot act through normal democratic methods, but must go underground. The Communists are used to operating in the special conditions of the underground. As a result, much of the opposition to the regime tends to gather around them.

On balance, however, it appears that the Communists have no chance of taking over any part of western Europe in the foreseeable future.

Communism in China

While the Soviet Union was taking control of eastern Europe, Chinese Communists, with the aid of the Soviet Union but not under its direct control, succeeded in gaining power in China.

Background: The Chinese Revolution

In the early years of the twentieth century, the ancient empire of China had fallen on evil days. The government, which had at one time been the most efficient in the world, had become weak, inefficient, and corrupt. Western European powers saw China as a fit area for colonialism, and claimed large areas of China as their own "spheres of influence." Not surprisingly, many patriotic Chinese were disturbed by the weakness of their country and by China's being exploited by the Western powers.

The Chinese Revolution, which began in 1911, overthrew the Chinese empire and established a republic. The new republic, however, was no more effective than the emperors had been, and it soon lost control of large areas of China. Each of these areas was governed by a "war lord," who maintained his own private army, fought constantly with neighboring war lords, and mercilessly bled the people under his control. In 1912 the great Chinese revolutionary leader Sun Yat-sen organized a political party, the Kuomintang (National People's Party), which had an army of its own and which attempted to bring the war lords under its control. But until the 1920's the Kuomintang enjoyed little success.

Sun Yat-sen appealed to the West for help, but for the most part the major powers paid little attention to him. But after the Bolsheviks came to power in Russia in 1917, they were not only willing but eager to help Sun. With the aid of the Bolsheviks, Sun was able to reorganize the Kuomintang and its army, and the Kuomintang began gradually to bring China under its control.

But while the Russians were helping Sun to organize his party, some young Chinese in Paris and later in China itself were organizing the Communist Party of China. Thus, the Soviet Communists were organizing one political party in China, and the Chinese Communists another. The two parties did not trust each other; each hoped to take over the other. For several years they attempted to coöperate with each other, largely because the Russians insisted upon it; but the uneasy alliance collapsed in 1927, and the two parties became bitter enemies.

Chiang Kai-shek vs. Mao Tse-tung

After the death of Sun Yat-sen, the leadership of the Kuomintang passed to Chiang Kai-shek, Sun's trusted aide. Chiang, though trained and aided by the Communists, had no intention of being dominated by them. He therefore turned against them, and drove them to southern China, where they reorganized their army. It was in southern China that Mao Tse-tung became the undisputed leader of Chinese Communism.

The next ten years were difficult ones for Mao and the Chinese Communists. At that time, Chiang and the Kuomintang were more powerful than they would ever be again. Mao feared that if the Communists remained in southern China, they would eventually be destroyed by Chiang. He therefore led the Communists on the 6,000 mile "Long March" to a remote area in northwestern China, near the Soviet border. After the "Long March," Mao concentrated on building a strong army and on working out a party program that would attract the Chinese peasantry. Mao realized that the Chinese Communists could come to power only through the peasantry, because China was an overwhelmingly agricultural country.

The struggle between Chiang and Mao was complicated by World War II. World War II began in China long before anywhere

Mao Tse-tung (1893–   ),
a powerful member of the Chinese Communist party since the 1920's, absolute leader of the party since 1935, and dictator of mainland China since 1949.

else. The Japanese attacked there in 1931, and fighting continued throughout the 1930's. In 1937 a cease-fire was arranged between the Communist and Kuomintang armies so that both could concentrate on fighting the Japanese invaders. But throughout the war, Mao was unwilling to use his army to fight the Japanese. He was waiting for the end of the war, when he could turn the army against the *real* enemy, Chiang; in the meantime he would not risk losing his soldiers. Chiang fought the Japanese occasionally; but he, too, held a large part of his army in reserve, waiting for an opportunity to destroy the Communists.

When World War II finally ended in 1945, the Kuomintang forces took control of most of the territory that had been held by the Japanese. But the country that they controlled was a ruined country. Much of China's industry and many of her cities were in ruins. The Chinese people were starving. Moreover, the Kuomintang, the victim of years in power, was riddled with corruption. In local areas throughout China it had lost control. Its leader was an old man who had lost much of his vigor and his former determination to bring reforms to the suffering people of China.

On the other hand, the Chinese Communists emerged from the war with organization, momentum, and purpose. They had weapons that they and the Russians had taken from the Japanese, and they also had Soviet weapons and military advisers. And they had a promise. Calling themselves "agrarian reformers," they promised the Chinese peasantry to take the land from its wealthy owners and distribute it among the peasants. It was this promise, as much as any other factor, that enabled the Communists to gain control of China. In the countryside, the Communists won the support of many Chinese peasants by promising to give them land.

The tactics used by the Chinese Communists in their native land were similar to those that they later employed in Korea, Viet-Nam, and Laos. They avoided pitched battles whenever they could. They rarely attacked a city, but preferred to surround it, cut off its lines of communication, and leave it to wither on the vine. Then they would move on to the next town. In this way the Kuomintang was bottled up in the cities; and the countryside, with its food supplies, was taken over by the Communists. In those areas which they did not permanently occupy, the Communists would from time to time send guerrilla detachments to terrorize the populace and to seize grain and prospective young soldiers.

On January 8, 1949, Peiping fell to the Communists; and within a year every other important Chinese city was in Communist hands. On October 1, 1949, Mao Tse-tung proclaimed the Chinese People's Republic. By May, 1950, all the remaining Kuomintang forces had been driven from the Chinese mainland. Most of them retreated to Formosa, an island 120 miles off the coast of China. Because the United States Navy protects the island from Communist attack, Chiang and the Kuomintang are still on Formosa. There they wait, hoping that someday they will be able to storm the mainland and return to power.

The Chinese Communists in Power

After Mao had taken over in China, he set about winning over the peasants and destroying the middle class. In 1949 he gave the peasants the land that he had promised them. Three years later, however, he began taking the land back; and within four years all the peasants had been forced into collective farms. The peasants, of course, did not like the change. Some of them reacted as violently as had the Russian peasants twenty years earlier. But Mao was able to push the change through.

Despite much evidence of peasant resistance, by 1956 Mao had convinced himself that the Chinese people stood behind him and approved of his policies. It was because of this belief that in February, 1957, he invited a "hundred flowers to blossom, a hundred schools of

, thought contend." He was telling the people to go ahead and express their complaints against the regime. He was certainly not prepared for the flood of hate which soon poured down upon the Communist party. Within a month Mao had to clamp down.

At the same time that Mao discovered that he was not loved, he also became convinced that China's economic situation was dangerous and required prompt action. The farms and industry simply were not producing enough for China's needs. It was under these circumstances—and with Mao learning that the peasants didn't like him anyway—that the *commune* was born. The Chinese Communists believed that the commune would be the key to their success, a speedy path to Communism. They thought that through the commune they could reach Communism even before the Russians, who had been struggling in that direction for forty years.

On the collective farm, the Chinese peasant had still had a small plot of land of his own. Under the commune, he had none. But he lost more than his land. He also lost his farm tools, his kitchen utensils, his house—and his family. Men and women lived in separate barracks. Children were sent to boarding schools. Husbands saw their wives a few hours a day at the most, and children saw their parents even less frequently. The barracks arose at six o'clock to the blast of a bugle. According to Communist propaganda, they awakened happily in the service of the state. Immediately they ran to the exercise area, and after their calisthenics they marched off to breakfast. They then marched to the fields, where the men often worked 16 to 20 hours a day. In their spare time they were supposed to do volunteer labor on the commune roads, receive instruction in Marx, Lenin, Engels, and Mao, drill in the militia, and study.

The Chinese people did not like the communes, and the communes did not succeed in increasing agricultural production. As a result, China's economic situation today is even more desperate than it was when the communes were begun. Many of the most objectionable features of the communes, such as the separation of families, have been eliminated. In some instances, small plots of land, 2½ yards by 2½ yards, have been returned to the peasants. But the damage to the lives and morale of the Chinese people cannot be so easily repaired.

At the same time that they were attempting to increase agricultural production through the communes, the Chinese Communists attempted to raise industrial production through enthusiasm. The campaign was to be known as the "Great Leap Forward." Its idea

The foundation of the Communist "People's Republic of China" on October 1, 1949, was celebrated with enthusiasm by many Chinese. Above, despite a heavy rain, students march through Shanghai carrying a portrait of Mao.

was that if all the people could be swept up in the excitement of a tremendous production effort, great results would be achieved.

The struggle was to concentrate on increasing steel production. According to some reports, over 3,000,000 small smelting furnaces were built in China. Farmers were to make steel in their "spare time." Nurses were to make steel in furnaces located in the back yards of their hospitals. Teachers and students were to make steel after school hours.

Bannisters, pots and pans, streetcar tracks, and lampposts were melted down and shaped into ingots. All of China was made a steel factory.

The Chinese Communists had high hopes for the "Great Leap Forward." But making steel is not a simple process in which tens of millions of people are capable. The steel that was produced was weak and unsuitable for industrial purposes; moreover, using up all their scrap metal left the Chinese with no raw materials for their next "leap." The "Great Leap Forward," like the commune, was a dismal failure.

Communist China Today

Despite all the efforts made by the Chinese Communists during their years in power, they have succeeded only in making the lot of

195

In 1961, twelve years after the Communist takeover in China, food was so scarce in many parts of the country that people were forced to rummage through garbage heaps in the hope of finding something to eat.

the average Chinese worse in many ways—and they have little in the way of positive accomplishments to point to as an excuse for all the misery they have caused. As we shall see in the next chapter, they have not even been able to keep the friendship of the country that should be their best friend, the Soviet Union.

Today the Chinese Communists are the greatest force for conflict among the Communist countries. Although they are not so strong as the Soviet Union, they are nevertheless strong enough to sometimes be able to force the Russians to accept their ideas. The Chinese accuse the Russians of being "soft" and afraid of the United States; and, to prove that they are not, the Russians sometimes are driven to actions that endanger world peace.

It is correct to say that China is the second most powerful Communist power in the world. This is true in spite of China's horrible food shortages and low industrial production. China is feared by friend and foe alike because of her huge, rapidly growing population, now almost 700,000,000—more than three times that of the Soviet Union. She is also feared because of the tremendous land mass that she occupies. Population and size, however, are not threats all by themselves; it is what might be done with them that counts. China may have tremendous *potential* for growth. It is this that sometimes frightens both the free world and the Soviet Union.

The Korean War

After the Communist takeover in China, the Communists continued their efforts to make all Asia Communist. One of their first efforts resulted in the Korean War.

Korea after World War II

Korea is an Asian peninsula, connected to northern China and pointing toward the Japanese islands. Korea was once an independent country, but Japan had taken it over in the 1890's. During World War II, the allies decided that after the defeat of Japan, Korea should again become an independent nation. Until the new government could be organized, the Soviet Union was to occupy the northern half of Korea; the United States, the southern half.

Soon after the war, it became evident that the Soviet Union did not intend to allow free elections in the part of Korea that it occupied. A puppet government, controlled by the U.S.S.R., was established in North Korea. In South Korea elections were held, and a democratically elected government was established. The United States then withdrew its forces from Korea.

Halting North Korean Aggression

Suddenly in June, 1950, the North Koreans invaded South Korea. The United States immediately appealed to the United Nations for action against the North Korean aggression. The U.N., the United States declared, must uphold the rights of South Korea. In an emergency session, the U.N. Security Council agreed to adopt the American proposal. Fortunately the U.S.S.R.'s delegates were absent from the Security Council, so they could not veto the action.

For the first time in history, a world organization voted to use armed force to stop a military aggressor. Although the United States furnished the largest number of troops and equipment and the principal leadership, Australia, Turkey, Great Britain, and other nations also supplied men and equipment. The army that freed South Korea from Communist attack was a United Nations force.

In the first weeks of the war, the North Korean forces almost succeeded in driving the South Korean and United Nations forces from Korea. As the U.N. strength increased, however, the North Koreans were driven back; and by September, 1950, the North Koreans had retreated north of the 38th parallel, the original boundary between North and South Korea. The United Nations forces continued to press forward, and by November, 1950, they had almost reached the Chinese border.

At this point a drastic change took place in the fighting: the Chinese Communists entered the war. Taking the U.N. forces by surprise, they threw huge numbers of troops at the front lines. Within two months the United Nations forces had been driven back into South Korea. But the offensive was finally halted, and the U.N. troops once again drove the Communists north of the 38th parallel.

Ending the Korean War

The Communists hurled several desperate offenses against the United Nations lines, but in each case they were thrown back with heavy losses. In July, 1951, the Russians suggested that a truce could be arranged between the two fighting forces.

Two years were required, however, before a truce was finally accepted by the Communists. The chief disagreement was the disposition of thousands of soldiers captured by the U.N. forces. The Communists wished these prisoners returned, but many did not wish to return to China. President Eisenhower, who had taken office in 1953, summed up the American position: "People that have become our prisoners cannot by any manner or means be denied the right on which this country was founded . . . the right of political asylum against the kind of political persecution they fear. . . ."

An agreement was finally worked out in which prisoners on both sides were given a chance to decide for themselves whether or not they wished to return. An armistice was signed July 27, 1953, at Panmunjom, where the negotiations had been conducted.

The Korean War marked the end of a phase in the Communist attempts to take over the world. Under Stalin, the Soviet Union had taken over much of Europe, largely by using military force. Other Communists had taken over China—again by using military force. But by the end of the Korean War, Stalin had died. His successors would depend more on other means in their drive for control of the world.

The Communist Offensive Today

With Communism halted in Europe, and its expansion through war halted in Korea, the Communists turned to new methods of attempting to win the world. Their major efforts were now devoted to attempting to win the peoples of the underdeveloped countries—the countries of Asia, Africa, and Latin America.

Military action of the kind that had won them China continued to be used in the areas bordering on China: Viet-Nam and Laos. In 1954 the northern half of Viet-Nam fell to the Communists, and guerrilla warfare in southern Viet-Nam and Laos continued into the 1960's.

For the most part, however, Communist efforts in the underdeveloped countries concentrated on attempting to convince the people (and, where possible, their leaders) that the best way to stop being an underdeveloped country was to embrace Communism.

Communist Appeal in Underdeveloped Countries

It would seem reasonable that no one who knew of the black record of Communism in the U.S.S.R. and, more recently, in China, could want Communism for his own country. The murders, confiscations, brutalities, and suppressions of freedom carried out in the name of Communism would seemingly make it very unattractive. Yet Communism does have attractions for many of the peoples of the world, particularly in backward non-European areas. There are two important reasons for this appeal.

The first reason is the Communist claim to be against colonialism. Until quite recently, most of the Asian and African countries were colonies of the major European powers; a few still are. The people of these countries have struggled for their independence for many years, and many of them distrust their former masters. The Soviet Union says that it is opposed to colonialism—though in reality it has its own oppressive brand in eastern Europe and in Soviet Central Asia. The Soviet Union says that it is against the exploitation by Europeans of the black, brown, and yellow races; it puts itself forward as their protector, and does everything it can to strengthen this image. Because much of the thinking of the former colonies is colored by their hatred for and suspicion of their onetime masters, the Russians are able to gain support on this point.

A second reason for the Communist appeal to the underdeveloped countries is the often-repeated story of Soviet industrial development. The Communists are constantly telling how the Soviet Union, which forty years ago was a weak nation, became one of the world's great powers under Communism. To deliver their message, the Soviets distribute millions of pamphlets and make thousands of radio broadcasts in dozens of languages.

To many of the leaders and educated people of the backward nations of the world, the failure of the Soviet Union to guarantee civil liberties is not important. Its lack of free elections, its purges, its Secret Police, and its slave-labor camps are of relatively minor concern. What counts with them is *power*. How can they gain it? How can they build their weak and underdeveloped countries into mighty nations like the United States, Great Britain, or France?

199

Khrushchev has made several good-will trips to Asia as part of the Soviet effort to attract the people and their leaders to Communism. Above, Khrushchev and Indonesian president Sukarno are surrounded by flower-bedecked dancing girls on the island of Bali, Republic of Indonesia.

To this question, the Communists offer the solution of Communism. The Soviet Union, they say, has become powerful by adopting Communism; and, they say, so can you.

The Communists, of course, leave out a few facts. They fail to mention that in 1913, before the Communists came to power in Russia, that country was already the fifth largest industrial nation in the world. It had some skilled manpower; it had a relatively large number of educated people; it had industrial experience; and it had one of the richest reserves of natural resources in the world. Russia in 1913 was waiting to burst forth as a mighty industrial nation.

The same is not true in most of the underdeveloped nations. They lack experience, trained manpower, education, and natural resources. Yet they aspire to build skyscrapers and dams, to have the automobiles and appliances—and food—of America. The Communists promise that they can bring all these things *soon*. Even though their arguments are for the most part untrue, the promise is so attractive that many are tempted to follow.

The United States, of course, has everything that the U.S.S.R. possesses, and much more besides. But, say the Soviets, the United States has had much more time to develop. They try to identify the United States with the former colonial powers, such as France, Britain, Holland, Belgium, and Portugal, who are our allies.

Although certain conditions in the underdeveloped countries work for the Communists, there are as many, perhaps more, working in favor of the United States. The United States is recognized as the leading nation of the world. This makes some people dislike us; but it also causes them to respect us and our methods. And most leaders in the underdeveloped countries recognize that the United States has given them more help than has the Soviet Union.

One of the strongest factors working for the United States is our revolutionary tradition. The United States was born in revolution. We were the first nation in history to gain independence from the colonialism of Great Britain. Our history and our leaders have been an inspiration to the leaders of the new countries. Our revolutionary heritage is a powerful weapon in the struggle to keep the underdeveloped nations from going Communist. Unfortunately, we have often failed to recognize its value.

Communism in Latin America

Latin America today is in turmoil. It is in desperate need of reform. It is divided into a few rich and many poverty-stricken. Democracy can succeed only where there is a large middle class, and this simply does not exist in Latin America. Our government today is attempting to encourage those in power to change their ways, to give the poor a better chance. But many of the wealthy refuse; and, in so doing, they open the way for Communist subversion.

Events in Cuba since 1959, when Fidel Castro took over the Cuban government, provide an example and a warning of what might happen in other Latin-American countries.

When Fidel Castro first appeared in the Sierra Maestra mountains of Cuba, attempting to lead the Cuban people against the government of dictator Fulgencio Batista, the majority of Americans cheered. They knew of the widespread corruption and brutalities of the Batista administration. They knew how well a few lived in Cuba, and how poverty-stricken the majority were. They thought it was time for a new day for the people of Cuba.

When the Castro government took over in Cuba in January, 1959, it was wildly acclaimed by the Cuban people. Castro was a national hero, and his bearded soldiers were embraced by the mobs. Castro had promised a program of democratic social reforms, and these the Cuban people eagerly awaited.

But by the middle of 1960 it was apparent that Castro's "democratic social reforms" were far from that. Moderate politicians were forced out of office. People that Castro didn't like were executed. Foreign-owned companies were taken over by the government; then

Cuban-owned companies were taken over as well. Cuban textile mills, paint factories, department stores, and even the land became government property. Nationalization had not been a plank of Castro's program, but now it became one. At the same time, Castro drew closer and closer to the Soviet Union. He shipped his sugar and pineapple to them, and received guns, tanks, and fighter planes in return. He suppressed books that the Russian Communists did not like, and he closed down newspapers that disagreed with him. Castro made a speech in which he shouted, "Glory to Vladimir Ilyich Lenin!" He altered Cuban agriculture to conform to the Soviet model; and he made peace with the Cuban Communists, who at one time had rebuked him and his movement as "petty-bourgeois." In short, it became quite evident that Cuba was being turned into a Communist satellite state.

Observers disagree on the reasons that Castro led his country toward Communism. Some believe that Castro had been a Communist for many years. According to this theory, Castro hid the fact that he was a Communist so that he could gain the support of Americans and of Cubans who were anti-Batista but also anti-Communist.

Others have a more complicated explanation for Castro's behavior. They reason that when Castro was fighting for power, all that he thought about was getting rid of Batista. He had no definite plans for what he would do after Batista was gone, and he had no idea of how to organize a government. When he suddenly found himself in power, he was convinced by some of his aides that the Communists had a good plan and that they knew how to organize a government. Castro bought the idea, and thus the Castro program became a Communist program.

As we have already seen, however, the Communists coöperate only in order that someday they may take over completely. If this theory about Castro is correct, it is likely that the Communists will get rid of Castro as soon as they feel that they have the power to completely take over Cuba for themselves. At the moment they cannot afford to do this: Castro, though less popular than he once was, still has wide support among the Cuban people, particularly the young. Apparently Castro, however, fears the future; and it is probably this fear that caused him to boast in 1961 that he had been a Communist for many years—a statement which probably is not true.

As Castro's coöperation with the Cuban Communists increased, he also increased his dealings with the Soviet Union. Cuba began shipping her sugar and pineapple to Russia in exchange for oil, trucks, cloth—and weapons. At first, these were guns and tanks and

Fidel Castro (1927–   ), Cuban dictator who turned his country into a Soviet satellite, with Khrushchev at the 1960 meeting of the United Nations General Assembly.

United Press International

weapons carriers; they were the kind of weapons that, as both the Cubans and the Russians insisted, could be used only to defend Cuba, and not to attack anyone else. In 1962, however, the Soviet Union attempted to establish guided-missile bases in Cuba, from which atomic bombs could have been delivered to most parts of the United States and Latin America.

In addition to its military threat to the United States, Communism in Cuba poses a great political threat to the rest of Latin America. Castro and the Communists have agents working in every other country in Latin America. These agents do their best to stir up anti-American feeling wherever they can and to promote revolutions like Castro's in other Latin-American countries. There is probably a great danger that in some places they will succeed.

Many of the poor of Latin America feel that they have little to expect from the United States. We are always portrayed by the Communists as a colonial Uncle Sam who has traditionally squeezed the smaller and weaker Latin-American countries. The promises of Castro seem to have impressed many Latin-Americans. They know little of Communism, of Castro's firing squads, of the greatly lowered standard of living in Cuba under Castro, of Castro's dependence on the Soviet Union. But propaganda has convinced many that the United States is an enemy and Castro a friend, and that by following Castro they can achieve a better tomorrow. At the present time, it is probably in Latin America that the greatest danger of new Communist successes exists.

Communism in Asia and Africa

Generally speaking, the present-day leaders of the Asian and African countries are middle-class people who are basically opposed to Communism and what it stands for. These leaders, however, will sometimes act more friendly toward the Soviet Union than seems wise to Americans. They sometimes accept large amounts of Soviet aid and invite numbers of Soviet and satellite technicians to help them build their countries. They accept Soviet aid because they are naïve or because they fear becoming completely dependent on the former colonial countries. These leaders are not likely to lead their countries into the Communist camp. If they should fail to improve the conditions of their peoples quickly enough, however, they (or their successors) might be more sympathetic to Communism.

The leaders of some of the Asian and African countries have been willing to coöperate with the Russian Communists, but at the same time have suppressed the Communists of their own countries. This is particularly true of Nasser of Egypt, who has accepted huge Russian loans and spoken frequent words of friendship for the Soviet Union, but who often throws Egyptian Communists into jail. Other leaders, such as Touré of Guinea, have realized that they were getting so close to the Communist fire that they might get burned.

In Africa the strongest Communist party is in the Union of South Africa. Many of the people who belong to it do so not because they approve of Communist economic and social doctrines, but as a protest against the racial policies of the government, which are among the most restrictive in the world.

In Asia, Communist armies operating out of China and North Viet-Nam have been active in Laos and South Viet-Nam. In these countries, the outcome is still in doubt. In the other countries of Asia, as in Africa, the future of Communism will depend upon the success or failure of the present leaders.

In Asia and beyond, much of the attention of the smaller nations is focused upon the struggle between China and India. They are the nations with the two largest populations in the world. Both are incredibly backward. Both are ambitious. India is trying to build itself up using the institutions of Western democracy. China is thoroughly Communistic. Can the freedom of India raise the standard of living of the masses of India more rapidly than the totalitarianism of China? All of Asia—and beyond—is waiting to see. The fate of Asia, and perhaps of much of the rest of the world, hangs in the balance.

Check the facts

1. Why was the Comintern established? Why did its activities continue after it had been "abolished"?

2. Why did Stalin negotiate the Nazi-Soviet Pact of August, 1939? What were the terms of this pact? What lands did the Soviet Union gain as a result?

3. What success did Hitler's armies have in their war with Russia? Why were many captured soldiers from the Red Army willing to join the Germans? Why did Hitler refuse to use them in his forces?

4. How were the people of occupied countries treated by the Germans? What methods did civilians use to oppose the Germans? How much aid did the United States give Russia in the fight against Germany?

5. Name the three major conferences held between Great Britain, the Soviet Union, and the United States. What agreements were made at these conferences? To what extent did the Soviet Union keep these agreements?

6. Describe the process by which the Communists took over the governments of the countries of eastern Europe. To what degree were these "people's democracies" dependent upon the Communist Party of the Soviet Union? Name the countries that in this way became a part of the Russian empire. How were these satellite countries treated by Russia? What is the "Iron Curtain"? What is its purpose?

7. What conditions after World War II made some countries interested in Communism? How were the Communist threats of control in Greece and Italy defeated? Name the policies adopted by the United States to halt the spread of Communism in Europe. Give the content of each policy.

8. Why do many people in France vote for the Communist ticket? What conditions in Italy prevent the Communist party there from gaining control? In what type of country does Communism have the best chance to establish itself? Why is prosperity one of the potent weapons against Communism?

9. What were the causes of the Chinese Revolution of 1911? Why was the Kuomintang organized? What aid did Russia give Sun Yat-sen after 1917? What events brought Mao Tse-tung into control of Chinese Communism?

10. When did Japan attack China? How did this war affect the struggle between Mao and Chiang? Why were the Chinese not more effective in fighting Japan?

11. Why were the Chinese Communists able to gain control of China after World War II? What tactics did they use to force the Kuomintang from the Chinese mainland? What promises did they make to the peasants? How well were these promises carried out?

12. What is a commune? Why did Mao establish them? Describe the life on a Chinese commune. What was the "Great Leap Forward"? How successful was it? Why is Communist China feared by both Russia and the West?

13. Why was Korea divided into two parts? What was the cause of the Korean War? Why did the United Nations enter it? When and why did the Chinese Communists take part? Why did it take two years to arrange a truce?

14. Name two reasons for the appeal Communism has for people in under-developed countries. What arguments do the Communists offer in behalf of each? What facts do they omit in promising underdeveloped countries that they can quickly become industrial powers? What conditions in these countries work in behalf of the United States? Why is the revolutionary tradition of the United States a factor in its favor?

15. What were the conditions in Cuba that brought Castro into power? What evidence is there that Cuba has become a Communist satellite? Why did Castro adopt Communism for Cuba? What is the main danger from Communism in Cuba?

16. Why have the leaders of Asian and African countries sometimes co-operated with the U.S.S.R.? Why is attention today focused upon the struggles in China and India to industrialize and to raise the standard of living?

Know word meanings

Define and use correctly the following words:
partisans   satellites   commune   puppet government   Kuomintang

Use the map

1. On an outline map of Europe locate (a) the Communist countries: Poland, Rumania, Czechoslovakia, Bulgaria, Yugoslavia, Albania, Hungary, East Germany; (b) the former independent nations, now part of the Soviet Union: Lithuania, Latvia, Estonia; (c) Finland, Elbe River, Yalta, Potsdam, Greece, Italy.

2. On an outline map of Asia, locate China, North Korea, South Korea, North Viet-Nam, Formosa, Peiping, Panmunjom, India, Laos.

Do something extra

1. Compare the experiences of the Soviet Union and Communist China with collective farms. In what ways are their experiences similar? How do they differ?

2. Read and report on the Nazi-Soviet Pact of August, 1939. A detailed account is given in chapter 15 of Shirer, William L., *The Rise and Fall of the Third Reich.*

3. Read and report on the German invasion of Russia and the Russian resistance to the German armies in chapters 23, 24, and 26 of *The Rise and Fall of the Third Reich.*

4. Consult the *Readers' Guide to Periodical Literature* for magazine articles concerning the crucial election of April, 1948, in Italy. Note the efforts made by Italians living in the United States to influence the outcome.

5. Read and report on the outbreak of the Korean War.

6. A story that deals with the drive to exterminate sparrows in Red China shows some aspects of life under Communism. It is "Sparrow Shall Fall," by S. Han, *The New Yorker,* vol. 35, pp. 43–50, October 10, 1959.

7. Make reports on (a) the agricultural crisis in China, (b) industrial progress in Red China.

8. Report on the work of the Peace Corps in underdeveloped countries. What have its members accomplished?

Josip Broz Tito (1892–   ), Communist dictator of Yugoslavia, broke with the Soviet Union but kept his country under Communism. Tito's break with the Kremlin was the first of the important events that have shaken the unity of world Communism.

United Press International

10

WORLD COMMUNISM TODAY —AND TOMORROW

The most notable recent development in world Communism is the Soviet Union's loss of its absolute control over every Communist party in the world. The Soviet Union and its Communist party are still by far the most powerful force in world Communism; but Communist parties of other countries—Yugoslavia, China, and Albania—have tried, and succeeded in, breaking away from the control of the Kremlin. In other countries—Poland and Hungary— attempts have been made to break away from the Kremlin, and have failed; but even these failures have brought some improvement to the lives of the Poles and the Hungarians.

At the same time that world Communism began to display its weaknesses, however, the Soviet Union itself continued to grow stronger. The confidence of Khrushchev and the Russian party leaders was reflected in the Program of the C.P.S.U., which was issued in 1961. In the program, Khrushchev promised that within 20 years the Soviet Union would have reached the first stages of Communism—that is, the ideal society predicted by Karl Marx. The promise has aroused enthusiasm in many people of the Soviet Union—but there is almost no possibility that the promise will be achieved.

The Break with Yugoslavia

The first break in the Soviet Union's absolute control of world Communism occurred in 1948, when Tito of Yugoslavia broke with Stalin.

Background: Yugoslavia as a Russian Satellite

In most of the European satellites of the U.S.S.R., the Communist leaders resented the demands placed on their countries by Stalin. They resented having to buy from the U.S.S.R. at high prices and being forced to deliver goods to the U.S.S.R. at much lower prices. They resented industries in their own country being run by Russians for the benefit of the U.S.S.R. They resented the demand that Soviet operations be exempt from local laws. In short, they resented the ravaging of their countries by the Soviet Union. They were Communists; but they were also Poles and Bulgars and Hungarians. They could do nothing, however, because they were unpopular leaders who could stay in power only because they were backed up by the Red Army.

The Communist Party of Yugoslavia, however, was not so dependent on the U.S.S.R. as were the other satellite states. The head of the Yugoslav party, Marshal Tito (real name: Josip Broz) was a national hero. During World War II he had led a strong partisan movement that had delivered heavy blows to the hated Nazis. Although the Red Army had helped, Tito's forces had played a major role in driving the Germans from Yugoslav soil.

The Yugoslavs, and Tito in particular, resented the demands made by the Soviet Union. Yugoslavia had suffered greatly in the war, losing one sixth of her housing, one third of her industry, and one half of her railroad mileage. Why should the Yugoslavs have to contribute so heavily to the rebuilding of the U.S.S.R. when their own country was in such need of being rebuilt itself? The Yugoslavs also were angry because Russians occupied key posts in their party, their secret police, and their army. Why should the Yugoslavs, who had fought on the same side as the Soviet Union, be treated as if they were a defeated enemy?

These points of resentment held by the Yugoslavs did not appear all at once. But little by little the Yugoslavs began to express their displeasure. They no longer jumped to carry out Moscow's orders. They recommended policies to the other satellites that were not acceptable to Stalin. They made cutting remarks about the Russians.

Stalin was not used to this kind of behavior on the part of the satellites, and he had no intention of putting up with it.

The Break with the Soviet Union

In February, 1948, the Soviet Union began to apply pressure to the Yugoslavian government. It delayed the signing of a new trade treaty. It threatened to withdraw Soviet technical and military aid.

It began a merciless propaganda offensive against Tito. Stalin believed that pressure of this kind would force the Yugoslav Communists to give in to the Soviet Union. But Tito would not give in.

For several months, charges flew back and forth between the Russian Communists and the Yugoslav Communists. Finally on June 28, 1948, a unanimous declaration by the principal Communist parties of the world was issued somewhere in Rumania. "The Central Committee of the Communist Party of Yugoslavia," said the declaration, "has placed itself and the Yugoslavia party outside the family of the fraternal Communist party, outside the united Communist front." The Yugoslav Communists had been expelled from the world Communist movement.

Stalin believed that the break would force Tito to reëstablish his dependence on the U.S.S.R.—on Stalin's terms. He was certain that Tito could not preserve Communism in Yugoslavia without the aid of the Soviet Union. To further pressure Tito, Stalin hinted that the U.S.S.R. might invade Yugoslavia. He launched a tremendous propaganda campaign against Tito. In the other satellite states, Yugoslav diplomats were insulted, their embassies attacked, their homes broken into, their mail opened. The non-Yugoslav Communists agitated among the many national groups that make up Yugoslavia, hoping to cause conflicts within Yugoslavia. They tried to convince members of the Yugoslavian Communist party that Stalin was certain to win and that they had best be on the right side.

The Soviet Union used economic pressures as well. Trade agreements were cancelled. Factories and materials for which the Yugoslavs had paid were not delivered. The Czechoslovakian government delivered only 60 per cent of the automobiles for which the Yugoslavian government had paid—and they left out essential parts, so that the cars could not run.

Obviously, the Yugoslav Communists were fighting for their lives. But they were prepared to do just that. Unlike the Communist puppets of the other satellites, they were national leaders who had placed and kept themselves in power without the assistance of Soviet armed might. For this reason, Tito was somewhat more popular in Yugoslavia than other Communists were in other countries. After the break, Tito's pose as little David valiantly standing up to the Soviet Goliath won him even more popularity among the Yugoslav people.

Another factor aiding the independence of the Yugoslav Communists from Moscow was that Tito had built his own party organization in time of war. He controlled it himself, and loyalty was to

209

him. This made it difficult for the Russians to penetrate the Yugo-slav party. Furthermore, the Yugoslav Communists had confidence in themselves, because they had successfully fought the Germans and taken over the government of their country. They were expe-rienced men who had fought against unfavorable odds before, and won—and who believed that they could do it again.

Yugoslavia since 1948

The events of 1948 did not free Yugoslavia from Communism; Yugoslavia remains a Communist dictatorship. But the Yugoslav Communists realized that in order to stay in power they must present themselves to the people as Yugoslav nationalists rather than as Communists. Tito has played down the fact that he is a Communist; instead, he emphasizes his role as head of the Yugoslav nation. Today Tito seldom even mentions Communism; that role is left for others lower in the party.

Tito also recognized that he would have to gain the support of the Yugoslav farmers, who are the majority of the population. These people were against the idea of collectivization, which had been begun shortly after the war. To win their support, Tito would have to give in to their wishes. In 1953, therefore, collectivization was abolished, and the peasant was told to "feel secure on his land." The Yugoslav Communists said that they favored collectivization; but they would not make the mistake of trying to enforce the Soviet Union's system of collective farming.

At the same time, the Yugoslav Communists attempted to prove that they were better Communists than the Russians. They admitted that they, like all Communists, were indebted to the Soviet Union for the 1917 Revolution. But, they said, the Soviet Union has wandered from true Communism since Lenin's death. It has become a prison ruled by force; it has chosen the path of brutality rather than that of socialism. As one of the leading Yugoslavs wrote, "No one in modern times has so much betrayed the noble ideals of socialism and Communism, for the development of which all peoples have contributed so much, as has the Soviet Union."

After the death of Stalin, and particularly after Khrushchev was firmly in power, the Soviet Union made several attempts to patch up its quarrel with Yugoslavia. As a result, the Soviet and Yugoslav governments are now on friendlier terms than they were in the early 1950's. But the Yugoslav Communists have refused to allow their country to come under Soviet control; they still do not trust the Russians.

On the other hand, the Yugoslav Communists have not sought any kind of alliance with the United States or the western European countries. Rather, they have attempted to place themselves at the front of the "neutralist" nations of the world, those that belong to neither the Communist nor the Western alliances. Their association with other neutralist countries, many of whom the Soviet Union is attempting to be friendly with, makes the possibility of a Soviet attack on Yugoslavia unlikely. And Yugoslavia's position as one of the leading neutralist nations helps Tito gain the support of the Yugoslav people, who are pleased that their small country has become important in world affairs.

The Significance of Yugoslavia   211

The Yugoslav Communists, perhaps somewhat to their own surprise, have maintained their independence from the domination of the U.S.S.R. Although they have wandered from the Soviet brand of Communism, they remain Communists.

Yugoslavia is a small country—very small in comparison to the U.S.S.R. Yet the Yugoslav Communist party has had a tremendous effect on the Soviet Union and on world Communism in general. The Yugoslav party was the first Communist party in power to successfully defy Soviet control. It decided that it had a better idea of what was good for its own country than did the Soviet Union. It was at first not happy at being separated from world Communism; but when separation was forced upon it, it proved that an independent Communist state could exist without being controlled by the Soviet Union. Its experience provided an example for other Communist states and parties throughout the world. At the time, few were in a position to follow the Yugoslav example; but when the time came, they would remember.

It was Yugoslavia which in 1948 first split the absolute unity of world Communism. In time others would follow.

1956: The Year of Revolt

By ousting Tito's Yugoslavia from the Communist camp, Stalin thought that he was ridding himself of "Titoism." To the Soviets, "Titoism" is the sin of putting the welfare of one's own country before the welfare of the U.S.S.R. To make sure that "Titoism" would not spread to the other satellite states, Stalin arrested anyone that he thought might someday follow Tito's path. The men who were arrested were loyal Communists, but they were men who thought of themselves as Poles or Hungarians or Rumanians as well as Communists. They did not doubt the leading role of the Soviet Union in world Communism, and they were not followers or admirers of Tito. But their own experiences sometimes caused them to resent putting Russian interests before their own—so Stalin threw them in jail.

But "Titoism" could not be wiped out so easily. Stalin's iron-fisted tactics kept all the satellites (except Yugoslavia) firmly under Soviet control. After Stalin's death in 1953, however, the Soviet leaders who succeeded him were forced to pay more attention to their own problems within the Soviet Union. National pressures built up within the satellites. Then, in 1956, came Khrushchev's "Secret" speech. According to the Soviet text, Khrushchev's speech caused "movement," "commotion," and "indignation" in the hall in which it was given. In the satellite countries its effect was more profound: it gave rise to revolution.

Poland in 1956

Under Stalin, Poland was an occupied country. Every government department had two or three Russians in it. In the armed forces the uniforms were Russian, and the instruction manuals were translated from the Russian. In the schools the textbooks were translations of Soviet books. Every main street in Poland, except one, was given Stalin's name. Soviet films, books, articles, and radio programs flooded Poland. The largest building in Warsaw was an exact copy of four buildings that stood in Moscow.

The Russian domination of their country angered the patriotic Poles, who had struggled against the Russians for almost 150 years until they received their independence from Russia at the end of World War I. Under the tight controls of Stalin, the Poles could do nothing. But beginning in 1954, occasional voices were raised against the Secret Police, the poor living conditions, and the general shortcomings and inefficiency of life under the Communists. The protests were not loud or insistent, but the fact that they were made at all, at times even in the newspapers, clearly suggested discontent and the desire for change.

It was in the midst of this growing discontent that Khrushchev's "Secret" speech burst upon the Polish scene. Khrushchev had hoped that the "Secret" speech could be kept secret; but the speech found its way into American hands and was widely reproduced. (See page 104.) What Khrushchev had to say about Stalin was worse than even the most anti-Stalin Polish Communists had imagined. It is said that some Polish Communists were so shocked by the revelations that they fainted. Older men, Communists who had built their whole lives on a belief in Communism and its great leader Stalin, suddenly found that their world had collapsed around them. Young Communists became suddenly and permanently disillusioned.

The Khrushchev speech took the starch out of Polish Communism. The Polish Communist party was divided into two groups, those who supported the policies of Stalin and opposed widespread reform, and those who preferred reform.

Unlike the Communist party members, the Polish people knew what they wanted: reform. And gradually changes began to occur in Poland. The changes probably would have continued to come about gradually had it not been for the events that occurred in the industrial city of Poznan.

The Poznan Riots and Wladyslaw Gomulka

In June, 1956, in a demand for higher wages and other concessions, 16,000 workers filed out of the Stalin Engineering Works in the Polish industrial city of Poznan. The workers marched toward the center of the city in a fairly orderly formation. On the way, however, the rumor spread that their leaders had been arrested. What had started as a peaceful demonstration turned into a howling mob. The headquarters of the Secret Police were attacked, and their files were burned. As the crowd became more daring, the Soviet flag was torn down. Members of the Polish armed forces joined in. Three days passed before the rioters were silenced, and only at the cost of 54 dead and more than 200 wounded.

Khrushchev's "Secret" speech had wounded the Polish Communist party; the Poznan riots came close to destroying it. The government was able to keep the story of the riots from spreading throughout Poland until after the rioters had been put down; otherwise all of Poland would probably have arisen against the Communists. As it was, hundreds of thousands of Polish Communists abandoned the party after they heard about Poznan. Estimates of the number who lost interest run as high as 90 per cent. What remained of the party was disorganized and dismayed.

Clearly, the Polish Communist party was on the verge of collapse, and by October the Polish people were on the verge of rising up against it. The Soviet Union, however, had no intention of allowing the Poles to bring an end to Communism. Red Army units in Poland readied themselves for action, and Soviet troops were rushed to the Polish border. On one occasion Soviet and Polish troops are reported to have exchanged fire. And on October 18, 1956, Khrushchev announced that he and several other high Soviet officials would arrive in Warsaw the next day.

The Polish Communists were terrified. The Polish people were threatening to rise up against them; Khrushchev was threatening to bring all the might of the Soviet Union against their country; and they were caught in the middle. Only one man among them, Wladyslaw Gomulka, seemed to have any idea of what to do. Gomulka was a "Titoist" who had been under arrest for several years; now, suddenly, he was placed at the head of the Polish Communist party.

When Khrushchev arrived at the Warsaw airport, he was met by Gomulka. Khrushchev looked at him and said, "Who are you?" Gomulka looked back and answered, "I am Gomulka, whom you put in prison." And with this unpromising beginning, Khrushchev and Gomulka sat down to negotiate.

Khrushchev tried to apply every pressure at his disposal—and he had large Soviet forces in Poland and along her borders. But Gomulka always returned to the fact that if Khrushchev did not accept a government led by Gomulka, there would be no Polish Communist government at all. Instead there would be war. Khrushchev could not allow a war to break out; it would have been an open admission that the only way the U.S.S.R. could control Poland was through naked force. Khrushchev therefore backed down. War was averted, and Gomulka became a great popular hero.

Poland since 1956

Gomulka recognized in 1956 that Poland was at the mercy of the Soviet Union. It could never hope to stand against the Red Army. While it could in many respects go its own way, it could not afford to do anything that would bring about Soviet intervention. Gomulka's problem was to determine just how far he could go without antagonizing the Soviet Union.

Gomulka also realized that to keep the Communists in power in Poland, he would have to make concessions to the people. Gomulka was (and still is) a Communist; but he was also a realist. He recognized that some of the demands of the people would have to be met, or the people would rebel. He therefore saw his task as advancing Communism, and at the same time avoiding antagonizing either his own people or the Soviets.

For Gomulka the task has not been an easy one, but he has carried it out with great ability. He is by no means so popular today

Photo from European

When Polish Communist party leader Wladyslaw Gomulka successfully defied Khrushchev, he became a hero to many of the Polish people. Above, soldiers and civilians applaud Gomulka in Warsaw, the Polish capital, in October, 1956, when he announced his great victory.

as he was in 1956, but no one threatens his position. He and his people have come to realize that in Poland today there are limits on what is possible. Neither the people nor the Communists can have all that they want. The people realize that if they attempt a revolution, there will be Soviet intervention. The government realizes that if it goes too far, the people will rebel. Every aspect of Polish policy today is determined not by what one side or the other thinks is desirable, but by what each side recognizes to be possible. Sometimes there is disagreement on the limits of the possible, but a rough balance is kept.

Today Poland is the freest of the Communist states, though it is far from being a free country. It is certainly not so free today even as it was in 1956. American and British newspapers can be purchased at some newsstands in Warsaw, but the writers and scientists of Poland cannot say everything that they want to say. Most schools are parochial, 97 per cent of the Poles being Catholic; but the leaders of the church must be careful not to speak too strongly against Communism. Forced collectivization of agriculture has been abandoned (and food production has increased steadily since 1956); but the farmers are heavily taxed.

Poland remains a Communist country, but it is a country where Communism is on the defensive. Marxism-Leninism has been shoved into a corner; Polish policy is largely determined by nationalism, by the pride of being a Pole, by consideration of what is possible.

The Hungarian Revolution

No sooner had the possibility of a revolution ended in Poland than an actual revolution occurred in Hungary.

Before October, 1956, Hungary had undergone few of the changes that had taken place in Poland since Stalin's death. It was still a closely-guarded police state. Its leader, Erno Gerö, was a Soviet puppet who ruled Hungary largely through the terror of the Secret Police. He was backed by a Soviet occupation force of more than 20,000 men and 600 tanks.

The Hungarians were deeply moved by what had happened in Poland. The Polish radio and other sources had provided enough information for the Hungarians to gain a general idea of what had occurred. Some Hungarians began street demonstrations, demanding that Hungary be granted the same concessions as Poland. The demonstrations were peaceful until the night of October 23, when the police fired on the demonstrators. The police interference was followed by pitched battles between Hungarian students and workers on one side, and the Secret Police and the Red Army on the other. By October 25, the Red Army had triumphed and order had been restored. Most of the fighting had taken place in Budapest, the Hungarian capital.

After the riots had been suppressed, the Soviet government decided that some concessions had better be made to the Hungarian people. They probably hoped that a workable compromise such as had been reached in Poland could also be achieved in Hungary. Gerö and the other Stalinist leaders were therefore dismissed. They were replaced by two men who, like Gomulka in Poland, had spent years in prison.

Under Imre Nagy, the new premier, far-reaching changes were made. The political parties that had existed before the Communist takeover were allowed to become active again, and their members were included in the new government. The Secret Police system was abolished. A degree of freedom of the press returned. The Communist party was reorganized. Nagy even demanded that Russian troops be removed from Budapest, and Khrushchev gave in to the demand. Clearly, the changes in Hungary had gone far beyond those in Poland. But it seemed that Khrushchev feared that further uprisings in Hungary might lead to even more trouble in other countries, and was therefore willing to accept the new Hungarian system. He probably hoped that the old system could slowly and quietly be restored.

Hungarian freedom fighters move into action in Budapest in November, 1956. Although their cause was doomed to almost certain failure, the Hungarian rebels fought the Red Army to the bitter end.

Photo from European

But the people of Hungary—particularly the students and workers of Budapest—had had a taste of freedom, and they demanded more. Nagy therefore withdrew Hungary from its military alliance with the Soviet Union and the other satellites. He demanded that all Soviet troops be withdrawn from Hungary. And he announced that Hungary would thereafter be a neutral country, no longer associated with the Soviet Union or with world Communism.

The Soviet Union could not accept these last changes; to the Russians, the Hungarians had gone too far. They therefore ordered the Soviet troops to gather around Budapest; and at dawn on November 4, 1956, the Red Army attacked. The youth of Hungary fought bravely, often with kitchen knives and clubs against tanks, flame throwers, and mortar fire. In the workers' quarters the resistance to the Red Army was particularly determined and stubborn. But the outcome was never in doubt. Within 24 hours freedom in Hungary was completely crushed, and a new Soviet puppet government was established.

In the fighting, which was mostly confined to Budapest, almost 3,000 Hungarians were killed and about 12,000 were wounded. Hundreds of thousands of Hungarians escaped across the border to freedom in Austria. Most of the able members of Hungary's youth either escaped or were killed. Hungary became a dead country of the old and the beaten.

A Hungarian soldier and his bitterly weeping wife cross the border into Austria after the brutal Soviet suppression of the Hungarian revolt.

United Press International

Hungary today has repaired most of the damage of the 1956 revolt, but the memory of it remains. The puppet government established in November, 1956, remains in power—but only because it is backed by the Red Army. From time to time the government attempts to gain the support of the Hungarian people. It is clear, however, that the government rules only because the Hungarians, like the Poles, have concluded that revolt is impossible.

The Soviet Union was able to force the Hungarian people to their knees, but only at a fearful cost. The brutal Soviet tactics shocked the world. Soviet prestige was dealt a serious blow, and tens of thousands of Communists left the party. The Soviet Union attempted to place the blame on "reactionaries" who, they said, had seized control of the Hungarian government. The world, however, knew better.

The End of Communist Unity

In many ways world Communism has never recovered from the events of 1956—and probably it never will.

In the free countries of the West, the Communist parties lost thousands of members, shocked by the disclosures of Khrushchev's "Secret" speech followed a few months later by the Polish and Hungarian uprisings. Men and women who had accepted the lies of

Communist propaganda for decades were no longer willing to listen. The image of the peaceful, worker-loving Soviet Union held by fellow travelers was destroyed by the photographs of Red Army tanks firing at helpless civilians in the rubble of Budapest.

In the Communist countries, the effect of 1956 was perhaps even more significant. When Stalin was alive, he had managed to run the satellite countries as if there were only one country—the Soviet Union. Only Yugoslavia had escaped from his control. But after Stalin's death, the absolute control of the Soviet Union began to be challenged; and after November, 1956, the absolute unity of the Communist world was dead.

The unity of the Communist world has collapsed because the Communists in power have adopted an attitude that Marx and Lenin hated—*nationalism*. The Communists of Yugoslavia and Poland and Hungary and China have found themselves to be not only Marxist-Leninists but also nationalists. They have discovered that often they must put the interests of their own countries before the interests of the U.S.S.R. What Khrushchev has decided is best for the Soviet Union has come into conflict with what Tito thinks is best for Yugoslavia and what Mao thinks is best for China. Out of this conflict has come the breakdown of unity that now threatens to grow into an actual split in the Communist world.

Of the conflicts that now divide the Communist world, by far the most important is that between the two Communist giants, the U.S.S.R. and China.

The "Have" Nation vs. the "Have-not" Nation

The basic difference between the two giants of Communism is that today the Soviet Union is a "have" nation and China is a "have-not" nation. In other words, the Soviet Union is a powerful, highly industrialized nation whose people have one of the higher (though far from the highest) standards of living in the world; whereas China is a poor country that has few factories, and whose people are terribly underfed.

China, however, is a very proud country. For centuries she considered herself the center of the universe, and everything beyond her borders was thought of as wilderness. But today China is weak. The Chinese—and particularly the Communist rulers of China—want above all else to restore China to a position of power and influence in the world. The Chinese Communists are ambitious, and they are in a hurry. And because they are in a hurry, and because they are so far behind, the Chinese Communists feel that their fellow Communists in the Soviet Union should go all out to help the

Chinese rise to the level of the Russians. Then, they say, they can all move forward together.

The Russian Communists have a somewhat different idea about strengthening Communist China. They would rather concentrate on building their own country than on building the strength of China. One reason for this Russian attitude is that the future—so far as the Soviets are concerned—looks bright for both the Soviet Communist party and the Russian people. The Soviet Union is now a powerful country, and it is moving forward at a rapid rate. But this position was not achieved easily: Russian industry was built on the backs of the Russian people. Now the people want to enjoy the results of their work; they do not want to struggle for another 40 or 50 years while China catches up with them.

A second reason for the Russian reluctance to help the Chinese is that the Russians fear the Chinese. China is a huge country, with more than three times as many people as the Soviet Union, and it is growing rapidly; it is estimated that the population of China will be more than one *billion* by the year 2000. If China were highly industrialized, it would—simply because of its size—become a more powerful nation than the Soviet Union. The Russians fear that if that were to happen, the Chinese would try to dominate the Soviet Union, or perhaps even attempt to take it over.

For these reasons—desire to build their own country, and fear of China—the Russians have greatly cut back the aid that they once gave to China. At one time, the Russians sent China large amounts of industrial equipment and military supplies, and there were thousands of Russian technicians in China. Today the industrial and military shipments have almost stopped, and the technicians have all gone back to Russia.

Traditionally, the Chinese have disliked foreigners. Their dislike changed to hatred in the 19th century, when European powers —including czarist Russia—took advantage of China's weakness. Today the actions of the Soviet Union have once again brought the Chinese hatred to the surface. For example, when the Russian technicians left China, they took with them the plans and blueprints for huge, half-finished projects such as dams and factories. The Chinese were left without plans or designs, without the know-how to make new ones, and without the equipment needed to finish the projects. The Chinese do not like this kind of treatment. It reminds them of the way they were treated by foreigners before—and they are angry. And they have made no attempt to hide their anger.

The Soviet withdrawal of foreign aid to China is only one example of how the goals of the two countries, the one a "have" nation

Although in 1959 Khrushchev and Mao appeared to be friendly, above, there were already great differences between the U.S.S.R. and China. Today their relationship is much worse, and Mao no longer hides his hatred of Khrushchev, which is an important factor in the Soviet-Chinese conflict.

221

and the other a "have-not" nation, have come into conflict. Another example, and one of far-reaching importance, is their different attitudes toward what, to any Communist, is a most important question: How should Communism be spread to other countries?

"Peaceful Co-existence" or Atomic War?

Before 1956 the Communist party line had been that all Communist countries should follow the example of the Soviet Union in everything that they did. After the changes that Khrushchev allowed to take place in Poland in 1956, it became necessary to develop a new Communist party line. The new line, which was urged by Gomulka and Mao Tse-tung, said that there was no "single road" to Communism. Although each Communist country was working toward the same goal, each of them had to work out its own problems in its own way. There were now "many roads" to Communism.

At first the Chinese Communists were in favor of this idea; indeed, they had done much to talk Khrushchev into it. Their unhappy experience in the "Hundred Flowers" campaign soon changed their minds. The "Hundred Flowers" campaign was an experiment in giving the Chinese people a certain amount of freedom of speech.

To Mao's great surprise the experiment turned into a disaster: the Chinese people quickly indicated that they hated Communism and their Communist rulers. Controls were soon brought back, more ruthlessly than before. (See page 193.) Mao concluded that what China needed was *more* orders, *more* commands, *more* unity, not less. China became similar to what Russia had been under Stalin.

At the same time, Mao became convinced that "liberalism," which was a mistake within China, was a mistake internationally as well. Mao argued that the Communist world needed greater unity and direction than Khrushchev and the Russian Communists were providing. The policies of Khrushchev, he argued, were causing the Communist world to dissolve, and they were also causing Marxism to lose much of its revolutionary spirit. Mao believes that each nation should *not* be allowed to decide what is best for itself; rather, the decisions should be made and carried out by the Soviet Union, the first and most powerful of the Communist nations. And, says Mao, it is the responsibility of the Soviet Union to do everything possible to bring Communism to the rest of the world. This must be done as soon as possible, and it must be done by using every possible method—including war.

Khrushchev, of course, is dedicated to spreading Communism by every means possible. But to him, a major war is not possible. Today, a major war would be a hydrogen-bomb war; tens of millions would be killed in such a war, and no nation would emerge victorious. The destruction would be so great that both the United States and the Soviet Union would be left in ruins. What good would it do the Soviet Union to destroy the United States if the Soviet Union, too, were destroyed?

In recent years, Khrushchev has talked much of what he calls "peaceful co-existence." As with most Communist terms, this one does not really mean what it says. Khrushchev believes in spreading world Communism; he considers all non-Communist governments to be deadly enemies that must be destroyed. He is even in favor of "little" wars—that is, civil wars or wars between small countries, in which atomic weapons would not be used. He calls them "wars of national liberation." But "peaceful co-existence," as Khrushchev uses the term, *does* mean that Khrushchev is quite opposed to atomic war. He has nothing to gain by it, and much to lose.

The Chinese Communists, on the other hand, have a quite different attitude toward atomic war. They believe that no method, not even atomic war, should be ruled out as a means of spreading Communism. They are willing to take the risk of atomic war because China is a backward, underfed nation of almost 700,000,000 people. The Chinese do not have nearly so much to lose as do the Russians. Of course, tens of millions of the Chinese people would be killed in such a war—but this does not particularly bother the Chinese Communist leaders. As one reportedly said, if half the Chinese population were killed, there would still be enough people to build up the country—and fewer mouths to feed. Moreover, the destruction in the United States and the Soviet Union would reduce them to about the same level as China; and China, which has far more people than the United States and the U.S.S.R. put together, would then be the most powerful nation in the world.

The Significance of the Russian-Chinese Conflict

The effects of this breakdown in Communist unity continue to be felt in the Communist world today. There have been several attempts to restore unity through negotiations or through discussions at Communist party congresses. All have failed. After some of the meetings, announcements were issued that promised both a "new" and a "continuing" unity, but it soon became apparent that these announcements were worthless scraps of paper. Both parties continue to go their separate ways. It seems unlikely that any new meetings will bring them closer together.

But, on the other hand, it is unlikely that there will be any complete Russian-Chinese split. Both sides recognize the propaganda value of staying together, and they recognize that they can still sometimes work together. Even if their relations are cool, they still have more in common with each other than they do with nations outside the Communist camp. And as long as they remain together within the Communist camp, there is always the chance that they will be able to resolve some of their differences. If they were to completely split apart, that chance would disappear.

As for the other Communist parties of the world, some have allied themselves closely with the Russians, others with the Chinese. Some have allied themselves with neither; they find that by playing one against the other, they can more easily do as they choose. and they can also increase their own bargaining power within the world Communist movement. Of course, it is also possible that some of these parties will split apart, with one part following the Russians and another following the Chinese.

Today it is apparent that the Communist world will not return to absolute unity. It seems likely that what is developing is a many-centered world Communism. But how many centers there will be— two, three, or a dozen—or what the relations between these centers will be, only time and events will decide.

The Future of the Soviet Union

Meanwhile, the Communist Party of the Soviet Union remains the leader of world Communism. The U.S.S.R. is no longer the unquestioned boss of the Communist movement throughout the world; but it is, beyond any doubt, the most powerful of the Communist nations. Thus, the successes and failures of Communism in the U.S.S.R. will determine the future of Communism for years to come.

Khrushchev's Promises

In recent years, Khrushchev has had much to say about the future of Communism in the Soviet Union. He has made a great many promises. Most of these promises are contained in the *Program of the Communist Party of the Soviet Union,* which was adopted at the 22nd Congress of the C.P.S.U. in the autumn of 1961. The highlights of the program are promises of an improvement in the standard of living and the establishment in the Soviet Union of what Khrushchev refers to as "democracy."

Since Khrushchev came to power, he has succeeded in noticeably raising the standard of living of the Soviet people. (See pages 99–101.) Moreover, he claims that in the near future, life in the Soviet Union will be even better. He has listed a large number of the improvements that, he says, the Soviet people can expect within the next 20 years.

These promises seem to have greatly pleased the Soviet people. And it is likely that Khrushchev and his successors will be able to further raise the Soviet standard of living. It is highly unlikely, however, that they will be able to completely live up to their ambitious promises. It should be noted, too, that even if the promises should be fulfilled, the Soviet Union's standard of living in 1981 would still be below that of the United States today.

As for "democracy," what the Communists call "democracy" is something quite different from what we think of when we use the term. To the Communists, it means that more people should take part in government and party activities. Khrushchev has taken steps to bring this kind of "democracy" about. But the chances that true democracy—government of the people—will be established in the Soviet Union are small. The real power will almost surely remain in the hands of the few men at the top of the party.

But Khrushchev keeps talking about democracy, and he is trying to put his own idea of "democracy" into practice. There are two reasons for his concern with democracy. The first is that the people want it, and they will probably be happier—and therefore work harder—if they can be convinced that they have it. The second reason for the constant talk about "democracy" is that the Communists are saddled with Marx's idea of the "withering away of the state." Marx says that the government will disappear when a Communist society has been achieved. Khrushchev says that the ideal Communist society is fast approaching. The time has come, therefore, for the state to begin withering. Khrushchev apparently hopes, and probably believes, that the "democracy" he is pushing will somehow bring about the "withering away of the state."

The Impossible Goal

Khrushchev has promised to Soviet people that by 1980 they will have advanced to the doorstep of Communism; and he has hinted that the ideal society that Marx predicted will come about shortly thereafter.

But will it? Will Communism, as Marx thought of it, ever become a living reality? Thus far, the Soviet Union has fallen far short of achieving its goal. Can the goal ever be achieved? The answer is: probably not.

What about the "withering away of the state"? We live today in a complex industrial society, made up of millions of people who produce millions of different kinds of items and perform millions of different functions. These activities do not take place in chaos. They must be organized and directed in some way or other. Much of the organizing and directing work can take place outside of government, as it does here in the United States. But that does not mean that we, or anyone else, can get along without a government. Without a government, how would our public policies—local, state, and national—be determined? Without government, how would we get our sewers dug, our highways built, our traffic laws enforced?

To all of these questions, Marx has the same answer: under Communism, man will become perfect. Because he will no longer lack food or clothing or shelter, his spirit will no longer be warped. He will be sweet and content. Government will not be required to protect the weak from the strong or the foolish from the shrewd. Men will organize their own affairs, and they will willingly coöperate with their neighbors whenever that becomes necessary. There will be no more need for government with its deadly red tape.

But Marx did not spell out how man's self-direction would operate in our complicated society. He merely stated, almost as an act of faith, that it would happen.

Communism believes that the man will be developed who will be completely self-controlled, who will not require any kind of direction from anyone else. Modern psychology, on the other hand, says that even if such a man could be developed, he would be hopelessly confused and frustrated, and miserably unhappy. Certainly the Soviet Union is far from having developed this self-controlled, coöperative sort of man. For years the Communists have been talking about the "new Soviet man," who will act in the proper Communist fashion simply because no other way of acting can ever occur to him; and for years the Soviet educational system has been attempting to produce this "new Soviet man." To most of us, such a creature would be nothing more than a robot. But the Communists have not been able to develop even these robots. There seems to be no chance, then, that they will ever be about to create the "perfect" man, capable of living in perfect peace with his brothers with no one to watch over him.

226

Just as improbable is the society that will operate on the principle of "From each according to his ability, to each according to his needs." This, too, would require developing a kind of men who would always do their best regardless of the reward. Some men, it is true, work largely for the pleasure that they get from their work; but this is far from true for all, nor is it ever likely to be. There will always be men who will work harder than others, and such men will almost always expect extra recognition—in money, prestige, or some other way—for their extra work. If they cannot work harder and achieve more, they will be quite unhappy. The idea of a society where no one desires anything better than or different from his neighbor, is a dream. In such a society, men would soon find new ways in which human weaknesses and superiorities could be expressed. Soon again the leaders would lead and the rest would follow, even as now.

Prospects for the Future

The Soviet idea of a rosy Communist future can never be achieved. But this does not mean that the Soviet Union cannot and will not advance to a higher level of development—though as it becomes more developed, its rate of progress is likely to slow down.

Undoubtedly the Soviet Union is already a powerful country and a dangerous enemy. If it could take over the United States and destroy our system, it would. The Communists still predict that they will someday do this.

But increasingly the Soviet people and their government look within their country, not outside it. They are becoming more concerned with their own lives, with what they have and with what they want. As they get more, they want to keep it. When one has nothing, he is willing to risk all; but when one has much, he is much less willing to take risks. We in the United States should therefore want the Soviet people to achieve a high standard of living and confidence in their government, so that both the people and the government may be satisfied and content. They might then be content to enjoy their own lives, and unwilling to attempt to destroy the ways of life of other countries. If this should take place, there is no reason why the United States and the U.S.S.R. could not live in peace and friendship—though certainly other enemies might appear.

But for the time being, the Soviet Union is the sworn enemy of the United States and all that it stands for. The Communists are convinced that they represent the future and we the past, and that their system will triumph over ours. They intend it. They have told us of their intentions. We must be prepared to meet the enemy on whatever battlefields fate may decree, and to continue the struggle until the enemy has stopped attempting to destroy us.

In this struggle, which will probably continue beyond the lifetimes of us all, we should be of good hope. Our arms are superior; our wealth is much greater than theirs; our influence is greater; and, most important, our principles, and our record of living up to our principles, far exceed theirs. If we act with wisdom and determination, we need have no fear for our future, nor for the ideas and ideals which we cherish and for which we stand.

aids to learning

Check the facts

1. Name three Communist countries that are no longer under the control of the Soviet Union. What demands of the U.S.S.R. were resented by the Communist leaders of the European satellite countries?

2. Why was Yugoslavia successful in achieving independence from the control of Moscow? Write a list of the events in this struggle. What is "Titoism"? What changes did Tito make in the administration of Yugoslavia? How does Communism in Yugoslavia differ from that in Russia?

3. What criticisms do the Yugoslavs make of the Soviet system of control? Why have the Yugoslavs remained Communists? What is the significance of the Yugoslav refusal to accept Soviet control?

4. How extensive was Russian control in Poland? How did Khrushchev's "Secret" speech of 1956 affect Polish Communists? What were the results of the Poznan riot? Why did Khrushchev have to accept Gomulka as leader of the Polish Communists? What is the present situation in Poland?

5. What concessions were made to Hungary after October 25, 1956? Why did Soviet forces attack Budapest on November 4, 1956? What effect did the Hungarian struggle have upon the Soviet Union? Upon world Communism?

6. Why has the unity of the Communist world broken down? How do Mao and Khrushchev differ concerning the promotion of Communism? What is the real issue between China and the Soviet Union?

7. Why does the Soviet Union no longer give large loans and other major aid to China? For what reasons do the Russians fear the Chinese? Why do the Chinese hate the Russians? Why is it unlikely that there will be a complete split between Russia and China?

8. Name the areas of Soviet life in which Khrushchev has promised improvements in the next twenty years. What is the Communist meaning of "democracy" at this time? How are they bringing this meaning into operation? Give two reasons why the Soviet Communists emphasize democracy. Why is there little possibility that the Soviet Union will become more "democratic" in the American meaning of the term?

9. What is Marx's ideal for Communism? Why is it unlikely that it will be realized?

10. Why would it be to the advantage of the United States to have the Soviet people achieve a high standard of living? What are the present Soviet aims concerning the United States? What assets does the United States have that make its future a hopeful one?

Identify names

What is the importance of each of the following?

Joseph Broz   Wladyslaw Gomulka   Imre Nagy   Janos Kadar

Do something extra

1. Read and report on one of these periods in the life of Tito: (a) Opposition to the German forces in Yugoslavia during World War II; (b) Defiance of Stalin in 1948; (c) Dictator of Yugoslavia. A useful reference is: Armstrong, Hamilton Fish: *Tito and Goliath*.

2. From newspapers and magazines of 1956, prepare an account of the riots in Poznan in June, 1956. Collect data concerning Gomulka and his leadership of the Polish Communists.

3. Using newspapers and magazines of 1956 give a report on the Hungarian revolts of October 25 and November 4, 1956, and the methods the Russians used to crush them.

4. Locate material and report on the Hungarian refugees of 1956–1957. What were their ages and their occupations in Hungary? Where did they go? What has happened to them?

5. Find out what action was taken in the United Nations concerning the Hungarian uprising.

6. Explain why the United States has given economic aid to Poland and Yugoslavia. How much has been given and in what form (money, food, etc.)?

7. Read and report on the 6,000 mile "Long March," 1934–35, of the Chinese Communists, from southern China to Yenan in northwest China.

8. Report on the conflict between the Soviet Union and Communist China 1960–1962.

9. Read and report on the *Program of the Communist Party of the Soviet Union*. The program is included in *The New Communist Manifesto and Related Documents*, edited by Dan N. Jacobs.

Armstrong, Hamilton Fish. *Tito and Goliath.* New York: Macmillan, 1951.
Armstrong, John A. *Ideology, Politics, and Government in the Soviet Union.* New York: Praeger, 1962.
Bauer, Raymond A., Inkeles, Alex, and Kluckhohn, Clyde. *How the Soviet System Works.* Cambridge: Harvard University Press, 1956; New York: Random House, 1960.
Berlin, Isaiah. *Karl Marx: His Life and Environment.* 2nd ed. New York: Oxford University Press, 1948.
Borkenau, Franz. *World Communism: A History of the Communist International.* Ann Arbor: University of Michigan Press, 1962.
Brzezinski, Zbigniew K. *The Soviet Bloc: Unity and Conflict.* Cambridge: Harvard University Press, 1960; New York: Praeger, 1961.
Campbell, Robert W. *Soviet Economic Power: Its Organization, Growth, and Challenge.* Cambridge: Houghton Mifflin, 1960.
Chamberlin, William Henry. *The Russian Revolution: 1917–1921.* 2 vols. New York: Macmillan, 1935.
Conquest, Robert. *The Pasternak Affair.* Philadelphia: Lippincott, 1962.
Crossman, Richard, editor. *The God That Failed.* New York: Harper & Row, 1949; New York: Bantam.
Curtiss, John Shelton. *The Russian Church and the Soviet State.* Boston: Little, Brown, 1953.
Dallin, Alexander. *The Soviet Union at the United Nations: An Inquiry into Soviet Motives and Objectives.* New York: Praeger, 1962.
Dallin, David J. *Soviet Foreign Policy after Stalin.* Philadelphia: Lippincott, 1961.
Dallin, David J., and Nicolaevsky, B. I. *Forced Labor in Soviet Russia.* New Haven: Yale University Press, 1947.
Deutscher, Isaac. *The Prophet Unarmed: Trotsky, 1921–1929.* New York: Oxford University Press, 1959.
Djilas, Milovan. *Conversations with Stalin.* New York: Harcourt, Brace & World, 1962.
Djilas, Milovan. *The New Class.* New York: Praeger, 1957.
Draper, Theodore. *The Roots of American Communism.* New York: Viking, 1957.
Fainsod, Merle. *Smolensk under Soviet Rule.* Cambridge: Harvard University Press, 1958.
Fischer, George. *Soviet Opposition to Stalin: A Case Study in World War II.* Cambridge: Harvard University Press, 1952.
Fischer, Markoosha. *Reunion in Moscow.* New York: Harper & Row, 1962.
Friedberg, Maurice. *Russian Classics in Soviet Jackets.* New York: Columbia University Press, 1962.
Granick, David. *The Red Executive.* Garden City: Doubleday, 1960.
Gunther, John. *Inside Russia Today.* New York: Harper & Row, 1958.

Gunther, John. *Meet Soviet Russia.* 2 vols. New York: Harper & Row, 1962.

Hazard, John N. *The Soviet System of Government.* Revised ed. Chicago: University of Chicago Press, 1960.

Hoover, J. Edgar. *Masters of Deceit.* New York: Holt, Rinehart & Winston, 1958; New York: Pocket Books, 1959.

Hunt, R. N. Carew. *A Guide to Communist Jargon.* New York: Macmillan, 1957.

Jacobs, Dan N., editor. *The New Communist Manifesto and Related Documents* (includes Marx: *Communist Manifesto;* Lenin: "Testament"; Khrushchev: "Secret" speech; Mao Tse-tung: "Hundred Flowers" speech; *Program of the C.P.S.U.*). 2nd ed. New York: Harper & Row, 1962.

Jacobs, Dan N., and Baerwald, Hans H. *Chinese Communism.* New York: Harper & Row, 1963.

Kennan, George F. *Russia and the West under Lenin and Stalin.* Boston: Little, Brown, 1961; New York: New American Library.

Leites, Nathan. *The Operational Code of the Politburo.* New York: McGraw-Hill, 1951.

Leites, Nathan, and Bernaut, Elsa. *Ritual of Liquidation.* Glencoe: Free Press, 1954.

Lenin, V. I. *State and Revolution.* New York: International Publishers, 1932.

Lenin, V. I. *What Is to Be Done?* New York: International Publishers.

Meyer, Alfred G. *Leninism.* Cambridge: Harvard University Press, 1957.

Moorehead, Alan. *The Russian Revolution.* New York: Harper & Row, 1958.

Mosely, Philip E. *The Kremlin and World Politics: Studies in Soviet Policy and Action.* New York: Random House, 1960.

Rauch, Georg von. *History of Soviet Russia.* New York: Praeger, 1954.

Reshetar, John S., Jr. *A Concise History of the Communist Party of the Soviet Union.* New York: Praeger, 1960.

Roberts, Henry L. *Russia and America.* New York: Harper & Row, 1956.

Salisbury, Harrison E. *American in Russia.* New York: Harper & Row, 1955.

Shannon, David A. *The Decline of American Communism.* New York: Harcourt, Brace & World, 1959.

Shub, David. *Lenin.* Garden City: Doubleday, 1950; New York: New American Library.

Stalin, Joseph. *The Economic Problems of Socialism in the U.S.S.R.* New York: International Publishers, 1952.

Trotsky, Leon. *Stalin.* New York: Harper & Row, 1946; New York: Grosset & Dunlap, 1958.

Ulam, Adam. *The Unfinished Revolution.* New York: Random House, 1960.

U.S. Congress. House of Representatives. Committee on Un-American Activities. *Facts on Communism.* 2 vols. Washington: Government Printing Office, 1960.

U.S. Congress. Joint Economic Committee. *Comparison of the United States and Soviet Economies.* Washington: Government Printing Office, 1959.

U.S. Congress. Senate. Committee on the Judiciary. *Expose of Soviet Espionage.* Washington: Government Printing Office, 1960.

U.S. Department of Health, Education, and Welfare. *Soviet Education Programs.* Washington: Government Printing Office, 1960.

Vernadsky, George. *A History of Russia.* New Haven: Yale University Press, 1954.

Wolfe, Bertram D. *Three Who Made a Revolution.* New York: Dial, 1960.

Zinner, Paul E. *Revolution in Hungary.* New York: Columbia University Press, 1962.

Aesopian Language, language whose meaning has been distorted.

Bolshevik, the term applied to the followers of Lenin from 1903 until shortly after his death; remained a part of the name of the Soviet Communist party until 1952.

Bourgeoisie, the middle class. *To Communists,* the dominating class of capitalist society, which must be overthrown in order to bring about the perfect society.

Capitalism, an economic system based on privately-owned property, hired labor, desire for profits, and a market controlled by consumer demand. *To Communists,* a system based primarily on exploitation of workers, and doomed to be overthrown by them.

Class Consciousness, *in Marxian theory,* awareness by the most advanced members of the proletariat of the nature of the class struggle and of their role in it as leaders of the Communist party.

Class Struggle, *in Marxian theory,* the continuing struggle between owners and those who must work for them, to Marx, the history of all society. *As used by Communists today,* the attempts of the Communist party to gain control of non-Communist countries.

Cold War, the struggle between the Communist and non-Communist parts of the world, in which actual warfare is usually avoided.

Communism, the beliefs and activities of the Communist party, based on the principles of Marxism-Leninism. *As used by Communists,* the ideal society predicted by Karl Marx. *Originally,* any social and economic system based on the ownership of property by the community as a whole rather than by private individuals.

Communist Party, *in Marxian theory,* a mass organization of class-conscious members of the proletariat, increasing in size and strength as the revolution approaches. *As modified by Lenin,* a small group of dedicated, full-time, professional revolutionaries. *Today,* the center of power in every Communist-controlled country; in non-Communist countries, a conspiracy dedicated to the establishment of Communist governments.

Counterrevolution, a revolution overthrowing a government that was established by an earlier revolution. *As used by Communists,* any activity against a Communist government.

Democracy, a political system based on rule by the people. *As used by Communists,* active participation by the people in government and party activities, but without their having any voice in deciding what those activities will be.

Democratic Centralism, *in Leninist theory,* the principle of open discussion within the Communist party, but of following the party policy without question after a decision has been made. *As used by Communists today,* obedience to the leaders of the party.

De-Stalinization, after Stalin's death, the removal by Khrushchev of some of the worst features of Stalin's rule of the U.S.S.R.

Dialectic, a philosophical theory which holds that the world is constantly being changed by struggles between new and old ideas.

Dialectical Materialism, the application by Marx of the dialectic to historical materialism; the basis of Communist thought.

Dictatorship of the Proletariat, *in Marxian theory,* a brief period after the revolution during which society would be reorganized prior to the entry into Communism. *As used by Communists today,* the dictatorship of the Communist party over the U.S.S.R., in effect since 1917.

Fellow traveler, one who supports the Communist party line but is not a party member.

Front organization, an organization that is not Communist in name, but which the Communist party controls or is able to manipulate for its own purposes.

Historical Materialism, a philosophical theory which holds that economic factors determine all human behavior and are therefore the moving force of history.

Iron Curtain, the heavily armed and fortified borders that separate the Communist countries from the non-Communist countries.

Kremlin, an ancient fortified area in Moscow. Because the most important offices of the Soviet government and the Communist party were there for many years, the Soviet government often is referred to as "the Kremlin."

Marxism, beliefs and attitudes based on those of Karl Marx. There are several varieties of Marxism, of which Communism is but one.

Marxism-Leninism, the theories of Karl Marx as reshaped by Lenin and further altered by men and events in the Soviet Union since Lenin's death in 1924.

Nationalization, the transfer of property from private ownership to ownership by the state.

Party Line, the position of the Communist party, and therefore of all its members, on any given issue at any given time; subject to sudden and frequent changes.

Peaceful Co-existence, *as used by Communists,* fighting for Communist domination of the world with every method except all-out war.

People's Democracy, *as used by Communists,* a Communist dictatorship established after World War II.

Planned Economy, an economy controlled by a state planning organization rather than operating according to the law of supply and demand.

Proletariat, *in Marxian terminology,* the working class gathered in cities by the Industrial Revolution.

Revisionism, *as used by Communists,* ideas or practices that claim to be Marxist but that oppose the Marxist-Leninist idea of violent revolution. *As a Communist swear word,* often applied to anyone who opposes any aspect of the party line.

Revolution, the overthrow of an established government. *In Marxian theory,* refers in particular to the seizure by the proletariat of the means of production, which brings an end to capitalism and establishes the dictatorship of the proletariat. *As used by Communists today,* any change of government that results in control by the Communist party.

Satellite, a supposedly independent country whose government is in reality controlled by the U.S.S.R.

Socialism, an economic system in which the principal means of production are controlled by the state. Not always Marxist, and often strong supporters of democracy, socialist political parties frequently are bitter enemies of Communism. *As used by Communists,* a stage within the period of the dictatorship of the proletariat leading to the establishment of Communism.

Socialist Realism, the Communist party line in painting, music, literature, and the other arts; demands that life under Communism be depicted as if the perfect society had already been achieved.

Soviet, the Russian word for *council. Originally,* applied to revolutionary workers' organizations used by the Bolsheviks in their seizure of power. *Today,* the basic (but powerless) unit of government in the U.S.S.R. *As an adjective,* of or pertaining to the U.S.S.R. or its government. *As used by Communists,* an adjective that indicates approval and praise.

Stalinism, belief that the policies and tactics of the Stalin era should be continued.

Titoism, *as used by Communists,* a swear word applied to non-Russian Communists who refuse to put the welfare of the U.S.S.R. ahead of that of their own country.

Totalitarianism, a system of government that attempts to control every aspect of the life of every person.

Withering Away of the State, *in Marxian theory,* the gradual disappearance of government during the dictatorship of the proletariat, to be completed with the establishment of Communism.

233

235

239

SD - #0014 - 160421 - C0 - 229/152/14 - PB - 9780282405922 - Gloss Lamination